Faith
Morality
Science

by
Cardinal Péter Erdő, Chief Rabbi József Schweitzer
and Professor E. Sylvester Vizi

Translated by:
David Robert Evans, "espell fordítás és lokalizáció Zrt."

DORRANCE
PUBLISHING CO
EST. 1920
PITTSBURGH, PENNSYLVANIA 15238

The contents of this work, including, but not limited to, the accuracy of events, people, and places depicted; opinions expressed; permission to use previously published materials included; and any advice given or actions advocated are solely the responsibility of the author, who assumes all liability for said work and indemnifies the publisher against any claims stemming from publication of the work.

Dorrance Publishing Co
585 Alpha Drive
Suite 103
Pittsburgh, PA 15238
Visit our website at *www.dorrancebookstore.com*

ISBN: 978-1-6442-6235-1
eISBN: 978-1-6442-6418-8

TABLE OF CONTENTS

LECTORI SALUTEM!

IT IS NOT EVERY DAY that the president of a national academy, the country's Catholic leader and its chief rabbi meet for a public and friendly discussion. However, this is what happened in Hungary in 2005; this book documents this unusual encounter. Three men with exceptional knowledge, who found much common ground beyond their personal friendship with one another, put this into a form so comprehensible to the lay reader that the record of their discussion became an immediate success on the Hungarian book market. Who best to discuss questions such as the points of connection between faith, science and morality in an accessible way but the country's leading authorities on these fields, who have not just acquired such knowledge, but are capable of passing it on in such a way that aids the progress of society and the whole of humanity?

As a Jewish leader, fate granted me the opportunity for a very particular public engagement in the last year: I met Pope Francis personally. In addition to welcoming the Jewish New Year, at the meeting we discussed the persecution of Christians in the 21st century. Today we live in an age in which the Christian community must endure the same religious persecution that we Jews, the 'elder brothers', have had to endure for three thousand years. This is why the head of the Catholic Church emphasized that for precisely this reason Christians must never forget the common roots that connect them to Jews.

Today we constantly hear about the conflicts between civilizations. So, it is particularly important and heart-warming to find that there are eminent scholars who are global in their thinking and who, while researching the foundations of human existence, also reinforce creative cooperation. For many Hungarians, it was liberating to read this volume. Now, in a new English version, in our present world so full of horrors, we can hope that it will again be a success. English speakers now can also experience the atmosphere of this unique meeting of minds: not merely one of friendship, mutual acceptance and reconciliation, but one proving the creative strength of the symbiosis of these three values.

András Heisler

President of the Federation of Jewish Communities in Hungary

PREFACE

THE THIRD VOLUME IN OUR SERIES addresses questions of Hungary's intellectual and spiritual health – questions that are at once topical and timeless. The themes raised in these discussions are of interest to us all, as they affect our everyday lives and human relationships. Those whose voices we hear in the book are among the most competent authorities in Hungarian intellectual and spiritual life: the cardinal primate of Esztergom, Bishop and President of the Catholic Bishops' Conference of Hungary; Hungary's retired chief rabbi; and the president of the Hungarian Academy of Sciences. It is no exaggeration to say that they are all scholars and thinkers known throughout Europe. In the following pages, the reader is given a glimpse into the discussants' family and personal backgrounds and how life prepared them for their missions at a national level.

We are always talking of individual responsibility, of the great challenges of the twenty-first century, in an age in which uniformization and the appearance of the dictatorship of taste constantly force upon us a certain type of lifestyle, says the president of the Academy. Not so long ago, the chief rabbi reminds us, it was possible to convince people that Hitler was the great liberator of the German people or that Stalin was the good father of the nation, although both were mass murderers. On the subject of faith and credulity, the cardinal is reminded of how Jesus was tempted by Satan and how, even for genuinely sober and polished rationality, traditions established over hundreds and thousands of years and validated by life as well as deep personal faith can be important.

In these pages, we can read how a flippant comment from a less than pious grandfather was proven true in the life of his grandson, who ultimately did not grow up to be a cigar-smoking capitalist, but did indeed become a bishop; about the ordeals and consolations of a religious family in the darkest period of the inhuman and anticlerical communist regime; about the life of a parish church on Bakáts Square, Budapest, or what a Piarist priest and teacher was like in the 1960s. The life of a Jewish family and community in the provincial Hungarian town of Veszprém in the interwar period is evoked, as is ten years in the everyday life of a Rabbinical seminary, its academic requirements and its difficult history, the emotional journey of the revival of the Jewish community in Pécs after the Holocaust and how it was liberated from one cruel dictatorship only to face another. We learn how a young man from a trading family in the village of Apostag could become a student at a well-regarded school for girls, and how his journey could lead from the depths of communist terror and deportation to the heights of academic life both at home and abroad. We will also learn about the Sisters of the Sacred Heart, who Károly Tihanyi and Gyula Kaposy were, and what the cruel reprisals were like in Pécs after the 1956 Uprising.

Looking towards the future, there is talk of 'pure' scholarship, of the inescapable importance of research and scientific inquiry that does not offer immediate reward for an individual or community that wants to live and think in the long term. There is mention of the vital adjunct for any new initiative, namely, to acknowledge, admit and confess that which is wrong or mistaken. There is also mention of forgiveness and how there is no future without mercy. We learn that one of the sources of authenticity is if someone says the same thing on the street as in the pulpit, at home as at work, to their friends and to their enemies. Attention turns to two types of institutions under attack in the modern world that nevertheless regard the preservation and creation of values assisting humanity's survival to be their calling and the reason they survive: the world of science and our scholarly academy, on the one hand, and the institutions of historic churches, on the other. Tradition, the richness and preserving force of our national culture, and the respect for the bishop's throne, are all great reserves for us to have for the future. Just as a heavy price was paid for the selfish infighting and narrow-minded behavior that preceded the Battle of Mohács, so too will the birth and serious acceptance of a possible social consensus on basic ethical norms and values, going beyond particular denominations, become a blessing not just for all of us but also for our children and grandchildren.

Our objective: One objective of this volume, in a rapidly changing world and in a stream of information of varying weight and importance, is to direct attention to thoughts and truths that have stood the test of time and that might provide more secure footholds for our everyday lives and questions.

The abbreviations used in the book should be obvious:

PE – Péter Erdő,
JS – József Schweitzer,
ESV – E. Sylvester Vizi, as well as
PLK – Péter Lajos Kovács and
SS – Szabolcs Sajgó.

We would like to wish all our readers rich and fruitful hours reading this book.

Szabolcs Sajgó SJ

I.

THE WORLD OF FAITH – THE FAITH OF THE WORLD

SS: Many people can't see clearly on the question of faith and religion. They say that they can accept faith, but not religion. How do you see this problem, Professor Schweitzer?

JS: Faith is a metaphysical gift, while religion, a system of laws, comes – by divine inspiration – from the Bible. But throughout the history of Judaism, theological scholars of the various ages have expanded this system in line with life circumstances. Perhaps one can say that religion is the pouring of faith into actions and a system. Let's take Abraham as our example: in our eyes – and I think we share this conviction –, he is the first monotheistic personality, indeed even Islam accepts this, as they also call Abraham *Avinu* or 'our father'. Abraham has no doubts when God tells him to 'Get thee out of thy country [...] unto a land that I will shew thee [...] and thou shalt be a blessing' (Gen 12:1-2). We do not hear of Abraham questioning even for a moment how and why this call came to him, and whether it was authentic or not; he just obeyed it. The Jewish exegesis then explains the fact of submission, the fact that Abraham left, that is the second part of the sentence, 'thou shalt be a blessing', in different ways. In such a way that the word *beraha* means blessing, but if we pronounce the punctuation differently, and read *bereha* instead of *beraha*, then it simply means 'be a source'. If I slightly stretch the point and refer to the Middle Ages, then I have to mention that the *Fons Vitae*, meaning 'Fountain of Life', written originally in Hebrew by Ibn Gabirol as '*Mekor Hayim*', was unknown at the time, and it was thought that it was an Arabian scholar called Avicenna or Avicebron who translated it into Latin. (C. Sirat: A History of Jewish Philosophy in the Middle Ages, Cambridge, 1985). At least the Biblical precursor, the expression 'thou shalt be a blessing', is there in the first book of Moses in connection with Abraham being sent away, as mentioned already. So, in this Biblical passage, the mission is to leave, and the task is to 'be a blessing'; the purpose of the mission is the action. To be a blessing is a question of faith; it also involves action. Of course, with regard to Abraham, the biggest problem for a reader of the Bible is the one I am so often asked: how can Abraham have exiled his second wife, Hagar, and her son, at Sarah's behest? To which we usually reply that this wasn't understood in the same way as today. According to the law of Mesopotamia in effect 150 years before the Code of Hammurabi, the second wife had to be sent away together with the son she had borne, who could not inherit from his father (The Torah. A Modern Commentary, Union of American Hebrew Congregation, New York; Gen 21:9-10). The Scriptures, however, call the exiled son Ishmael, that is, 'whom God hears'. We know that the Almighty made a promise to make the people of Ishmael a great people. (M. Guttmann: Sefer Mafteach haTalmud I, 1906, s.v. Abraham ve Ishmael. Guttmann discusses the legal interpretation of the problem at the time in greater detail in Das Judentum und seine Umwelt, Philo Verlag, Berlin, 1927. The 'Notlüge' was judged differently at the time. 10, and related notes.) As such, man's action – the exile – was righted by God's mercy. Here we should quote Amos, the great writer-prophet, when he says 'you all stand before me as *Cushi*, as "the blacks"'. That is, there is no difference between human being and human being. Perhaps this is the relationship between faith and religion. Faith is an internal conviction, and religion is, to a certain extent, the system of this conviction.

SS: So faith is a personal connection to God, while religion is...

JS: ...the community connection which appears in the form of rites.

PE: The question of the relationship between faith and religion is one very much rooted in the Christianity of the twentieth century. As one example, we could mention Dietrich Bonhoeffer's strong emphasis on the distinction between faith and religion, and of course there in the background was the historical difference between the national church and the Confessing Church, which caused considerable tension in Germany at the time. Our Catholic conviction tells us that faith is not merely trust, not merely reliance on God, and neither is it merely a belief, as in the everyday phrases like 'I believe this' or 'I think that'. Rather, it is one source of true knowledge (the other is science or scholarship). So faith is not just about mere personal behaviour; faith has substance. It means a behaviour which accepts truth as truth out of respect for the words of some kind of authority; that is, it requires this authority whose words we believe, and it also requires the object that we believe. So of course it brings with it trust, and also implies a personal decision.

In Christian parlance we can also say that faith is a virtue, and a divine virtue at that; this means that we are not able truly to believe God and that which he wants to tell us purely out of human strength. Yes, but faith by its very substance cannot be individual; that is, for a Christian, faith itself depends upon communal communication of that substance and communal witness. For precisely this reason, religion cannot strictly be separated from faith; rather, it joins it to form an organic whole: faith feeds religion, while it is with the framework of the religious community and religious life that we pass on our faith. This relationship pours light on an anthropological faculty: we develop culture in general, language, and all our other abilities via the medium of another human being, even though the talent is inside us, and we are born with it. This is why people say that man is a creature born to believe. And yet, the uniquely Judeo-Christian type of faith is related not just to human community but also to a God who reveals himself, as ultimately it is from him that we believe what we believe.

In this regard, that is, we consider ourselves a religion of revelation, and we live in the conviction that there is communication between humanity and

God, and that there have been fundamental events and facts of this communication over history which provide the basis for and the corroboration of our faith. Thus, for our liturgy and faith system, the fact of the Exodus or the person of Abraham, or later, and only for the New Testament faith, the life, teaching, suffering, death and resurrection of Christ, are facts which we regard as the source of divine revelation, and on which we base our faith. This means that for us the problem of the relationship between faith and religion leads to the question of how we are able to acquaint ourselves with divine revelation, us, personally, today. And this is to a great extent a historical question, namely the question of the sources for the experience of revelation, and that of the authorities bearing witness to the authenticity of these sources or the authority of the sources themselves.

For us, the continuity of the conviction of the religious tradition, the church community, the Christian community, is given, and this is the totality of the Scriptures, authorized by tradition, but also written on the basis of tradition and inspired by our conviction. For our church, the designated foundation for awareness of faith and knowledge of the revelation is the Holy Scripture, and the complete Holy Scripture, at that. And there are historical reasons for this: the first Christians always used the Scriptures they had at hand, that is, the Old Testament, as the indispensable means of passing on their own faith; it is in reference to this that the most important statements of faith in the New Testament include the phrase 'according to the Scriptures' almost as a refrain, while elsewhere we read: 'This day is this Scripture fulfilled'. The writings of the Old and New Testaments have thus been in a deliberate and organic connection from the outset, and this is precisely why, for us, the authority of the Scriptures is an authority based on historical foundation, which connects us through divine revelation.

The question could of course be broadened in the direction of the difference between the books of Scripture and apocryphal literature, that is other works from Antiquity about Jesus or about Old Testament subjects that people still like to talk about today. And, in my view, the foundations of the Christian answer to this are also in the liturgy, which I will return to at the next question. Here all I would say is that, according to this, the relationship and difference between faith and religion means that personal religious conviction – which is communicated by society – and the acts which express and implement it belong together, and yet there can be a certain distinction between them, perhaps even a tension, even if, naturally, we do not think this ideal. The objective possibility of experience, historical experience, is thus for us one of the pre-requisites of faith: if human beings were incapable of experiencing objective historical truth, then there would be no bridge capable of connecting us to revelation and the sources of revelation. In other words, a relativist rejection of the possibility of objective historical knowledge is a serious problem for our faith. This is one reason why Pope John Paul II emphasized the cognitive potential of the human mind so strongly in his *Fides et ratio* (Pope John Paul II, Encyclical letter, Fides et ratio, 1998, IX, 14, 3-4).

At one time it was highly fashionable to attack the Christian religion and historical religions in general with the charge that they are not rational enough, and that sources investigated with the techniques of historical criticism do not fully verify their content. Currently the tables have turned: it is more or less on the basis of our religious faith that we have to rush to help the confused people of today and tell them to trust their own ability to experience things, and to trust in the opportunity objectively to glean true knowledge of the past with historical-critical methods. Thus I believe that the possibility of gaining objective historical knowledge is a sort of anthropological prerequisite for faith, at least for us, and I think that at the same time this is precisely one of the difficulties for people today to accept our faith with trust.

JS: Revelation is the bridge along which human beings travel to meet God. By revelation we usually refer to the revelation of the Ten Commandments on Mount Sinai in chapter 20 of the second Book of Moses. This begins with 'I am the LORD thy God, which have brought thee out of the land of Egypt'; that is, revelation refers to a historical fact. In the medieval Jewish exegesis, indeed perhaps even in the ancient one, the question arose of how broad the references on the first pages of the Bible are: they refer not to a people being driven out in a particular historical period, but to the whole world being created. The answer to this is that this is true, but this is also hard to comprehend and accept. According to the Scriptures, this revelation occurs in the third month after the Flight from Egypt, and we have to say, so the old exegesis says, that the simplest little girl, who does not have the capacity to understand abstract ideas like the creation of the world, can easily understand the fact that with Moses' help and following God's orders they left Egypt and were free. We experience revelation prior to this, with the vision of the Burning Bush, when God personally addresses Moses.

SS: Professor Schweitzer, could you say a few words about the 'I am who I am'?

JS: The '*ehyeh asher ehyeh*'. This *ehyeh* in the burning bush scene is really *futurum*, the future. *Ehyeh*, 'I will be'; *asher ehyeh*: 'the person I will be'. But this is a kind of *futurum perfectum*, one that is already achieved. Generally, we interpret this as 'I am who I am'. To return to what we were talking about: history is the dependable bridge along which everyone can become acquainted with the liberating force of God. Once this liberating force has been established, the laws are laid down, the Ten Commandments, where the interesting thing, already here, in Deuteronomy, is that most of the commandments are in the plural: you should all do this, you should all not do that. There are very few laws which are in the second person singular: honour thy mother and father, thou shalt not steal, thou shalt not kill, and so on. This is how the Scriptures want to express, so the exegesis tells us, that no one should be able to say that these are nice ideas expressed in a general way. They are in the second person singular, and so affect the person reading or hearing them *in concreto*, individually, and so there is no way out, so to speak. The second thing that needs to be said about the law is that according to tradition these stone tablets which they engraved are such that the first five commandments are on one tablet, and the second five on another. Yet today all Christian depictions have a four-six division rather than a five-five one; the elders of the church separated them on the basis that the first four are about God, including 'Honour thy father and thy mother', and those on the other tablet, refer to human beings. The Jewish interpretation, on the other hand, emphasizes the fact that the fifth commandment, 'Honour thy father and thy mother', is on the first tablet together with the obligations towards God because the obligation to one's parents is as serious as one's obligation to God. Law in general is an obligation. According to a scholar named Simlay in the third century (this is at the end of the Makos tractate in the Talmud), there are 613 commandments in the Bible to which people are obliged. Some of these are prohibitions; the others are calls to act. That is, obedience to God is realized via implementing the law or by abstaining from a specific act. There are many theological views which see Judaism as a legislative system, a religion of the law, and Pharisaism is usually included in this school of thought. There were hypocrites among the Pharisees, there are hypocrites everywhere, but the notion of Pharisaism is not in itself at all judgmental or dismissive, as it is derived from the Hebrew word *perushim*, which is from the verb *parash*, and simply means 'explain'. So they are those who paid very close attention to the Scriptures, so that, for example, at the time of Jesus, in addition to the existing obligations, it would be possible to create new religious laws, for example for the field of trade, on the basis of deduction from the Scriptures. It is in this religion based on the law, *mitzvah*, that is the legal system, that Michael (Mihály) Guttmann, one-time rector of the Rabbinical Seminary in Budapest, sees the characteristic that defines the essence of Judaism. The essence of the religion based on law is that we draw close to God and serve God through submission, that is by obeying the law or by not doing a given action. Its nature as a religion is defined not by the number or form of its rituals, but rather by the intention and religious content of those rituals (István Hahn: Mihály Guttmann (1872-1942), Lebanon, year 3, 1942, IV, 97-99). They took great care to observe the Levitical cleanliness laws, and would take pains to avoid Levitical uncleanliness. The Hebrew word for this caution is *parash*, which means 'to separate'. It is from this Hebrew verb that we get the expression 'Pharisee', which often has negative connotations. The Sadducees stood opposite the Pharisees, and often observed a different exegesis and religious law. The Sadducean interpretation of Passover was different from the Pharisean one, for example. So there are exegetical differences, but the point is that in the Jewish religion they did not, so to speak, make it the subject of the commandments that you should believe in God – as this was our starting point – because this was assumed to be the case *ab ovo*. As

Cardinal Erdő was kind enough to state, the Scriptures and history are not two distinct fields; rather, the Scriptures include historical parts which today are easy to investigate. So we can deduce the fact of when the Flight from Egypt took place; but that God's revelation took place on Mount Sinai is based not on philosophy, but on historical fact.

SS: Could we say in rather more brash terms that someone who doesn't obey the law or only obeys it now and again is actually an unbeliever?

JS: It would be hard for me to dare to make such a pronouncement, because the law itself can be interpreted in different ways. And our starting point was our distinguishing a faith in God as a metaphysical gift or realization, and considered religion and religious observation as putting that faith in God into a systemic framework.

If someone cannot say of all principles of faith or religious laws that they can completely believe in them, I cannot call them an unbeliever; at worst, I would say that their emotional and intellectual world or their need for religion is different from ours. Obeyance of the law is a religious duty; there can be exemptions from this under grave pressure, with three exceptions. These are the worship of idols, carnal immorality, or being forced to kill another human being. In these three instances one must accept death (TB. Sanhedrin, 74a). You cannot know whose blood is redder, the Talmud says, that is, whose life is more valuable: your life or that of the person the enemy is condemning to death. So if someone has to be taken to their death, if immorality has to be committed, or monotheism has to be denied, then you must accept death. With all other pressures, one can weigh up what kind of pressure is present. To give a practical example: if you are called up to be a soldier, but you cannot eat the food you are given, you cannot die of starvation, not to mention that if you continue not to eat, this may be read as some kind of political or anti-militarist declaration for which you would be hanged. So, please, you have to eat what they give you, because this is an absolute need, but this does not absolve one of the three things I just mentioned.

ESV: Much has been said about the relationship between faith and religion: I would like to discuss the relationship between faith and science. According to Aristotle, experience is not needed to learn about the world; thought is enough to know truth. A world based on faith is characterized by the acceptance of phenomena without proof. It is no accident that Plato still thought that a larger stone would fall more quickly than a smaller one. However, Saint Thomas Aquinas considered the experience of phenomena to be important: *nihil est in intellectu, quod non prius in sensu* – nothing is in the intellect that was not first in the senses. Indeed, Galileo went even further and felt obliged to extend the abilities of our sense organs; for example, this is how he discovered Jupiter's moon, using the telescope he himself built. However, in the leaning tower of Pisa, Galileo wanted to prove his theories with experiments and reached the conclusion that our thoughts must be tested. With this came the end of *ex cathedra* truths. Galileo Galilei, the man who regenerated human thought, had no choice but to give in to violence. The old physicist was taken by force to the church of Santa Maria Sopra Minerva in Rome to retract his theses under the pain of the Inquisition, but after the age of seventy, he again put to paper all that he knew of the Sun and the Earth.

However, in his own era, Galileo did not have to (or did not only have to) confront what the scientists and scholars of today often have to confront – namely, that a discovery that overwrites previous academic results, and the researcher behind it, will be received with skepticism, even ignored, by those representing the previous position.

Thus, Galileo had to confront not only the earlier community of scientists – and their geocentric worldview – but also the dogmatic 'defenders' of the faith: faced with the Inquisition, he had to retract his theories, the results of his discoveries. It was then that, according to tradition, he mumbled to himself during this procedure: *Eppur si muove!* (And yet it moves!) Alas, we find many examples like this in the history of scholarship: the authorities put violent pressure on scholars, and scholars do the same to scholarly truth.

However, if I have introduced this example, then I should add that in 1992 – some 359 years later – Pope John Paul II apologized and officially retracted the Inquisition order against Galileo. With this, it was finally decided that the era in which Giordano Bruno was burned on the stones of the Campo de' Fiori was never to return.

In fact, it was not only the defenders of the tenets of faith who had trouble understanding Galileo but also many of the representatives of what would become the new science, as countless members of this circle believed in the omnipotence of science and thus forgot or ignored Galileo's thought on the subject: 'This vain presumption of understanding everything can have no other basis than never understanding anything'.

Positivism, the social scientific theory developed in the nineteenth century, tells us that the working of the human brain, some three hundred billion nerve cells, is capable of uncovering every mystery of the world and of society. Now it is entirely clear that the entirety of truth cannot be grasped, only partial truths. Many say that first there is knowledge, and for those things I cannot work out or explain, there is the kingdom of faith. But there is also a view, to which I subscribe myself, that faith comes before science, as you must believe that there are still partial truths we are not aware of; you also have to know that real discovery is unexpected – something that cannot be predicted in advance. This is the alpha of science. And there are those who say that they have worked out what laws will govern society and nature. This is a mistake. The real discovery is something that is unknown, but where I have faith that I will be able to find something new. So faith comes before knowledge and before the first steps of science. It was exactly the Papal encyclical, the *Fides et ratio*, that referred to the rising of the human spirit as being on two wings. This rise is essentially the rise in society: in everything, we rely on both faith and reason. There are very many of us who believe what I have just said, that faith must come before knowledge. For example, Michael Polanyi, who had previously been a member of the Galileo Circle in Budapest, became a Christian believer under the influence of the writings of Tolstoy and others, and he clearly established this position in his philosophical writings. Saint Augustine 'makes an appearance' in Polanyi's views: *Nisi credideritis, non intelligetis*, that is, 'you will not understand unless you will have first believed'. Later, in the 17ᵗʰ century, John Locke would turn this view around and say that faith is the shortage of knowledge (An Essay Concerning Human Understanding, Oxford, 1690).

SS: Does faith come before science, or is it a source of knowledge independent of it?

ESV: Faith comes before science. A scientist must believe in what he hypothesizes. I have a metaphor for this: All scholars, I mean real scholars, able to think in abstract terms, who genuinely want to learn what the world is like, will eventually be confronted with their own littleness and powerlessness. If I compare knowledge to a sphere, and the surface of the sphere touches the unknown, then the greater my knowledge, the greater my encounter with the unknown will be, and the smaller I will feel here is this world, this fantastic thing, because of how little of it I am able to be acquainted with.

So the realization of one's littleness is what really leads to other parts of faith, which can be called faith in God, the Creator, the Prime Mover, or whatever you like. Many great scientists and scholars only reach this point at the end of their lives. Not dogmatically, not from a primary school catechism (as I learned at the Sophianum of the Sacred Heart in Budapest, quite a different thing), but quite simply when someone thinks, "My God, how wonderful this world is, and I am only able to encounter such a tiny part of it, and the more that I know, the more that I see the contents of this incredible unknowable thing!"

SS: Faith by its very nature precedes any kind of knowledge, as it means the acceptance of suppositions about things which I was not able to prove for myself; science cannot really get going without this, but here we are primarily talking of the unique area of faith which is related to the transcendent, to a faith in God. We are picking apart the relationship between this faith and religion.

ESV: A fundamental characteristic of science is that it is quantitative in attitude: results and knowledge can be measured and are truly measurable. Modern science, based on facts, grew out of the European culture, which had, in turn, emerged from Greco-Roman philosophy and the Judeo-Christian tradition. In old cultures, such as the Hindu, Indian, Egyptian and Babylonian cultures, the development of science was limited. In India, for example, Buddhism and its predecessor, Brahmanism, placed peace and agreement at the center of its thought, whereas the European culture based on Judeo-Christian religion emphasized the clear distinction between good and evil, between that with value and that without value, which is essentially the ethos of the Ten Commandments and also suited scientific thinking well. Although the religions of the Far East were meditative in nature, and their way of thinking was mostly characterized by synthesis, in Christian Europe, public thought and scholarship would become dominated by thinking based on value and thus were analytical in nature; this was true of industry and is currently true of the economy as a whole. This is why Europe would be the cradle of modern science as we know it.

Faith, on the other hand, is in the category of quality, not quantity. It cannot be measured, but it has qualitative consequences. This is the same category as human thought, relationships between human beings, the relationship between man and the environment, humanity and human morality. However, it is not the category of the quantifiable.

JS: In some places the behaviour of faith can be measured, for example in the acceptance of martyrdom. I am thinking of the great Hungarian poet János Arany, whose famous 'Bards of Wales' accepted martyrdom not out of faith but out of loyalty to their king. 'Five hundred went singing to die / Five hundred in the blaze / But none would sing to cheer the king / The loyal toast to raise' (trans. Peter Zollman). Faith is potentially measurable in critical cases.

ESV: I accept that, but this is more the qualitative change in someone's behavior.

JS: But what motivates someone to such a qualitative change?

ESV: Faith or conviction, obviously.

SS: How should we understand the long-established science of faith?

ESV: Theology. The Hungarian Academy of Sciences has always had a dispute with the canon of bishops: we wanted to incorporate theology, but they said it was not an academic field.

PE: As regards faith and science or faith as science, and apart from a few authors in the patristic era, who may also have referred to spirituality or experience in the field of faith as *sacra scientia*, by theology we understand the academic study dealing with faith, while we accept that faith and religion can be approached academically from different perspectives. From the moment I begin to study an existing system of thought, social system or system of religious behaviour, I enter the world of demonstrable knowledge, from which it is already possible to construct a system. Whether from a theological or a natural scientific perspective, or from a historiographic perspective, it can of course be said that this claim is not justified, that this conviction is correct, that it become widespread in this or that period, because I can prove that two hundred years earlier it had been confessed to in some other place. When the subject is whether it is true, or not true, then naturally it is about the content of the convictions of various religions. If something is stated as a religious claim which specifically refers to a scientific fact, and the system of science can be used to prove whether it is true or not, then naturally there can be agreement or contradiction.

What I mean is that the difference between theology and the study of religion is not in the subject of the two, but in their method. The study of religion asks not whether they are right or not, but rather what their social role is, or what their relationship to some part of human reality is, or how they relate to each other phenomenologically, and so on. Theology is determined according to denomination, and puts into an ordered system the elements of a given religious community or world-view within that faith, and looks for answers to new questions for this community within its faith. So here there is proof, too, if you like, there is something to measure against, just that the point of reference is tradition, the tradition of Scripture and the church, which we can document historically. In other words, in the science of theology and in our view there could justifiably arise the question of whether a certain statement or conviction is consistent with the Catholic faith or not, and we can show on the basis of historical sources whether it is or it is not. So the question is not that of whether it is scientific or justified or not, but we can go as far as to ask whether or not it is consistent with the system of faith within the given religious community. I believe that back when the Hungarian Academy of Sciences was founded, the statement of foundation included an interesting comment: it states that the Academy of Sciences deals with all fields of academic study with the one exception of theology. We can take this to mean that it does not question the academic nature of theology in terms of its structure, but as this is determined according to denomination, and the Academy sees itself as a neutral scholarly body, it does not want to take up positions on such questions. So I think that it is very much appropriate for the activities or horizons of such a body as the Academy, for example, to include the academic treatment of religion as a phenomenon or as a reality, but neither the state nor a public body is competent to judge, for instance, which theologist is more Reformed Church than the other.

ESV: We have re-established religious studies at the Hungarian Academy of Sciences; Cardinal Erdő is a member of the board. The old order has been restored.

JS: It was a very pleasant surprise that when Professor Vizi said the term 'Prime Mover', he looked at me, because I was thinking about how Professor Vizi worked on the religious philosophy of Maimonides. Theology was different at the time of the Talmud and at the time of the Bible, and different in the Middle Ages, and my sense was that when Professor Vizi looked at me when he said the words 'Prime Mover' he was thinking of old Maimonides. His very significant claim was, in Hebrew, the *matsuy rishon*, the prime mover, who himself moves, and moves the others in the chain, but there is nothing that moves him. He is the Almighty.

ESV: This question is a terribly difficult one for scientists: How can it all be explained? How can we explain miracles?

JS: One can only be pleasantly surprised to hear a scientist say such things.

PE: If I may add something to what we were discussing earlier... There was talk about the relationship between religion and ritual, that is between religion and liturgical life; our Christian notion of tradition and our notion of Scripture is closely connected to liturgy. It is connected to it because even in the New Testament, as we see in the light of the history of this genre, there are established formulas in liturgical use (Cf. e.g. Martin Dibelius, Die Formgeschichte des Evangeliums Berlin 1969; Heinrich Zimmermann, Neutestamentliche Methodenlehre, Leipzig, 1967), for example the Eucharistic formula, which has been preserved in a number of places. There are hymns, there are details, which present to us the confession of faith in the Resurrection in a form simplified for the liturgy, while in what follows we know of the confessions that the earliest Christian creed surviving in written form are from baptismal confessions, for example what we now refer to as the Apostles' Creed. So the liturgy of baptism was the *Sitz im Leben*, which was also the basis for the formulation of the creed.

For us, the Scripture, and its canon, which distinguishes the books of the Bible from apocryphal literature, is very much of liturgical origin. The point is that the Christian community held its own meetings in a way similar to the Jewish synagogue liturgy. We know that Jesus himself and Saint Paul originally and on repeated occasion spoke in synagogues, and just as part of the Torah was read, afterwards an explanation accompanied the *Haftarah*. Jesus says, 'This day is this scripture fulfilled in your ears' (Luke 4:21), or Saint Paul repeatedly stands up and bears witness to the prophecies of the prophets coming true, with which he often stirs up debate among the rows of the faithful (Acts 13:14–42). But the Christian community itself recognized that it had taken on the notion and the spirit of the Scriptures, just as we see in Peter's second letter, which talks about how Saint Paul's letters are often misinterpreted – to their loss, 'As also in all his epistles' (2 Pet 3:14–16). The writings – *graphai* – referred to the books of the Old Testament Scriptures. So Christian congregations on the one hand read details of the Old Testament, because it was so natural to do so, in particular with the objective of showing that its predictions had come true in Jesus. On the other hand, they began to read writings containing their own traditions referring to Jesus' life and teaching, his death and resurrection, and so is it possible that the second Epistle of Saint Peter groups the Epistles of Saint Paul together with the other writings. Similarity and continuity also exist in the way that the church makes use of pericopes, that is it reads various parts of the Scriptures according to a pre-arranged order, just as the weekly sections had existed in the liturgies of synagogues. The Christian scriptural liturgy also takes the former synagogue ceremony as its model in that it distinguishes details from the Scripture in two ways, and on more festive occasions three ways. Modelled on the Torah and the *Haftarah*, there are the readings and a gospel reading, or there is an Old Testament reading, a New Testament reading and a gospel reading. All of this, not to mention the creation of psalms, the liturgy of the hours, the evensongs, is closely connected to the old Jewish service, and this is the environment in which the list of the books which have to be read or which are allowed to be read in a Christian service comes to be solidified.

Alongside this is also developed a list of books which are not allowed to be read out. In practice these can be traced back to the turn of the second century, so these are not the celebratory, universal synodic-level canonical lists of the fourth century, which were the first to collect the authorized books of the Christian Scripture in a single place; rather, they are authorized by liturgical practice that has developed from the outset. So the faith and conviction of the community are in a continuous interaction with the sources which contain the revelation, that is, the books of the Scriptures. This helps us to build a bridge towards the sources and to interpret them properly.

JS: Cardinal Erdő referenced an Aramaic word that perhaps not everyone is aware of: *Haftarah*. The *Haftarah* is the prophetic lesson; in Judaism this exists such that the Torah of Moses is divided into the Saturdays of the calendar year, and every Saturday a certain part of the chapter is read from this. There is a prophetic lesson in some kind of relationship with the lesson of the Torah, and this is the so-called *Haftarah*, which in point of fact merely means 'conclusion', because originally the service was concluded with this. As far as the psalms are concerned, there are psalms in many places in the liturgy. I would give just one example: when Friday evening brings the start of Saturday, then the psalm for Saturday is read out. Another similarity, if you will allow me: according to the Eastern calendar, the next day begins not at midnight but when the first stars appear in the night sky. As far as I know, a memory of this has survived in Christian liturgy, on Christmas Eve, which, as the name suggests, begins not on the morning of December 25, but on the evening of December 24, and in this it follows the Jewish liturgy, in which a festival always begins on the evening of the previous day.

SS: Yes, every Sunday and more important feast day has its celebratory eve beforehand, the vigil.

JS: On the relationship between faith and the law, I would just add obeyance of the law is always a documentation of faith. Actions prescribed by the law were recorded in legal codices. The most famous such book of laws is the Sulchan Aruch ('The Tablecloth'), edited by Rabbi Joseph Karo. It was published in Safed, which was the greatest centre for Kabbalist, or mystical studies, in what was the Jewish land at the time. In point of fact this is the thought that every moment and action has to be blessed by a law, from the moment of awakening, when hands must be doused, to the moment of going to sleep, which is also accompanied by a confession of faith, by saying the *Shema Yisrael* ('Hear, Oh Israel'), because this, said Kabbalist Joseph Karo, helps us towards Divine revelation by the road of obeying the divine law. In its ultimate consequences the religion of the law leads all the way to Messianism.

ESV: The similarities between Judaism and Christianity can indeed be beautifully analyzed, but academic thought also played a role in the studies of Jesus Christ, not just remaining within the boundaries of one national religion, but becoming open and available to everyone. Paul the Apostle's work in Greece and his travels played a role in this, as it was an acquaintance with the Athenian school, Greek philosophy and Greek science that drove the Christians to make their religion open to the people, the *demos*. This is how it stepped out of Judaism's national boundaries to expand into a world religion, and this became the secret of its success.

SS: I think it would be good to return just a little bit to the question of faith and religion, as the conversation so far could easily allow someone to think that religion is nothing other than the continuation of past connections. And then we could think that someone who accepts this tradition, the historical facts, the existing prayers, the laws, and lives by them, is religious and a believer, and someone who doesn't is not a believer, or at least there are serious questions to be raised about their belief. I would like to drive our attention towards the point that God is a living God.

ESV: If I might interrupt: We have the faithful and the religious. Do all believers have to be religious? I do not think they do: religiosity is really just a confirmation that I belong somewhere; this is what *religio* means, whereas faith is the confirmation that someone believes in revelations, believes in God. I think the two are separate categories; of course, if the two were to meet, that would be the optimal outcome.

PE: You have put that very nicely, as far as I am concerned. We ourselves traditionally distinguish two basic types of religion: natural religions and religions based on revelations. This despite the *gratia supponit naturam*, that is our faith says that the revelation, the Divine mercy, which speaks to us does not rid us of our common sense and our natural knowledge; rather, it supposes it, and builds on it.

Natural religions can be communal in nature, they can sustain traditions, but we accept that someone can find their way through the world of natural reason to the awareness of God, to a conviction of the existence of God, and so on (Cf. Rom 1:20; First Vatican Council, Const. Dei Filius, 2; Heinrich Denzinger-Peter Hünermann, Enchiridion Symbolorum: A Compendium of Creeds, Definitions, and Declarations of the Catholic Church, 2012). It really is true that individual research, individual experience and individual conviction have a serious role and space here. And yet religions founded on revelation inescapably include a communal element. I would return to the word 'obligation': I would debate whether these historical elements which we discussed with Chief Rabbi Schweitzer would principally be obligations. Today, in ordinary parlance, it has become fashionable to use an ugly expression to describe the mind-set of people today, that they are looking for something to cling to. Not obligations, but safe points to cling to. For we look for a relationship with a revelatory God, and in this, if we are believers in a religion based on revelation, we require historical mediation. So I believe that religious law, liturgy and even the life of the community are all such an opportunity for us.

SS: I'll put the question differently: are we museum guards, or do we carry one form of life in us? So is faith something simply derived from the past, or is it a force that is seminal, uplifting, cleansing in the life of today? In both Judaism and Christianity, the God speaking in the Bible, the God appearing in church history and the God present today are all in harmony; if we focus only on the present, we lose the past, but if only on the past, we lose the present!

ESV: Please allow me to help with an example from the field of science! Science and scholarship have grown incredibly quickly, exponentially, in the last century, whereas ethics and morality since Greco-Roman times and on the basis of Europe's Judeo-Christian traditions, such as the Ten Commandments, have developed linearly, at best, or, I fear, not even that fast – I am thinking of the horrors of the twentieth century. People feel increasingly insecure because they hear of the incredibly bad but also supposedly good use of atomic energy; they hear that we, medical biologists, are able to produce living creatures, perhaps cloned human beings, via asexual means; they hear that the wrong use of an atom bomb or the creation of a human clone by now are merely moral questions: yes or no. I note in parentheses: this is why humanity needs faith, religion and morality. This very rapid development in science and technology has resulted in the average person starting to be afraid: they do not know what is going to happen – here are these mobile phones, which have transformed our everyday lives, our family life, everything, human relationships, or here is this television, whose programming decisions have confused everything. The ordinary person wants to believe, if credible people tell them so, that atomic energy can be good, that mobile telephony can be good, that the extraordinarily fast progress of the information revolution can be good for them, as they can do everything from home on their computer and do not have to go anywhere. However, this is all a question of faith because they do not know what this technology really brings with it. At the same time, another school of thought has appeared with phenomenal strength, which misleads this society and very simply tells it that it should not believe in all this, thereby generating insecurity, and then it is the job of academe and academics to come to people's aid, to explain what lies behind these phenomena and what good this phenomenal progress of science can do. At the same time, the attention of ordinary people must be drawn to the terrible things that these innovations can be used for. Here, I am thinking of the letter by Albert Einstein and Hungarian-born physicist Leo Szilard written about the atom bomb. So, a scientist has a double responsibility: to strengthen the people's faith in the belief that what is good is good. This is a question of faith: most people cannot grasp the fantastic results of physics, chemistry, biology or medical science in a scientific way, so fear is generated, and they need things to cling to. In other words, every single person looks for things to cling to from a scientific point of view. However, cling to what, and why? So they can believe and so they have the courage to at least partially understand what is still unknown to them. Thus, faith does indeed play an incredibly large role in our everyday lives.

JS: If I may continue the point about things to cling to… We cannot expect a single one of our believers to know the history of prophetism or to know this and that, and here is where the role of religion today comes in, that we are not only museum guards. I had this idea when I was first in Prague, where the teaching of Judaism faced very real challenges. In the Jewish Museum we saw the beautifully laid festive table, the Seder table for the Exodus, the feast of Passover. My wife and I would agree on how sad it was for us that our children would only know the Seder table from seeing it in a museum. In order for us not just to be museum guards, here is the key importance of relating and preaching the Word. We work for the future as well as the present, and it is the Scriptures which guide us in this.

ESV: It is when someone is faced with major problems in their life, with illness, with death, that they really look for the things to cling to. So, I think that every person needs something to cling to sooner or later; faith may be it. As I claimed, the rapid progress of science and scholarship demands that every member of society believe that this is in their interest, really is a good thing because otherwise, the results of science will make them anxious. It is very interesting to observe that among people with faith, anxiety and various psychological illnesses are much less prevalent. If someone believes that everything will all be all right for them and that they will be helped, this is something that has a very strong influence, especially for those left on their own.

SS: Our conversation seems to include and mix the concepts of natural faith, supernatural faith, human faith and divine faith. This is natural, because while the subject of all of these faiths may be different, it is ultimately the same human being who is believing. Scientists also mix various faiths and various prejudices. And it is not irrelevant to what hypotheses one subscribes. I am reminded of that example from St. Exupéry, in *The Little Prince*, of the Turk whose European fellow scientists don't listen to his great discovery when he is in his traditional robes, only when he changes his clothes. They do not expect to hear anything serious from someone in an Eastern robe.

We can think of Einstein and Leo Szilard and others for whom faith, and thereby a responsible, moral life, is important when it comes to science and to using science.

PE: I would begin again with the expression that we are museum guards. First of all: if the museum needs to be guarded at all, that is a good sign, because that means that it has things of value inside it that many would like to access. I also think that Chief Rabbi Schweitzer is entirely right, that our task is not merely to preserve a tradition, and that we at the very least are museum guides. We need to explain things, introduce them, and turn them into a relevant message that influences the life of today. This is our obligation. Professor Vizi's comment is very fundamental in this regard: what we guard are religious values, not just old values. It is distinct from many other fashionable cultural phenomena not just in this regard, but in what it applies to, something that is very basic at a human level. I think that great Hungarian poet Mihály Babits plays with the words for electricity and star, saying that electricity is true, a star is bold, electricity is new, a star is old (Mihály Babits: *Evening Arrival*). In this 'bold' and 'old' there is something fundamental, something that is always relevant. So if our historical heritage applies to something that is fundamentally a human question, then this has a message. I think this will be something that will lead us further, the issue of what the role of religion is, what message it can have. I am convinced that it has a role in the answering of basic human questions. There are always newer and newer basic human questions such as these, as for example science progresses, but in these our own traditions and humanity's basic fundamental experiences are a help, and, according to our faith, the encounter with revelation is among these. We do not stand with empty hands when new questions are raised. The reference to new questions brings to mind Nicolas of Cusa and his major work, *De Docta Ignorantia* (On Learned Ignorance, 1440). This tells beautifully of the way that as human knowledge grows, each new element of knowledge content generates new questions, so we can hardly surmise that our human, individual or collective reason could solve all problems in the universe or become acquainted with it from every possible perspective. And yet this all contains the confidence, especially on the basis of our faith, that we are able to attain the knowledge we need. So the reason that it is worth humanity becoming ever better acquainted with the world is not that we are able to learn about everything perfectly, but because we are able to attain knowledge which is indispensable for our individual and our communal lives. This again takes us a long way, and belongs more to the domain of science.

SS: Let me mention again that God is a living God, and both faith and religion refer to this, and the whole of history is about the consequences of this fact, as do the Scriptures, and yet God's voice is present now, too. In one dimension, this is what I meant when I said we are not museum guards. We not only guard God's past voice, but God speaks to us today, too. If we could also talk about the experience of this.

JS: We are in a very simple situation with regard to precisely the great tragedy I don't want to talk about, when on that certain Passover Seder evening we read in the Jewish Passover narrative that they have turned on us in every era. We respond not just to a historical past, but those of us who are older also seek a response to our own horrible experiences.

SS: Do we respond, or does the Lord God respond?

JS: This is the question of Auschwitz theodicy.

ESV: This is not a good question for God. Human beings were given complete freedom. People have the right to decide; people are responsible. If I put the question otherwise, then I am acquitting human beings for carrying out the Holocaust, or saying they had the right to deport tens of millions of people to Siberia to meet their deaths. The fifteenth-century philosopher Pico della Mirandola said in one of his parables that the Good Lord created the world, then when the living creatures appeared, he gave the lion strength, the fox cunning. He gave each of them something, then man was left for last, but God had nothing left to give him, so God had the idea of letting man decide what he wanted and how he wanted it. This free will must not be confused with thinking that someone else is responsible, as otherwise I would acquit human beings of all the consequences of their actions. This is morality, which in the whole of the living world is a characteristic exclusive to human beings.

SS: This response is a very important one, and it is much needed by many, and yet it does not render redundant the question of whether it should just be human beings who answer for things, or God as well. When creating man, did God take a vow of silence, and condemn himself to inactivity, and now the Earth spins, and the Creator can rest, or does the Almighty work alongside man?

PE: The question was whether God speaks in the present as well. On this, Catholic theology says that revelation, in both the communal and direct sense of the word, was completed. Revelation was completed with Christ and the age of the Apostles, and private revelations are not on a par with what God wanted to tell humanity through his son Jesus Christ. At most there can be an aspect to it, detail relating to a few particular situations, which individual people can see more clearly through special inspiration or as a divine gift. In other words, we are not entirely untied as regards the content of our faith, the essence of the content of the revealed faith, and the situation is not one in which someone can emerge next year and say that the Scriptures make them think of entirely different things, and they have written a new book of Scripture they would like to add to the existing ones. In this sense, that is, we do not see this as a free-for-all, and yet Christian theology says that the Holy Spirit works in the world. Especially in the church, and he speaks directly to individual people, and teaches us all that Jesus said to us (John 14:26).

There is a tension of this kind. Precisely in the period after Pentecost, sections of the Scriptures repeatedly deal with this; on the one hand, Jesus says 'I have called you friends; for all things that I have heard of my Father I have made known unto you' (John 15:15), that is, all things God wanted to tell us; on the other hand, he says 'I will send you the Comforter who will guide you into all truth' (John 16:13). And elsewhere: 'he shall [...] bring all things to your remembrance, whatsoever I have said unto you' (John 14:26). This means that he is not promising a new understanding, and is not improving our memories for us to remember him more precisely; rather, he is promising clarity of sight in how to apply this to particular situations.

ESV: Ergo, he leaves the decision up to us! That is the crux of the whole thing!

PE: Yes, we are responsible, and the revealed faith or truth we have inherited we have to apply to our lives today.

JS: If I may add something to round off or close this subject: what Professor Vizi said was said and written by no less a figure than Lord Jacobowitz, Chief Rabbi of the British Empire, who was apparently of Hungarian extraction...

ESV: Everyone is Hungarian...

JS: He was a scholar, and in his writings I read exactly the same thing: the question about Auschwitz is not that of where God was, as God gave man free will; rather, the question is where man was. And another sentence from a German rabbi who became a professor in Canada: if we come to the conclusion that everything we stood for was lost at Auschwitz, then it is not we who have won, but rather we have handed over victory to Hitler and his accomplices. It is a tough question, because now, sixty years on, it is easy to talk about us, but when Rabbi Sándor Scheiber, director of the Rabbinical Seminary in Budapest, told me, as a young rabbi, 'You, Schweitzer, you go and be a rabbi in Pécs', I was only 23 years old, and my face was still full of a rash from starvation. I replied to him, 'But Professor Scheiber, there the congregation was destroyed, thousands were killed, and a little boy like me is going to preach to them and draw them back into the synagogue?' He replied that I should study the Scriptures, and that there was always the telephone. And with that he sent me off.

SS: We have raised the issue of faith and credulity. What are our thoughts about the phenomenon of faith and credulity from both an academic and a religious perspective?

ESV: This question is equally important in academe and social life, as in both we make great use of human credulity. Businesses and political parties are built on it. For example, it is very interesting to observe that the most 'discoveries' in the world are related to curing cancer. Someone who is ill would like to believe that he can be cured. Again, I use this word 'believe', because if he knew, he would not turn to methods that are not proven to heal. One very important task for science, in academies across the world, is to spread knowledge, so that the correct position of science be communicated to people in a comprehensible way. In Hungary, the Society for the Dissemination of Scientific Knowledge, founded in 1841 by members of the Hungarian Academy of Sciences, including Ányos Jedlik, had the same goal as the Academy itself: to present the scientific results of the age, in Hungarian, in an accessible way for everyone. Those who exploit credulity, who continue to reap enormous financial gain from this, must be stopped.

JS: I apologize for saying something that it is not directly relevant to this, but it is something very important for those learning to be priests or rabbis. We are talking about credulity. A doctor knows that a patient cannot be cured. The doctor tells me, and I talk to the patient. What should I do?

ESV: In a patient-doctor relationship, it is very important that a patient continues to believe in their own recovery and to have faith in his doctor. There is statistical evidence that a patient's attitude towards his illness, his strength of will – that is, his neuroimmune system – is a very important factor in recovery. Therefore, it is vital that if a patient so desires, a priest, rabbi or psychologist will visit him in the hospital, so he can feel that he is not left to his own devices, and thus, recovery is possible. Professor Michael Balint, a Hungarian psychoanalyst who lived in England, considered the relationship between doctor and patient to be of key importance to the patient's successful treatment (cf. Michael Balint: The Doctor, His Patient and The Illness, 1957).

JS: It is worth knowing that in those days we were banned from visiting hospitals. There were few of us, so I got the better of them and went in official visiting hours. The professors I talked to, like Professor Hámori, for example, all said I shouldn't pay attention to this nonsense, because what I do is good for the patients. Let's say they never said so *ex officio*, but they were very glad if we went.

SS: So it is not clear for everyone where faith ends and where credulity begins.

PE: I think we have reached another crucial question. According to our Catholic convictions, but in the eyes of most religions, faith has an objective truth content. While on the one hand our church is a full believer in freedom of worship, and ever since the Second Vatican Council settled this in a declaration (*Declaratio Dignitatis humanae*), I think this has become even deeper in Catholic thinking, this does not mean that for us 'it does not matter who believes in what, or that all that matters is that they honestly think what they think'.

Rather, there can be content that is objectively true or false, from the trustful acceptance of reality through to a credulity that is threatening to our very selves. Many phenomena can occur. We respect someone's right to choose, or their freedom to think about religious affairs, because of their personal dignity, but we do not do this because we think there is no objective truth content here, but because we think that personal human dignity demands, in particular in matters of faith, that everyone freely choose their own convictions. Outside force should not influence them in this. I think that if we take this attitude on board then we can look for objective criteria with which to distinguish superstition and more realistic or more comprehensive faith.

There is another thing people easily forget, namely that religion generally covers the entirety of life, and offers an organic view of the world. Old lexicons told us so rather nicely. They do not merely offer ideas, suppositions or convictions to fit one or two particular situations; rather, they are comprehensive. If, for example, I only believe that there are three old statue fragments in the stone fence around the external wall of the primate's palace in Esztergom, stone heads which will heal me if I put my hand on them, if this is all I believe, then this is not a religion. This is a typical example of a belief being associated with something, and which can be examined to see if it has a foundation or not; if someone claims it offers physical healing then, God forbid, it can be subjected to scientific investigation, but this is not in and of itself a religion. In the context of the freedom of worship, what creates a bridge between the search for objective truth and the freedom and variety of religious faith? If I say that one must respect the dignity of the individual in this regard, that they must be free to choose, and I also say that there are objective truths in this area, that these are possible, then what guarantee is there that people will choose these, and not base their convictions on something false, highly inhuman and very destructive? This is why it is important for them to glean true knowledge of the world around them. The First Vatican Council placed particular emphasis on teaching that even the existence of God, what of God is invisible and never-ending and divine, can be recognized with human reason on the basis of created things on (Cf. Rom 1:20; First Vatican Council, Const. Dei Filius, 2; Denzinger-Hünermann, no. 3004).

This respect for human reason, this respect for natural human common sense, is what connects freedom with objective truth, even on religious matters.

ESV: Not so long ago, we visited Padua, and inside the Basilica, there was a queue by Saint Anthony's tomb. I looked at the people there. All of them touched the side of the tomb, and it was obvious that they all believed. They believed their problems would be solved, they believed they would be healed. To this, as a natural scientist – in particular, one who addresses the nervous system and the working of the brain – I can precisely connect the results of medicine and natural science. The psychological state is a characteristic of human beings that has a tremendous influence on the condition of our nervous system and, through our nervous system, on our immune system. It matters a great deal whether it releases one type of the so-called inner endogenous materials, one type of the cytokines, or blocks its releases, or it releases another type. One type, for example, increases the reproduction of cells. In other words, it helps cancer. The other restricts it. The effect of faith, of the fact of faith, which can be objective, influences the immune system, and thereby the patient, his illness, and his recovery from that illness. I will give an example. The level of stress and frustration present in society, whatever its origin, be it at the workplace or at home, this constant stress has the effect of blocking the release of those types of cytokines that would restrict the growth of cancerous cells. This blockage could cause a greater risk of developing cancer. So, there is now a scientific explanation that connects the two things.

SS: We experience the positive effects of faith. But do they differ from the inner psychological processes of the credulous person? Is there a difference, and if so, what is it?

ESV: Believer, credulous… I pay great heed to Cardinal Erdő's explanation that there is no objective foundation for credulity. They make someone believe something when there is no such connection, as in the example I just described.

SS: That's one side to it. The other side is the creative potential there inside people, what they think, fantasize, clutch at, all that works to some degree with creative power. There is a great trend nowadays in turning to all kinds of bracelets, crystals and other items in the hope of their healing powers, for example. On the one hand there is no concrete basis for these things; on the other hand, this kind of 'credulous faith' could set in motion some kind of psychological transformation.

ESV: Yes, because people look for something out of ultimate desperation. I could provide a list of examples, of world-famous professors in the last days and weeks of their lives turning to all kinds of things. A believer knows from the outset, *eo ipso*, who and where to turn. Credulous people do not have this type of certainty. Anyone in the house who says something, that they know some magic cure, will be believed. This is the difference between the two. One of them knows where to turn, whereas the other…

SS: Turns to a placebo.

ESV: Not so much to a placebo as to anything that is offered to them.

JS: May I take the discussion in a different direction? So far we have talked about well-intentioned things. Well-intentioned in faith, or well-intentioned in credulity. In the twentieth century we saw that it was possible to fire people up to be excited about and convinced of doing entirely wild things. It was possible to make people believe that Hitler would be the great liberator of the German people, while he was in fact a mass murderer. It was possible to make people believe that Stalin was the good father of the nation, while in fact he sent masses of his citizens to their deaths. How could this duality happen? Either everyone was lying, and only clapped because they had to clap, or else they really did believe in these absurd things. This is the second question here.

SS: That's right. The case of faith and credulity if someone lives their life with good intentions or bad intentions. The two types of attitude may have similar consequences, but they are not the same. When does credulity become destructive, and when does a person's credulity turn against them?

ESV: If we have gotten this far, then I would continue this train of thought and raise the issue of individual responsibility when one is alone and when one is in a crowd. Psychologically, this is a very difficult question. It has been hardly fifty years since everyone clapped together rhythmically… In a crowd, one does not feel that he is responsible for anything, whereas inside the individual, there is a sense of responsibility. In the majority, everyone leaves the criticism of thoughts and actions to someone else. This is what Stalin exploited, as did Hitler: that a crowd can be fanaticized. It is possible to rob a person in a crowd of their moral behavior. The person in a crowd thinks that individual responsibility is spread among the others. I agree with those who say that everything has its unit of measure, and this includes ethics, and everyone gets as much as everyone else. Fanaticizing leaders are dangerous because they spread this unit of ethics, whether among ten thousand people or a hundred thousand.

JS: I would like to quote an old favourite of mine from twentieth-century Hungarian master of the grotesque, István Örkény. He writes that once upon a time writers were required to go and meet the people. Once, on Saint Stephen's day, the national Hungarian celebration of the first constitution on August 20, he went to Sztálinváros [Stalin Town], now Dunapentele, where he was welcomed by the local party secretary. Comrade Örkény this, Comrade Örkény that, as the official showed the writer round the local points of interest. Oil will flow out of this tap, hot water out of that tap, and this out of the other tap. Then he invited Örkény to a coffee, where he said, 'Comrade Örkény, your face is very familiar, and I'll tell you where from: the Österreicher Pharmacy'. Örkény told him that pharmacist was his father. And the party secretary replied: 'You know, Mr Österreicher, like hell is any of that stuff going to flow as I told you it would.' Emotionally this is a precise depiction of the difference between the behaviour of the person in the crowd and the individual.

PE: The topic of faith and credulity reminds me of the section in the New Testament in which Jesus is tempted by Satan. Satan takes him up to the pinnacle of the temple and says, 'if thou be the Son of God, cast thyself down' (Matt 4:6). As it is written in Psalm 91, says Satan, that 'He shall give his angels charge concerning thee: and in their hands they shall bear thee up, lest at any time thou dash thy foot against a stone' (Ps 91:12). But Jesus replied to him, 'It is written again, Thou shalt not tempt the LORD thy God' (Matt 4:7; cf. Acts 6:16). So it seems that there is no foundation in the Judeo-Christian tradition for one to believe in amazing natural phenomena just as they see fit, and according to their own need, and to be free to do so at will. We are not dealing with magic; we are looking for God's will. Again I will return to tradition, which on this question gives us a kind of objective orientation, and which has stood the test of time, too. Thus anyone who has followed the concept of the faith, who has followed the religious conviction of this community, has not fallen from the pinnacle of the temple, but rather has found an Ariadne's thread by which to lead their life, which, if you like, has been proven right at some kind of social level. Otherwise it is interesting that according to Gregory of Nazianzus the tempter did not continue the quotation from the psalms because he did not dare to do so. He was frightened by the lines that follow, which include 'Thou shalt tread upon the lion and adder: the young lion and the dragon shalt thou trample under feet' (Ps 91:13; cf: S. Gregorius Nazianz. Homil. 40, 10: PG 36, 370–371). It is as if these lines hint at the tempter's failure in advance. I think that in Jesus' reply, 'Thou shalt not tempt the LORD thy God' (Deut.6:16), which again is a quotation from the Old Testament, there lies the believer's response to superstition.

JS: Magic is something denounced and banned in the Scriptures. It is not possible to mention magic and religious behaviour in the same breath.

SS: This is exactly the subject I wanted to mention. If we look around, the world is full of such returning old phenomena, which strangely are nonetheless called New Age: we can encounter esotery, gnostic things and this kind of thing, and sometimes it is wrapped up in a package which says that God gave us medicine in all kinds of grass and trees, and so has allowed us to dream up these abilities so we can fulfil our potential. My question is: from the perspective of faith and religion, what is everyone's opinion of this rich variety of esoteric phenomena appearing as a kind of substitute for religion?

JS: I don't know these things; I have never come across them. At best I could say something about the Gnosticism of Antiquity, but nothing of its modern version, so I'd rather take a pass on the question.

ESV: Let me return to the previous thought: the only thing in my mind is what I sense. Modern science tells us that I believe what I see – that is, objective facts need evidence. According to the American historian of science Thomas Kuhn, science occasionally experiences a paradigm shift, but delusions can appear at any time. Science is able to prove its claims; parascience can only make claims. John Maddox, a former editor of *Nature*, writes in his excellent book that progress in science is always the product of a battle between claims and counterclaims (John Maddox: What Remains to be Discovered, 1999).

PE: As it happens, medicine really is there in all kinds of grass and trees, of course it is there, but that does not excuse us from the work in hand. What does the pharmaceutical industry make medicines out of if not ingredients found in nature? But here is where we see man's responsibility we were just talking about. The Creator doesn't want to help us in some magical way; rather, he granted us reason with which to study the world around us, and to use this to look for and find solutions to our problems. This is an even greater responsibility for a believer, as it emphasizes the human behaviour that we cannot expect miracles from God just for our benefit. Thou shalt not tempt the Lord thy God: the solution does not fall into our lap without effort on our part, because God wants to help only through the use of his people. And the chief commandment for love of God and man, which Jesus himself mentions as the first and most important commandment, as well as the second, which is similar (Matt 22:37-39; Deut. 6:5; Lev 19:18), show that we should express our love for God with our love for our fellow human beings, and that God wants to love us through our fellow human beings, too. Our religious faith does not relieve us of our complete personal responsibility or of the toil that life represents.

ESV: The two main commandments are clear: our love and respect for God and for our neighbors. This also means, for the believer, that he has an obligation. We are constantly discussing the responsibility of the individual, and I think this is the great challenge of the twenty-first century, an age in which globalization and the tendency towards the universal, uniformization, the dictatorship of taste – the arrival of the taste tsunami, as I tend to call it. Just look at movies, TV programs and the latest directions in literature. All these things try to force upon us a certain type of lifestyle. For today, 'everything is uniform'. They want to lessen individual responsibility, and this can lead to the loss of morality.

JS: I would like to reflect on what Cardinal Erdő said about loving thy neighbour. We know that this is Leviticus chapter 19, which begins, 'Ye shall be holy: for I the LORD your God am holy'. This is a difficult exegetical problem for us, because let's compare it with Isaiah chapter 6, Isaiah's first vision, in which God takes us up to his celestial throne room, where we see the seraphims floating all around the divine throne, and then he says the Sanctus. (The prophet comes later than Moses.) The prophet says that God is holy, while Moses demands that we be saints. This is something that looks like a contradiction, which the Jewish exegesis resolves by stating that holiness is an ideal. As an ideal, it involves that which cannot be realized. We come forever closer to it, but we can never reach it. But the following sentences show how we can approach this ideal, and here we can read that you should love your neighbour as yourself. This is such a serious demand that it cannot be made universal; in the Hebrew text, if we translate *kamocha* precisely, it means love your neighbour because he is just like you. And this essentially means that he has flaws, but so do you, so it is not about self-sacrifice, but it does imply the tolerance that is necessary for people to be able to live together. Yet this is a different kind of love from that which we owe God. According to the Jewish exegesis, this means all the moral characteristics which appear with the prophets, for example Hosea – fairness, justice, love, and mercy – exist in God at a maximal level unattainable by man, as they are ideals, but people must strive towards this, and this can be realized by loving another person with the same faults as one has. For us, one group of people are described as holy: those who suffer martyrdom for their religion. They say of even the most religious and exemplary of rabbis: *tzadik*, someone who is righteous. Holy is said of someone killed for being Jewish.

ESV: Let me make an analogy, even if a slightly forced one. Both these major religions are about the relationship between the individual and the community and that between individuals. Science and scholarship always build on the brilliant discovery or world of thought of some given individual who wants to share the discovery with others, which is why that individual publishes it. For example, it is no accident that Erasmus of Rotterdam, who wanted Europe to be united, recommended that Europe's language be Latin and that it be directed by academics – this would have been a big mistake, of course – and that they should establish contact with one another not just through correspondence, but in person, and share their knowledge with one another because then scholarship and the contents of knowledge would develop more quickly. For us, it is also natural that if I recognize or discover something, then I will share that with others. In natural science, this is taken for granted, and it is in the fire of debates that we crystallize not the complete truth, but the greater discovery. This is also the basis for the progress of today's science, that each idea is subjected to criticism. At first, everyone is in a minority – that I am the only one to think this way – then, more and more people join me, until finally, the whole of scientific society accepts it. Thus, scholars seek truth and try to act together with others, ideally striving for perfection. They try to avoid a bad or erroneous solution: indeed, they dispute it.

PE: Coming close to the truth and to holiness and the idealistic nature of this contain a very interesting tension, which appears clearly in Jesus' teachings, in a way that I would call almost paradoxical. On the one hand he says you should be perfect, just as your Father in Heaven is perfect (Matt 5:48). It is obvious that we cannot reach God's perfection, so what is he trying to say with this? His figurative speech helps us through this difficulty, happily, as he himself says that the Lord 'maketh his sun to rise on the evil and on the good, and sendeth rain on the just and on the unjust' (Matt 5:45). The tolerance we heard about in Chief Rabbi Schweitzer's explanation is Jesus' commandment, too: that we should learn to live with each other, and follow the example of the Creator, who turns to us in his infinite goodness. Of course we cannot say that we can become equal to him, as even Jesus responds, when someone calls him 'Good Master!': 'Why callest thou me good? There is none good but one, that is, God' (Mark 10:17-18). This tension is wonderfully present in Jesus' teachings, and Judeo-Christian moral values really do include an obligation to work towards an ideal. He is a realist. He knows that we are not perfect, and that on this Earth perfect beings do not exist, but I think that Pope John Paul II gave a perfect description of the resolution to this tension: how can I be obliged to follow something I cannot reach? Pope John Paul II said the key is God's mercy, which illuminates this situation (Pope John Paul II, Enc. Dives in misericordia, 1980. XI. 30, no. 89–91). We are obliged to strive for perfection, we are unworthy, but God is merciful. So human imperfection is not a design fault or dysfunction, it is not a material deficit; rather, it is something which belongs to the personal relationship between man and God. It can be improved, there is space for improvement, for forgiveness; this is what today's public opinion struggles to accept, or else it denies the problem, saying things are fine as they are, or else it rejects flawed action, together with the person who acts in a flawed way, perhaps together with a whole community, branding them as having come off the right path.

ESV: If we were all perfect from a biological and medicinal point of view – that is, if our genetic make-up were completely uniform, if there were not even the minutest differences between us, if we all thought in exactly the same way – the world would never develop. Complete uniformity is an obstacle to progress. I would express this by saying that if the differences were generated by errors entering the biological systems or growing with historical development, or by errors that were present at the outset, then they are at once the motors of progress.

PE: Let me reflect a little more on the concept of holiness and the holiness of human life, which Chief Rabbi Schweitzer so clearly showed in the Jewish case primarily means martyrdom. In the history of the Christian church it originally referred exclusively to martyrdom, but later there appeared alongside the martyrs the ascetics, virgins and confessors, who suffered for their faith, but were not killed for it. They formed the newer types of saints. Yet to this day we have never in the global church formally named a living person a saint. The canonization process can only begin if the individual in question has been dead for at least five years. There was recently an exception to this, when after the death of Pope John Paul II his successor bowed to public pressure and allowed the inquiry procedure for beatification to begin at once, and not wait five years for this. This also shows how a person's life, while we are still here on Earth, is not complete, not even in a moral sense. None of us is perfect, but there is an ideal we have to follow, and there are people who we look to as examples, after their death.

ESV: Let me add to both of your ways of thinking – which, as it happens, I agree with – because there has been a need over history for us to set examples. Why? Because we are not identical, because this error, this difference, is genetically inside us in every respect, as well as the erroneous engrams acquired in our upbringing, the erroneous social reflexes, the erroneous individual thoughts. This is why upbringing is so important. There is a need for role models. The secularized world has created beat singers, excellent athletes, and brilliant artists. Nations need role models whose prestige is cared for. Why? Because we are all different. We all have this error inside us, in ethical terms, too. A healthy sense of the nation is important for the community.

SS: Otherness… The topic of martyrdom reminds me that when the persecution of Christians came to an end, it was a real problem to work out how someone would now become a saint. They started to ponder the notion of everyday martyrdom: everyday very tough ascesis, dying for the ego, dying for oneself…

PE: There were even those who provoked persecution just so they could be martyrs, even though there was no pressure!

ESV: Did the flagellants in the fourteenth century – whose name comes from *flagellare*, 'to whip' – do it specifically to become saints?

PE: As an act of attrition and penance.

PLK: I would like to raise an everyday question: which poses the greater danger for people today – a lack of faith or a lack of religion?

PE: I think the two things are related. We have tried to connect the two phenomena, to show the organic bond between them in Judeo-Christian thinking. I would not put the two at odds here, either. I would say, of course look at the subjective side of this, looking at the individual, that we have need of faith. But this faith does not develop in us in some special or accidental fashion; rather, it is born of social mediation together with our concepts and with our lifestyles, even if we end up with an individual perception of life. In other words: both as individuals and as a society, we need faith, but we also need religion. This does not mean that a society is only healthy if it has a single religion, and with this I return to what was said about freedom of worship. So I think there is a need for both, for faith and for religion.

SS: The question is whether a lack of faith or a lack of religion is the bigger danger. This is connected to the question that believers, if they look around in the world today, might put to themselves: if faith is such a treasure, if people need it so much, then why, especially in Europe and North America, is there such strong alienation from religion nowadays?

ESV: Although a basic genetic and biological structure can be inherited by one human being from another, this is not true of knowledge and morality. These must be taught and learned from one generation to the next, from father to son, from mother to daughter. Here, I am referring to the responsibility of the literate, of the churches, of the state because they forget that there is a need in society for certain norms in which to raise each generation from birth. Missing this can have serious consequences. In a secularized world – and in a Europe 'slipping towards anarchy' – and as the result of overblown permissiveness and overblown liberalism, a very significant antisecular movement has also come into being, forgetting the fact that, thanks to its past and history over many thousands of years – alongside all that it is responsible for – religion can be a great help to people. It seems that the equation for the twenty-first century is the following: knowledge + information = power. However, this leaves out an important factor – namely, morality. The role of the various religions can be enormous in the presentation of knowledge that can only be passed on with upbringing. This knowledge is the relationship of human beings to each other and to nature – that is, morality. Europe leads the way in the neglect of religion, of morality. I would not put North America directly in the same category. There are followers of this tendency in North America, but four-fifths of that country are members of some religion, some are strongly puritanical, and satisfy certain moral norms with great consistency.

PE: I would like to reflect on what Professor Vizi said about diversity. About the way we are genetically diverse, that there are as many types of people as there are people. We are individuals. We can approach ideal perfection in a number of ways, and so we need a variety of role-models. In the Catholic Church and the Orthodox Church this is expressed by a respect for the Saints – indeed, in these two churches, by a respect for images. Now, in 2006, when Pope Benedict XVI officially published the Compendium of the Catechism of the Catholic Church, and in it icons and images of saints, and in every edition, every translation, it is obligatory to include those same images in the same places. The first image, as a leading image, is an icon of Jesus Christ, and the theology of this icon is very important for us, too. Of course we do not adore the icon of Jesus Christ, it is God we adore, but our veneration for the icon of Jesus Christ is addressed to the person of Jesus and through him to God himself. At the same time we see in the saints that the ideal of Christ's life wants to materialize in a million situations and a million eras in history, always in different, individual ways. In other words, one feature of the Christ icon is exposed by each of them, and so the images of the saints must not be adored, but do deserve a certain veneration. I think that this is all a visual representation of the thought that, in its summary nature and its completeness, human perfection involves the presence of Christ; we strive towards it, and as a whole humanity can achieve something of it, but even this it does not do perfectly. The common ideal has many faces, and this also demands that we be patient, and look in another's visage for the features of that one icon. As Saint Paul so beautifully puts it in his ode to love in the first Epistle to the Corinthians: 'Charity suffereth long, and is kind' (1Cor 13:4). In reality it is hard to be patient and to notice these features and these values, but there really is a need for this.

SS: It is also an interesting question to ask what the trend is in spiritualism. Usually spiritualism puts faith and religion in brackets: 'Oh no, not faith or religion, but spiritualism, oh yes'.

JS: What do you mean by anticlerical spirituality?

SS: Discussion of spiritual matters which does not involve responsibility or obligation. For which human community, society, a sense of calling, and work, are not important. Which chooses according to its own whim between various faiths, religions, and which interprets and uses that which it has gathered together, separated from its sources, to satisfy its momentary need.

PE: In practice, the transformation of religious life into a commercial good. I think this is similar to the commercialization of other things, and let me put it quite bluntly and say that Rostovtzeff was right (Mikhail Ivanovich Rostovtzeff, Russian ancient historian, 1870-1952) that this is how the Roman Empire fell (The Social and Economic History of the Roman Empire, Second edition, Oxford, 1957). He looked not only at literary memory but at the culture of artefacts, too, and said that when, at a certain stage of economic development, certain practical objects became available to everyone, the quality of these decreased to such a degree that this mass demand for raw materials exploited natural resources so much that in the end this led to the collapse of the Empire. I would only mention this as an analogy for one side of the general human condition, and I think that in a great number of areas of life, from clean and healthy food produce through to clean and healthy artistic endeavour, that in many areas we can observe that something is made accessible to the masses, but not of the same quality as before. We know that however much photographic techniques improve, it is quite a different thing to go through the Uffizi at different times of the day and to see the paintings, from holding a catalogue containing reproductions of them. Just as it is different if I listen to a concert or watch a play by electronic means from participating in the live audience. What used to be the only opportunity in cultural forms, has become rare, aristocratic and great.Applying all of this to religion, I think that very seriously religious people can have experiences, if we consider spiritualism to be when we undergo as an experience our condition according to our religion or our personal connection to God. If this is so, this is a wonderful thing; I think that every theist religion has such a tradition. But if my understanding of it is that I feel fine at this moment, then I remain very superficial. If under the influence of some visual, musical or other experience, and perhaps dealing with some thought or other, but all this does not become some kind of coherent conviction, particularly not some communal conviction, then I have not obliged myself to this thing, and most of all I make no effort to deduce the consequences of this for my life, then my momentary emotional experiences can be very superficial, but I do not acquire all that is granted to someone by the real spirituality experienced within the framework of a religion. We are talking about it turning into a consumable thing.

ESV: Let me add the thought of a very good friend of mine, István Kovács, whom we called 'Doc'. Although, sadly, he is no longer with us, we were students together. He was the priest of a little parish, and he said that a priest represents a bridge between the individual and the Good Lord, but if I remove the priest's role, if I remove the individual's connection with God, then I consumerize it and make it such that it loses its most important element: the system of intimate relationships. This is how he always thought of the priest's calling, as mediation. The priest presents that which would otherwise be very hard to present. I also feel that the world's technological progress introduces many new techniques that can be applied in natural fashion. However, if this results in the loss of the individual's direct personal relationships, then there is a problem. Today, this is characteristic of the whole world.

JS: The rabbi's calling can at most be to show the means or the way to establish a connection with the Almighty. This connection can in some cases be really very relaxed. There are those who on the Day of Atonement drop in their business cards like a well-behaved guest and then don't even glance in the temple's direction for the next year. If someone says that we can be God's children wherever we are, they are right. We can pray to God anywhere. But if you want to be a child of Israel, all the while as a child of God, then you need the community. For us, community has great power, because it is one thing on the Day of Atonement for me to mutter a prayer of contrition on my own, and quite another if five hundred people say it together. The spiritual effect is different. We cannot entirely separate faith from institutionalized faith. The two are in alliance with one another. It is in a community that faith is fully realized.

ESV: In the Confiteor Deo, I confess my sins to my spiritual father so he may transfer the confession and attrition to God. The greatest mistake in public life is that we do not confess our sins, we do not accept our mistakes, perhaps our lies, and thus any possibility for forgiveness is lost.

JS: Professor Heller is someone who if he makes his big public confession then of ninety-nice per cent of it we say to ourselves, 'Thank God I didn't do that'. There are very few people like that, but Heller was one of them. He not only taught the Bible at the Rabbinical Seminary, he lived it. We make confession in the name of the community, too.

ESV: How much harder it is for Catholics, as we have to do it for ourselves…

JS: Jews have faced so much adversity already: the Catholics can face just a little…

PE: I think that Christianity also places great emphasis on the communal aspect of religion. Jesus says that 'where two or three are gathered together in my name, there am I in the midst of them' (Matt 18:20).

JS: This is a rabbinical example, because, for example, there are prayers to be said after eating where a longer prayer can be said if there are three people than if one is alone. The smallest unit which Jesus refers to, as I remember – alas I didn't learn the Strack-Billerbeck (an enormous series of commentaries on the New Testament on the basis of the Talmud and the Midras) for this occasion, though I should have – is three, and this because in Jewish tradition, according to liturgical guidelines, the smallest community is three.

PE: We started talking about how Christianity also places great emphasis on community. This can mean many things; it can mean the liturgical community side of things, or it can mean that when we carry out a liturgy in the name of the church, that is formally, then we claim that it is done by Christ and the whole church (Codex Iuris Canonici, Città del Vaticano 1983, can. 834. Cf. Second Vatican Council, Const. Sacrosanctum Concilium 7c). It is no accident that in the mass we remember the living and the dead. We pray for those who have departed, for those suffering in purgatory, we ask for the intervention of the Saints, because we believe that the Community of Saints, the *communio sanctorum*, comprises the departed, those in a state of suffering, and the members of the valiant and battling church here on Earth. This solidarity appears in various images in the New Testament. Saint Paul uses the ancient analogy of an organ which we know from Roman literature: there is one body, but with many members, and we are all members of Christ's body (1 Cor 12:12-26). This means that one cannot suffer without the other suffering, and that we can pray for one another, indeed we are all called upon to bear witness together as a church. This leads to the question of collective responsibility. Of course, we do not accept collective responsibility: everyone is responsible for their own actions. At the same time the church, as a community, bears witness, and every mistake and misdeed of every individual curtails this community testimony. So an apology to God for all our sins – in other words, atonement – is also part of our tradition. I think that these very powerful central thoughts in our religious conception are historically connected to what we have just heard.

SS: It is a very interesting issue that our faith does not apply to anything or anyone, but to God the Creator. What does God the Creator mean? What does Creation itself mean?

JS: What Genesis does is state a fact. It does not explain it. An explanation is more to be found in medieval scholarship, and our greatest medieval thinker, Moses Maimonides, has thirteen different branches of faith. These include the belief in the Creator.

SS: It is there at the very start of the Bible, at the start of Genesis!

JS: Yes, but it doesn't explain it, it just states it!

ESV: This is an enormous problem for science, as it is very hard to give an explanation for what is written in Genesis. Something comes from nothing. 'In the beginning God created the heaven and the earth' (Gen 1:1). If there was a beginning, there has to be an end, too. But what is that end? These are questions on which science has not yet been able to take a position, and there are huge debates. I am convinced that, for example, infinity is ungraspable to the human brain. We are unable to process the notion of infinity. Science uses exact measurements, and these measurements and systems of methods cannot be used to explain infinity. These are the areas in which scientists become uncertain; they lose their stable footing from which they claim that they can explain everything. They cannot. The infinite series of numbers, or the beginning. When is the beginning? And what came before it? The statements in Genesis, as Chief Rabbi Schweitzer said, only state what happened and give no explanation for it. We try to find an explanation, but do not have one yet.

PE: I think this is the point where our faith contains a very important starting point, as our creed begins: I believe in God, the Father, the Almighty, Maker of heaven and earth'. So the Christian form of monotheism and Creation are closely related things. What it says about the world refers to the world after the Creation. Years ago, the question of transcendence and natural science concerned Christian theological thinking differently from how it does today. Unlike what we see in the tabloid press, we, Catholic theologians are not particularly bothered by question of evolution. Long ago, back in the 1960s at Piarist high school, I was taught that the books of Scripture should be read as being in their own genre, and that they should be examined for their theological message, not used as a source for acquiring natural scientific knowledge. So we were not scared of natural scientific knowledge, but neither did we think that we had to explain to natural science what the results of its investigations should be. Forty or thirty-five years ago, as I say, our attitude was, almost instinctively, that for us this is in point of fact indifferent; relative to this the public mood has changed somewhat, because there is now greater theological interest in new scientific discoveries. In its own immanent system, science is not able to give an answer about Creation itself, or the things that came before Creation, or about the existence or lack of it of a transcendent reality. It cannot prove it or disprove it. At least, that is our understanding. So a conviction in a transcendent God, especially his personal aspects, his goodness and his relationship to the world, is the subject of religious faith, or a non-religious but faith-like conviction, but not one of natural science. In this sense we are not surprised that amongst scientists we find both believers and non-believers.

As regards Creation: we have to establish some kind of image of the world in order to live. In this construction of an image or this acquaintance with the world, in this process of learning to live in the world, we have to interpret and evaluate things. Both interpretation and evaluation are activities in which we bring one thing into connection or a relationship with another. It is through this relation that I interpret things, and it is through a relation that I mark their value. If I am looking for the meaning and value of the universe, then I am forced either to say that it has meaning and value, but I cannot establish what those are, or else, as a religious believer, I can say that there is a transcendent reality which, relative to the whole world, is the Other, the One, and that it is the relationship with the One which gives our whole created world its meaning and its value. Now, I think the most beautiful expression of this conviction is the belief in the Creator, which also means for us, that is for Judeo-Christian thinking, that the world has a purpose. So God did not create the world meaninglessly and without reason and an objective; rather, he did so out of love. As we read in the story of Creation: 'Let us make man in our image, after our likeness: and let them have dominion [...] over all the earth' (Gen 1:26). So the universe has a goal, our history has an objective, as does our individual existence, and for us it is the faith in Creation which lays the foundation for this.

JS: On the created world itself, we are more likely to find places in the Hebrew Scriptures, of course depending on author, age and attitude. If we look at Deutero-Isaiah, who argues with Persian dualism, then at odds with Persian dualism is *yotzer ohr*, God who creates the light, *boreh choshech*, who creates the darkness, *ose shalom*, creates peace, *u'boreh ra*, who creates evil. What's interesting in this? Centuries later the basic meaning of this text is that the Persians, with their dual belief in Ahriman and Ormuzd, are wrong. Good and evil come from God. In the age of Jesus, by which time there is an established liturgy, the authors who created the liturgy and those using Biblical texts regard it as blasphemous to say of God that he creates evil! So where in Deutero-Isaiah it reads 'created evil', in the prayer book it reads 'created all'. This is the same as in medieval Jewish philosophy: there is no bad, only a lack of good. The medieval philosopher cannot accept that God could create bad.

ESV: What does science say? It says that 13-16 billion years ago – that is, it cannot determine the time of the creation of the world more precisely, as there are enormous discrepancies – there was the 'Big Bang' and that ever since then the Universe has been expanding. How far can it expand? To infinity? And what does infinite mean? These are questions to which science is incapable of giving an answer at present, and so here faith comes in again. I think that nothingness or infinite smallness – quantum mechanics, the newest results of physics, approach nothingness – and the other extreme, the distance between the two, is a problem that is presently unsolvable for science, and I think this will remain the case forever. That is, as I mentioned before, our brains, made up of three hundred billion nerve cells and displaying incredible precision and abilities, are incapable of grasping this rationally. I could also add the longevity of mankind as a species – how long people have existed. In Genesis, we read that creation took place according to species. This does not mean the rejection of evolution, nor does it mean that it all started from one thing, as we change genetically during our development. For us, it is a huge and shocking recognition that we observe very similar mechanisms in the world of flora and in primitive living creatures as in human beings. The genome of a fruit-fly is half that of a human being, and yet consider how many things humans are capable of!

SS: To return to creation and creation out of nothing, one can also experience at a theoretical and practical level that what one wasn't capable of earlier, one is capable of now. What one didn't see an opportunity for before, one does see an opportunity for now. What didn't exist needed to be created. Human beings are able to do more and more with less and less raw material, and can continue down this road. As a theoretical question, God creates from his own self, as there is no such thing as nothing, so God makes the world out of himself. And here we see the importance of a Creator God, as if human beings are in the Creator's image then in some way they also have this ability to create something that doesn't yet exist from within themselves…

PE: Allow me to comment on the expression 'God makes the world out of himself'. Of course we cannot mean by this, at least not in a Catholic context, that the world is some kind of emanation from God. That the world be made up of his own essence, his own material, as this would make us pantheists. We draw an important dividing line between the whole of the created world and a transcendent God. When we in Catholic theology acknowledge a creation from nothing (2Macc 7:28; First Vatican Council, Const. Dei Filius, no. 1; Can. 1-5: Denzinger-Hünermann no. 3001-3002, 3021-3025), we accept the exposition in the wisdom literature of the Old Testament that God made the world of matter (Wis 11:17) in some way. But as to where this material came from: in our faith, it came from nothing. That is: 'And God said, Let there be […] and there was' (Gen 1:3 etc.). This is a very ancient form of expression of the creation from nothing. In line with the laws of this world we can deduce a Big Bang, but what was there before the Big Bang?! Perhaps later and with other techniques it will be possible to deduce something, but it appears that we really are at the boundaries of the human brain's ability to grasp things, and at the boundaries of its potential. We are not able to use the methods of natural science to go back infinitely beyond or outside the current universe. And it is to this fact that our faith in Creation refers.

ESV: Can I play devil's advocate here? Is it not the point that the human brain and the system of techniques for learning is limited in regard to answering questions such as those of creation and the end, and so human beings invented God as a means to an end, according to Maimonides the Prime Mover, to somehow resolve what for them was unknowable or unsolvable? In his book *Mein Weltbild*, Einstein writes of the perfection of nature that 'the harmony of natural law, which reveals an intelligence of such superiority that, compared with it, all the systematic thinking and acting of human beings is an utterly insignificant reflection' (Albert Einstein: Mein Weltbild, 1931).

SS: Asks the scientist of the theologians…

PE: I don't think that science is able, within its own area of competence, to give an answer to this question. And if human science leaves this question open, then from this point on there follows the world of images, and we have to take up a position on the basis of some authority and applying all our decision-making powers, and to find an answer, or else we have to decide not to bother with it. I think that religious faith contains very basic and deep human traditions which contain answers to this gigantically large human problem that is unsolvable using its own strengths.

PLK: So there are questions which can only be answered by faith?

PE: Of course.

PLK: And is that where science ends?

PE: Of course.

SS: And science does not just come to an end before getting to certain questions; it is not competent on them anywhere. It is not its area.

JS: '*Primus Motor*' is in reality *Primus movens*.

ESV: There is an explanation for how in ancient philosophy and later on, until we reach Newton, then Einstein and Heisenberg, there was a need, for example, when I say that something has a beginning, I accept the temporal start to the world (that is, that it was created), then that is a static state. Movement follows from this because movement is required for life, for progress, for everything. This is what Newton wanted to explain: in all three of his laws of motion, he relies in part on the original concepts of ancient philosophy. This is a beautiful aspect of the development of science, and in retrospect, when it is covered in textbooks, this developmental history is not mentioned. In addition, faith played a very important role in this, namely, that one believed what another stated or thought. Copernicus, Galileo: this is there in the whole developmental history of science. I was telling of the former Soviet, Georgian and Armenian astrologists who confronted the 'horrors' of the unknowable nature of the universe until they realized that something has to be in operation that set this whole enormous, perfect – we have not used the word 'perfect' yet – mechanism in motion.

PLK: Professor Vizi, is it not possible that it is faith and science that are on the two sides of Gödel's axiom (viz. that a statement can simultaneously be true and false)?

ESV: Faith has always played a role in the development of science and in scientific activity. Many deny this, but I must have faith that I want to recognize something that will move me forward, that is different, and faith plays a large role in this. Faith is significant in everyone's life, even in those who claim that they do not believe in anything. This a general human characteristic in all of us.

PLK: So science presupposes faith?

ESV: Each of us presupposes faith; faith is there in everyone. Without it, we cannot do anything. It may be that someone is not aware of this, most of us certainly are not, as elemental reflexes operate in our world of thought and in our actions, such that we do not even notice that faith is there in everyone.

PE: A propos the concept of the unmoved mover, I would like to mention that this is one of Saint Thomas Aquinas' five arguments for the existence of God (St. Thomas Aquinas, Summa theologica, I q. 2 a. 3), and that this displays the influence on him of Aristotelian heritage. Nowadays it would be worth thinking about this again: even from such phenomena of the created world as movement, we can reach the boundary of our possibilities for acquiring knowledge. Though it is true that Christian theology has in recent decades moved away or back to a different area in this regard, as well – perhaps a little disappointed in the issue of the use or problematic nature of science from a religious standpoint – and has instead placed great emphasis on the transcendental argument for the existence of God. We have talked about a knowledge of and search for the reason and value of the world as being a fundamental human characteristic, and in this sense I agree with Professor Vizi that this human search is indeed a great prerequisite for science. But that this need of ours shows that we need something which suits it, well, this is the transcendental argument for the existence of God, which itself affects the world of faith (Wilhelm Breuning, Proofs of the Existence of God, in Wolfgang Beinert, ed., Handbook of Catholic Theology; cf. also Leo Scheffczyk, Der Gott der Offenbarung. Gotteslehre, Aachen 1996, 62–63).

SS: As regards faith and religion I would be glad to address another set of issues which is also, so to speak, here around us: the question of a personal

God. People often feel themselves to be believers in the sense that they believe in some kind of impersonal force, some dualist system of forces, invisible forces. What we believe in is under no circumstances an impersonal force, nor is it a dualist source of that which there is, but rather a personal God: a challenge to all kinds of scientific interpretations of religion which reject this answer.

JS: The traditional Jewish understanding is that God is quite different, but we have no choice, and the Bible itself has no choice but to use human categories to talk about God, so that we may understand. Anthropopathism. God's anger. It is only like this that the Scripture is able to make God and matters of God understandable for us, by using concepts that people can understand. This is why there is mention of the voice of God, the hand of God, and so on. I don't think there is any example of an impersonal concept of God in traditional Jewish theology. I think there can only be talk of a personal God, and according to the Jewish understanding, and what Maimonides says, that God has no physical form, is not a body, is incomprehensible, but again I quote the Talmud: *dibra Torah ki'lshon bnei adam*; the Torah speaks such that a human tongue may understand. God is not a human being, is something entirely different, but the concept cannot be approached except to use notions familiar to human beings.

PE: I think that, similarly to Judaism, the divine Name or names have traditionally proved a problem for Christianity, too. An interesting piece of evidence on this is provided by the work *De divinis nominibus* by Dionysius the Areopagite (Dionysius the Areopagite, Works, London 1897, I, 1-127). The problem of the naming of God and of the expressions and names that may rightly be used with reference to God had as early as Antiquity raised the self-critical question of how much, when we talk of God, we are talking of him in anthropomorphic fashion, and, if so, how much we have a right to do so. This was extended or expressed within the Christian tradition, if sometimes stretching the boundaries of that tradition, by negative theology. That is, what we cannot say about God. Naturally we have to reject all our mundane concepts to some degree when talking of God, as he exceeds them, and yet we cannot talk about God without using these concepts.

JS: The Tetragrammaton is the Divine name which according to punctation we cannot speak out loud, and which is related to the second commandment, 'Thou shalt not take the name of the LORD thy God in vain'. There was one exception: in the sanctuary in Jerusalem, on the Day of Atonement, the high priest in the innermost sanctuary asked for triple atonement, for himself, for the people of his homeland and for the entire congregation of Israel. But the congregation could not go in, and waiting in the temple, the equivalent of the Assyrian *ekalu*, when they heard the high priest saying the Tetragrammaton, everyone threw themselves to the ground. This was a only a privilege for the high priest and for the Day of Atonement, however.

ESV: After the representative of the Old Testament and the New Testament, let me speak as the representative of the modern testament. Of course, I am only saying this in parentheses: I do not intend to lift science to this level. A great many scientists, world-famous ones, address this question. Stanley L. Jaki, Benedictine priest and winner of the Templeton Prize, wrote an excellent book, *Bible and Science*, which summarizes all those scientists who have dealt with the concept and existence of God. Science and academe in general can only address the created world. It cannot address what it cannot measure, observe and experience with classical empirical techniques. It would be judged unscientific were it to do so. However, it is an entirely different perspective if an individual, a scientist, addresses the question out of their own faith or conviction. I think that this is classically the task of theology.

SS: I would mention Michael Polanyi here, and the book he wrote in 1946. A person's psyche strongly determines science. If this is true, and if God is personal, then how much does the personal nature of God puts its stamp on our knowledge of him and on our knowledge that emerges from our relationship with him? Knowledge is personal, not impersonal, even *in extremis* in the case of the most scientific knowledge!

ESV: Michael Polanyi's complete philosophical writings were published in Hungary in two volumes. We should note that he began, as a member of the Galileo Circle, as an atheist. His family was an exceptional one and produced a Nobel Prize winner, too. (This is one reason the Hungarian Academy of Sciences maintains such a good relationship with the Polányi family.) In his works – and there is no doubt about this – Michael Polanyi brings up serious academic counterarguments to positivism and materialism and presents the role of faith and an image of God and the existence of God in academic activities and thought. However, I would like to emphasize that at the present time, it is not possible for the question of God's existence to be made a subject of science. I would say that our system of methods and measurement is not suitable for it. Nor is it a coincidence that modern humanism, on which science had a great influence, if only in strengthening its resolve, had to raise the question that Albert Camus phrased as follows: 'can man be holy without God?'

PE: This is precisely what the question referred to. When scientists ask something, this is always done within their own concepts. This is one of the basic discoveries of hermeneutics. When we ask about God, we also ask within our own concepts. We must be aware of the relativity of our concepts, and the Christian world is traditionally aware of this. I would like to make another comment about the notion of a person. We have talked about the way we often talk and think about God in anthropomorphic fashion. But how do we think about human beings? Where does our Western culture get its notion of the person? This concept was essentially produced by the great theological debates raging from the third to the fifth century, which we now apply to people retrospectively, primarily so that on this basis we can be anthropomorphic again and ask whether someone believes in a personal God or not. For during debates on the Holy Trinity the question would always arise of what it is that is one in God and what it is that is three in him.

Christianity was committed to maintaining the monotheism of Judaism, and yet at the same time it collided into the expressions and situations in the New Testament which partly suggest the divinity of Christ, and partly the divinity of the Holy Spirit. In this set of problems – to which the ultimate solution to this day is that it is a mystery, and not a problem that can be solved with logical explanation – at one point they reached a stage at which they stated that which they had referred to as three, they would now refer to with different names. For example, they called it hypostasis, or persona (cf. e.g. Wilhelm Breuning, Holy Trinity Studies, in Beinert, W: Handbook of Catholic Theology). Writing this down must have had repercussions on our attitude to human beings. Thus to say just how personal the faith in God is among certain peoples outside the Judeo-Christian world is to raise a question that may well be anachronistic. We could also say that, going as far as animism, ethnography finds something everywhere. Even in the religious world of the Chinese or the religious thought of the so-called natural peoples. What goes beyond this is what is related to the Judeo-Christian tradition in the culture of the Western World, that is, as we believe it, what is related to revelation. That is, that we are not just looking for God. Naturally we are not looking for a God whom we could not precisely imagine. We are also talking about how he has revealed himself to us, this is what we term revelation, and it is on the basis of this that we look back to, or try to deduce in retrospect, the source of this message.

ESV: God created man in his own image; meanwhile, man would like to see his own image in God. If you go to Africa, you will see a black God. If you go to China, God is Chinese. If you to Malaysia, he is Malaysian. People would like to see God as themselves. This presumes a two-way connection, and people would like to include themselves in this two-way connection.

SS: This description was there in Ancient Greek philosophy, word for word; the red-haired god of the Thracians, the curly-haired African God, and so on. Yes, perhaps we could say that we talk of God in an anthropomorphic fashion and of people in a theomorphic fashion. We mentioned the *via negativa*, or negative theology, in talking about God. This is just one of three classical ways of talking about God: there is also the *via affirmitiva*, the theology of statements about how God has all the values we have in the world, and the *via eminentiae*, that all the beautiful, good and true things we can say about God should be said such that they have to be perfect in a way we cannot ourselves grasp. Similarity to God's image also belongs here: the whole epistemological question of how we become acquainted with everything through what we have within us, and if God is not within us, if we are not made in his image, then it would be impossible to establish contact with him or become acquainted with him. It is through the God inside us that we get to know the transcendental God, just as we can translate the tradition of Greek philosophy for this subject.

II.

Faith is a Very Personal Matter
In Conversation with Péter Erdő

SS: This boy will become a bishop one day...

PE: Or a capitalist. The only thing he's missing is a cigar in his mouth. My grandfather said that when he saw my childhood photos of us as twins in our little bed.

PLK: Both of those had their precedents: on the one hand a bourgeois family, on the other hand a father who was well respected as an ecclesiastical lawyer...

PE: No, this is more of a family joke. My grandfather wasn't such a devout man as to expect me to become a priest, we can't say that. But it is true that I was a fat-cheeked little boy, and so the comparison was natural. There were many other things; when we were born as twins, we were not exactly identical. My father was in Miskolc at the time, and could not come to Budapest, when my grandfather called him on the telephone with the news: 'Sándor,' he said, 'you have two sons, one red-headed, one black-haired'. The red-headed one was my twin brother; the black-haired one was me. My maternal grandfather was a redhead; his name was András Kis. I don't know of any other redheads in the family; my twin brother went on to be blond, rather than red. His hair retains something of that blondness to this day, and I didn't become that black-haired, either. Obviously I was slightly darker than my brother was.

SS: Then let's talk about faith in the family.

PE: I think that faith is a very personal thing. It is not simply an attitude, a decision, a human action, *actus humanus*; this human action or decision has concrete content. It is not like an emotional state, not like a mood, and so one's will is engaged in the act of faith, so in acceptance there really is a free human decision, too. So there can be a place for human obligation in the area of faith. This includes a great many things, of course; the most important, which many people feel today, but many don't, is that faith is not just a mere impression, but rather it has concrete content. Christian faith has a very special content historically mediated by the whole knowledge of the Church. This is what we call the Christ event, together, as it were, with its theological message. Religious faith is significantly different from human faith in that I accept other people's statements depending on their qualities and professional abilities, while in religious faith it is on the basis of the authority of a revealing God that I believe a certain content or certain teaching. Well, for this it is necessary for the chain of human witness to lead to the certain historical events which announce the revelation. Historicity and historical mediation are very important in all religions based on revelation.

PLK: Here we could stop for a moment to ask how all this develops historically. Let's not stray too far – say until the sensualists. Here we have this certain Locke metaphor about the clean slate. Does faith originate in God, or not?

PE: According to Catholic conviction, there are at least two things which originate in God. The content of faith comes from God, because we believe the message of a revelatory God, the deposit of faith is itself of divine origin; at the same time there is also a merciful effect at work in the act of faith, in the human action of accepting that faith. So faith is mercy, faith is a gift, a divine virtue, and at the same time the expression of a free human action. On both sides, both the objective and the subjective side, there is equally something divine.

PLK: Can personal faith form and develop within someone?

PE: Of course the working of divine mercy within an individual is in part a great secret, and also something dynamic. It is not that there are those who are right and those who are evil, and that they already here on Earth become separate from each other. This would present a static state in which someone stays as they are, whatever they do, once they have wandered to where they are. Rather, someone is responsible for every moment in their life that is spent in a conscious state as a human being. There is no sector of human life, not even science, not even politics, not even many others, which is free of moral responsibility. So in one's every moment of life that is conscious and involves free will, that involves human action, one has a sort of moral responsibility. From here on natural human responsibility has to have a horizon.

Who am I responsible to? To a group, to society? In what way am I responsible? Legally? Morally, in the sense that certain types of behaviour are subject to general rejection? Am I responsible within the boundaries of convention, as a softer system of social norms referring to the area of politeness? If I use the wrong hand to pour wine, will people laugh at me? We claim that more is at stake, especially along the plane of morality, and that this is a social system of norms, which is rooted in human nature, the nature of the world, and as such in the will of the Creator. It is customary, according to our faith, to call this 'natural ethics'. I think that God's laws are also written into the hearts of gentiles. What goes beyond this, that which we know from the sources of revelation, does on the one hand enlighten these natural desires: other people can discover this or feel this, but we are convinced of this with even more certainty on the basis of the sources of the revelation. On the other hand, there can be principles and contents of the Christian moral ideal, and of the Judeo-Christian ideal – as the Old Testament already contains revelation – which go beyond the consequences of mere natural decency. At this point we can talk of supernatural ethical norms.

PLK: If I sense things right, Cardinal Erdő, you are talking of how faith and disbelief are both present in a person at the same time, and of how faith is divine in nature, while disbelief is human?

PE: I say that it is not disbelief that is present but rather that *gratia supponit naturam*: 'mercy presupposes nature'. This means that there is no person without a nature. By living, we are part of the world and of the human condition. One who observes their own nature and that of reality cannot be that far from the land of God, so to speak, just as Jesus said.

PLK: I would return to the personal aspects. Faith was present in the family. From what age did you sense this, and in what way?

PE: Ever since I can remember. At home we prayed together, we were taken to church from a young age, for the whole of the mass; I can't even remember how long we managed without making a noise or how much we bothered the others. What is certain is that from a very young age the family attended Holy Mass together, on Sundays, at least. Sometimes it would have a slightly funny side, as the family would be getting ready in the morning, and it is not so easy for a family of five to get ready all at the same time. We would go to church, let's say the Sacred Heart of Jesus church in central Budapest, but by that time they were saying the Creed there, and the Offertory was beginning. My father knew precisely how long we had to be at the mass for that to be valid, and as they had already said the Creed, we moved on to the Christ the King church. There the mass began half an hour later, of course depending on the length of the priest's homily. So there were times when they were about at the Elevation of the Host by the time we go there. On these occasions our last resort would be the Piarists. For at that time, in the chapel of the order there was not only high mass at the main altar, but the fathers always held other masses at the side-altars. So it was certain that on Sunday mornings there would be a mass at one of the altars every ten or fifteen minutes, and we never had to go back home without having been to a valid mass. Furthermore we would sometimes be witness to quite wonderful things. The Piarists, for example, had an excellent choir, and they would sing Advent songs beautifully. I remember there was once a huge crowd at the Piarists, and we could not go up the stairs to the upper floor; I asked my father why we couldn't, and he said it was because the famed Piarist leader and writer Sándor Sík was preaching.

PLK: This was in the 1950s and 1960s, wasn't it?

PE: Yes, that's right.

SS: Sándor Sík died in 1963.

PE: That was a memory from my early childhood. Someone I would listen to more consciously, as a schoolboy, was Edgár Artner. By that time he was not allowed to teach at the Faculty of Theology, but he gave very witty sermons at the Sacred Heart of Jesus church, and we could sense that there was much more in those sermons than we were able to understand. But they were witty and entertaining, so we were happy to listen to them. We had other similar experiences, of course; we are talking about the early years of elementary school now. No doubt our parents began by signing us up for religion classes.

PLK: Can you remember any pressure?

PE: More the pressure on them not to sign us up than to sign us up. In any case, they signed us up in the year 1958/59. True, it was a pretty varied affair, because every two or three months they would remove or relocate the priest who held the religion classes. In second grade there were still classes in school, of course only in the afternoon, and at some strange time, but there were some; from third grade no one signed up for them, and my parents also said that there was no point, as they wouldn't actually hold the classes, anyway. Then the church religion classes and catechisms began, which at first we did not attend very often. Mostly because we did not know when and where they were held, and it wasn't all very well organized. But my father said that he was responsible, that he would teach us. So on Sunday, when we returned home from mass, he took out the catechism by Endre Hamvas – the only one available at the time. Hamvas, the then president of the bishops' conference, was the only one in a position to publish such a thing, and it was from before the war; he was an excellent catechist, and so it was from this work that we studied religion all the way through our time at elementary school, led by my father. He gave us compulsory readings, and there were games, too. Father Imre Mihalik, who was also not allowed to be active at that time, would deal with families, and then organized a theology competition for the older children, and many other activities.

Later, when he lived in America, as a teacher in a seminary, for decades he wrote all kinds of Bible games and puzzles for Catholic newspapers. This was very good educationally, even if it was extra-curricular. It was also good how we were given compulsory reading, and could talk about these, like *The Jewish War* by Josephus Flavius, for example, and many other source texts relating to the origins of Christianity. We were given these at a young age, because my father was someone who thought that you could never start this kind of thing too early. Why should we later read discussions of them, when we had the original texts here? Ever since I can remember, as well as going to mass and family prayers, we also read the lives of the Saints of the church. We had the one by Polikárp Radó, the big *Lives of the Saints*, and my parents would read one of the biographies when we were little; later we would read them for ourselves.

Then came the lighting of the candles for Advent. Every Saturday in Advent we would light the candles on a plate. In those days they didn't have these prepared wreaths like today, but they would make them out of pine twigs and this and that. We sang Advent songs, and my parents would read out a section of Scripture, we would pray a little, and then something good would happen. I think they learned, perhaps precisely from Uncle Imre Mihalik and his family, how to arrange a family Advent candle-lighting ceremony like this. We cooked apples and did many other things which made it all memorable and atmospheric for us children. Not to mention the feast of Saint Nicholas! In our house Saint Nicholas did not just come all of a sudden on the morning of 6 December to leave something in our shoes (as is customary in the region)! We could write him a letter at least two weeks before, we could offer to do various good deeds, and sometimes we would find *szaloncukor*, the wrapped Christmas tree sweets under our pillows – not the ones in white paper as at Christmas itself, but the ones in red, especially for the feast of Saint Nicholas. One each. This was a Saint Nicholas pre-present, which meant that Saint Nicholas was dealing with us. If we would do what we had promised to do, we would get proper presents! This is how it worked, and it was very good-spirited and created the right mood. The celebration of Christmas and Easter was always a great event in our family, not just in church, where we would also go.

PLK: Can I ask what your mother's role in this was?

PE: Of course you can! My mother was a pretty significant leader in the Sodality of Our Lady, as a student of education. Although her social background was no obstacle for higher education, as her father drove a suburban train in those days, she proved to be too religious, and was told that she could study at the Academy for Fine Arts, but would have to join the Union of Working Youth (DISZ) and assume at least as important a function in it as she had in the Sodality of Our Lady. And she refused to go along with this. And so not only was she not accepted to the academy, but she was not really allowed to teach, either. She tried to find work as an administrator, and this is how she met my father, who for his part was unable to find work as a lawyer, and so also worked as an administrator.

PLK: Your father, Cardinal Erdő, was a university lecturer?

PE: After finishing university, as a young lawyer, he would have started teaching, in just the years when Professor Jusztin Baranyai was arrested. His activity was at about the same time that Professor Baranyai was removed, and Professor Heller completed that year, but afterwards they closed the canon law department down, and my father was the one who, as the last assistant to be working there, had to hand the key in to the porter. Afterwards, when in 1996 Cardinal Pio Laghi brought the founding certificate from the Holy See for our faculty – which to use state terminology we call a postgraduate institute – I had the audacity in my inaugural speech at Pázmány

University to say that the Holy See had just opened the door which back then my father had closed, and perhaps it was now more open than it had been before. We bear responsibility for ensuring that certain parts of human knowledge, perhaps parts of ecclesiastical knowledge, do not disappear from society altogether.

PLK: How did your mother deal with children?

PE: Oh, in many different ways. On the one hand as a teacher, and in any case she had the right temperament for it. She taught us to sing, she drew for us, cut animals out of cardboard, ones that were coloured and which stood on their own legs, that we could play with. We covered the big table with a cloth, and underneath it was the cave for the animals. These were terrific things indeed. My paternal grandmother, who also lived there, in the same house, was very good at sewing animals from textile fragments, which could then be stuffed. I don't know where from, but she had various cut-outs, a bear, a dog, an elephant, a whole zoo. The various holidays were in no small part about us being given animals like these. Of course, as there were now three boys at an age at which they could still be given presents, she always had to make them for all of us. My grandmother gave the animals distinguishing marks, so each boy could know which one was his, and of course we were all very proud and sensitive about our own animal collections. It counted as torture *in effigie* that my twin brother placed the foot of the bed on the head of my little brother's bear.

SS: Do I remember right that your mother was in contact with Valéria Dienes, the first Hungarian female university lecturer?

PE: She was in contact with a great many people, especially in her days at the Sodality of Our Lady and afterwards. She had a broad circle of friends, and a strong social nature, but she wasn't really able to experience this side of life, because society was not like that. And then we were born one after another, and my three younger sisters, too, so she was not in a position to play a great public role. But even now, fourteen years after my mother's death, I am still in touch with her friends, who invite me and I visit them. This was a solid group of friends. There were members of it who became godparents, for example my own godmother or those of my twin brother and little brother, who were also part of this same group.

PLK: It was a pretty tough world, back then. How did your parents experience it, and what were the consequences for the children?

PE: The basic expression for this would be that we somehow found these sad and negative things or these material needs to be natural. The same with the fact that we couldn't just go anywhere to continue our studies, or that my father couldn't get a job just anywhere; at that time, in that context, we took all this to be natural. This is the same sense of 'natural' as Imre Kertész uses in *Fatelessness*. It is no pose, the way he writes about this, it is for real: in one's own system of coordinates, one could experience this actually rather strange state of affairs as uncomfortable, but as relatively natural. We did have things to enjoy. Our parents called the local doctor, because they were worried at our necks being yellow. What is making the children yellow? After a thorough examination, the local doctor asked what these kids get to eat. The doctor, after examining us closely, asked just what food these children get. Well, carrot, either made like this or like that. And what else? Sometimes milk. And what else? Well, not much. Then that's why they're so yellow. On the one hand there was a problem like this, which also meant for instance that we licked the wall in the whitewashed or painted room up to our own height, because we were lacking calcium, as were so many things. They didn't have refrigerators in those days, and we didn't even have an old-fashioned ice-box; in winter we could put roasted meat in a jar, with fat above it; my mother would sometimes cut a slice and put in on the bread. How good that was! Nowadays hardly any-one can be glad over something like that! When it is so obvious! So, this wasn't all that terrible, while it was of course very negative. This was around 1956, and I remember my father returning home one time during the working day, very crestfallen. Then my godfather also came, as he had been fired from his work; they told him that there was no need for both him and his father to work, that one breadwinner was enough in one family. There were many things like that.

PLK: Did anyone in the family have their name tarnished? Or anyone in prison?

PE: Thank God, there was no prison. Why not, I don't know, because in those days they put people in prison who had done nothing at all! Perhaps it was Providence. I am talking about my close family, because one of my mother's older brothers was indeed imprisoned, and the other was taken to the Soviet Union, but they didn't take my parents or my grandparents. My maternal grandparents died rather early, and my paternal grandparents were not the type. Our family was not really the type to get into politics in general.

PLK: Was there no mention of political events?

PE: Of course there was! But my father was never guilty of carrying out any kind of political activity which might not have appealed to the régime. His only crime was being so religious. He never flaunted it, and publicly he did not even support the persecuted Prince Primate Cardinal Mindszenty, but he did attend church regularly, and sent us to religion classes; we had our First Communion, we were confirmed, we served as altar boys, and he made no secret of this, because he said there was nothing to keep secret about it. It helped things a great deal that, with the help of a few good priests, community relations were established between the religious big families. Imre Mihalik and his circle was such a closely knit group that I saw those members of it who are still alive at a wedding in early July this year; this is the third generation, we all met, and the descendants of the big families filled the Church of Hungarian Saints in Budapest. It was a great pleasure to see them and meet them. There are priests from the diocese from these families, so I think that this old community of friends has an influence in the church to this day. Perhaps not in quite such a direct fashion as some think it once had.

There were those who said that nonbelievers would not accept children, while good religious people would of course raise many children however difficult the circumstances, and then how religious society will become. Not everyone from such families will automatically become religious, of course – everyone has a free choice in their life. It was interesting to see, for example in the case of my siblings, and with regard to the conversations of various parents in the family community, how one or other of them would start to worry because one or other of their children was not very observant, or had lost their faith entirely and their life had led in another direction. There is such a thing as human freedom. Religious upbringing does not have an automatic effect, but it does have an effect.

PLK: I would be interested in hearing about your personal encounter with the experience of faith, Cardinal. What are your earliest memories of this?

PE: I can not really report what I felt or did not feel at a very young age. I am sure that we prepared very intensely for the First Communion. We had our First Communion at the age of six in those days, and we did not delay this without good reason, as is often the case nowadays. On the other hand, when I was about twelve, by which age I was often serving at mass as an altar boy and receiving communion, the fact that I was present at the masses began to be a big experience for me. What is happening there, in point of fact? This was connected to serving as an altar boy. I was close to the altar, I could see how the priest was conducting the mass; I served at masses for a number of priests, some old, some young, some who did the mass with extreme devotion, of course in Latin. One would learn the words while doing this, and say the responses nicely. Just as I would, with my elementary school view of the world, start to think about all this, it began to be very important for me. I started to read spiritual literature, and I had a very good spiritual adviser in this, who gave me books, like the Lives of the Saints, but by this stage not the Polikárp Radó version, but the Antal Schütz one in four volumes: 'The Lives of the Saints for Every Day of the Year'. This book has been reprinted recently, and thoroughly deserved to be, because it writes so beautifully and in such detail, every biography is pretty significant, and it is clear in it what is history and what is legend. Of course I didn't only read 'The Lives of the Saints' but also other things, mystical things. For example at the age of fifteen I read a lot of Saint Theresa the Great. All that was available in Hungarian. And Saint John of the Cross and Saint Francis de Sales in the same way.

PLK: At such a young age?

PE: My spiritual adviser recommended them, and I read them. I found it interesting, an experience. I would do so later, too.

SS: By then as a student of the Piarists.

PE: Yes, by then I was fourteen. So this whole thing began in elementary school, and it was a result partly of this experience that I asked my parents, purely of my own volition, if I could go to a religious school. This was connected to a class outing with my elementary school. We visited the Archabbey and Benedictine School in Pannonhalma, and I liked it so much, that I wanted to be a student there. My father was very happy to hear this, as he had been a Benedictine student himself, albeit in Budapest, not Pannonhalma. So he began to look into it: we were twins, after all, and if I wanted to go, my twin brother would no doubt want to as well. My father asked how much it would cost. It was 450 forints, which was a lot of money in those days. He told us quite directly: boys, I can't pay this much, but I know there is a Catholic high school in Budapest, the Piarist one.

We had a look around there, got to know a few Piarist fathers, went to serve at mass, and the end result was that we were very keen to attend the school. We had to start our application in seventh grade; Ferenc Pap was the principal when we had our entrance exams. My twin brother and I were both accepted to the Piarist High School in Budapest.

PLK: Who was your class teacher?

PE: My class teacher was Antal Fekete, while my twin brother was in a different class in the same year. And, now that the high school year book from the

1960s has been published after so many years, I see that almost all of the teachers had started working there before the war. They were first-rate secondary school teachers of the old school. Before the war, the Piarists had had a number of schools, but they were only allowed to retain two, so they strove to keep the best teachers on their lists, and let the others be pastors or go to the dioceses. I can say that my relatively old teachers were exceptionally good.

PLK: There were younger ones, as well, though, like István Jelenits, for example.

PE: Yes, he and István Salánki were the younger ones, but I have to stop to think if there was anyone else who was young. Those who are in their seventies now did not teach me. The ones who taught me have mostly passed away. Mihály Kovács, Lajos Makláry, László Szemenyei, and János Pogány was my mathematics teacher for a while. It was a great generation. Zoltán Somogyi, our history teacher, also had a great effect on me. He could present things elegantly and concisely, and taught us how to take notes. This was also a great achievement of Mr Jelenits, who taught his students how to take notes on the basis of a free-ranging lecture. And Mihály Medvigy! The things that Mr Medvigy taught us in the subject called moral studies we wrote in a notebook with squared paper. If we were to reproduce that notebook, I would gladly give it to anyone as a secondary school textbook in moral theology. I think these teachers really were greats, not just on the basis of their knowledge, but also their method. Lajos Kincs, our Russian teacher, even made us love Russian!

SS: If we look back on that era, how would you describe the typical Piarist teacher-priest?

PE: The Piarist teacher-priest was first and foremost someone who worked from morning till night. Of course the various monastic orders have their various styles and personalities. The Piarist teacher-priest wasn't particularly devout. Indeed, he would almost deliberately cause friction with his profanity, and yet one would know that they were faithful and upright men, though this was more obvious for example from how Mihály Kovács prepared his physics experiment for four hours beforehand, to be sure it worked. And it did. As they lived in the same building where they taught us, we could see that this was indeed their life. Actually this is why I didn't dare apply to become a Piarist, because I thought that profane subjects or fields presented such an obligation in the life of a Piarist teacher that I thought I would want to spend more time on holy concerns. And this was why I became a diocesan priest instead.

SS: What was your relationship with the local parish church like, if you were so occupied with the Piarist school and the life there?

PE: Of course I had a connection to the local parish church before I had one with the Piarists. We attended church, and while we would sometimes dash here and there for mass, everyone knew we belonged to the parish church of Józsefváros in central Budapest, then to the one on Bakáts Square not far away. This was our own parish church, where we went to serve as altar boys, and that is where we went in general, because it was where we would meet people of our age. They held Saint Nicholas there, Christmas, and all kinds of events; these represented the social life of the time. We liked our parish church; we knew who was who, who the parish priests and the other priests were. We can say that in those days in Budapest, on the basis of legal decree 1957/22, the permission of the state ecclesiastical office was needed for someone to become a parish priest. This is true. Yet at the same time the parish priests strove to see that there was a good ambience in the parish churches, and that there be life in the parishes. There were of course chaplains, young chaplains. For example, László Arnold in Józsefváros was very kind and had good ideas, and so did others. There were very lively young chaplains on Bakáts Square, like János Zimonyi, or Father Károly Futó, whom I met there. Róbert Hajnal was there for a time, or Father György Kiss, who later ended up in Szentendre, north of Budapest. Márton Györgydeák was also there. In short, we got to know many interesting priests, and older ones, too. Also assistant priests. And the various monks, who were banned from being active, but who existed on the periphery of parish life. In Józsefváros there was dear old Frici Molnár, for example. Uncle Frici was a good friend of Zsigmond Mihalovics, and so there was even a family connection there in the background, as well. He was a wonderful man! He was the perfect example of the good old Budapest pastor – retired by then. And Ferenc Pap, who taught us personally for our First Communion, and taught us singing. I am grateful to him to this day, as he did it all with such style. Without fussing too much about things, with momentum, with kindness. So I met a good variety of people at the parish church, and we liked it there. Meanwhile at Bakáts Square there was Bishop Mihály Endrey, not exactly under house arrest, but in the one place he was obliged to be. He wasn't even allowed to celebrate mass in public; this was allowed once a year, when Pastor Károly Draskovits negotiated for him to have this one-off permission to celebrate the services for Holy week, because it was more beautiful after all presided by a bishop. The church was always full, and he preached with his voice trembling from emotion, because this was the only time he was allowed to speak. His sermons were splendid, and it was obvious from the atmosphere that everyone loved and respected him. There were other retired fathers and abbots who conducted masses; they were active monks, like the Piarist teachers, or ones who were banned from being active, but who would appear at the side-altars in the mornings.

PLK: Was there, so to speak, any way in which this being hemmed in by the authorities could have encouraged you?

PE: I am sure there was, but I would add that life back then was much more intense. Hardly anyone had a television back then, for example, and social life worked quite differently. It has a different significance. Intellectual conversations. Conversations with my father. Or when we would visit Piliscsaba, more precisely Klotildliget, in the hills near Budapest, on holiday. There were two houses there on one plot, and one of them was given to us to use for many long years, and we went there on holiday. We would go over to visit Vilmos Nagy and his family. He was writing his memoirs at that time; sometimes he would read out from them, for the adults, of course, but we would listen in, too, to hear about what happened during the war. There was an intellectual circle there, there were old artists, old characters who had been squeezed out of the city, who were very clever, well-educated people. Writers, painters, and just a broad range of people whom we met.

PLK: It is obvious what the next question is: your call.

PE: It is strongly connected to what we have been discussing. As I awoke to religious life, the gravity of the whole thing became more conscious, more intense (I am talking about from the age of 13-14), and the greatness, especially of Holy Mass, but also the importance and seriousness of the whole work of a priest, and I began to wonder whether this might be my calling. Of course, at such a young age I did not kid myself by thinking I would become a priest, or that I had to become one. So I was not the type who built his own little altar and conducted a mass. I tried to be a good student at high school, and I did also think about what civilian careers I might follow. When in the last year of high school I had to submit the completed form about where I wanted to continue my studies, I put down my choice. I had spent the night before praying, and I wrote that I wanted to attend the Theological College of Esztergom in the north of Hungary. But this all happened at the appropriate time, at the appropriate pace, even if the thought had been there inside me all along. Then at high school I became a communicant on a daily basis. Of course, this was not a walk, but rather a run, as I knew that to make it for the communion it was enough to get there for the middle of the mass if not the beginning of it. Today we would say that I wasn't taking this entirely seriously, and ask why I couldn't dedicate another fifteen minutes to this, if it mattered to me. Back then, however, the proportion or relationship between communion and being present for the whole of a weekday mass was rather different. In the case of the Franciscans in Budapest, I think that the priests came out to give communion every half hour or hour. This does not mean there was always a mass, just that people came to confess and take communion.

PLK: Were there so many people coming to take daily communion in those days that this seemed necessary?

PE: I don't know whether those present came every day, but there is no doubt that the habit of communion outside mass was very much present. It is true that religious life still had the rhythm from before the liturgical reform; it is also that it is a very legitimate thing for it to be possible to take communion once a day outside mass. This is still around today, if not to the same extent. As there was confession all day, it was not possible to conduct mass all day, if only because there were no Franciscans there then as there are today! There was Richárd Horváth, the church director, and there were a few chaplains, who worked very hard, and there were the confessors, who only went to help in the confessional.

PLK: I was wondering how a young man aged eighteen was able to choose a profession that is rather tied down, closed, and which demands complete devotion.

PE: First of all there is the seminary training, which lasts for five to six years. Those who complete this can experience the nature of this way of life; the decision taken at the age of eighteen is but the first step. I would add that according to Hungarian law anyone over the age of 18 can get married. That is also a pretty serious decision, and people are not mature enough at that age for it. At the same time a human being is a biological creature. Whatever society does, even if it says that we acquire maturity at, say, the age of 50, we will still have human nature, which has its spring, its summer, its autumn and its winter; that is, there is the time for everything. There is the time to choose our way of life. Our teacher Mr Jelenits said in one conversation that it was not about the priesthood but choosing one's mate: if I wake up on a Sunday morning, I can decide where I would like to make a trip. Let's say to the Börzsöny hills. I go out to the train station, where I have to get one a particular train. If I get on the train that goes to the Börzsöny hills, then there is no point thinking about how it would be better to go in the other direction, to the Pilis hills, because I will ruin my entire day. I will have to think about where to get off, etc., and when the train stops, then I have to decide whether I will really get off or not. When I was a seminarist, the examinations presented the question of whether to postpone them or not. There were different ways of postponing them, and you could even make a scandal out of it: if in the June exam period you said you would only take the exam in the autumn, you would put yourself in a very bad light.

PLK: Which were the difficult subjects?

PE: The Biblical languages – Hebrew and Greek. The philosophical subjects were difficult until you learned the conceptual terminology, but after that it bacame easy, as you could use it as you liked. In almost all disciplines it took a whole term of hard study to learn the conceptual terminology. I always applied to take the exams in the first possible slot. My friend Szabolcs Sajgó would also sometimes apply for the first slot, but then he would then go down the dean's office to ask if it could be the following week instead. Then he would do very well in the exam, as did I, but this was his method. We were in Budapest by this stage. In the summer after the first year it was suggested that I be sent to the Central Seminary, which meant that I could continue to study theology, at a university level.

PLK: This was after the end of the first year?

PE: It could happen at any time after the end of the first year. It was called the Central Seminary, while the educational institution next door was called the Roman Catholic Theological Academy. This gave a university qualification, was recognized by the state, and the doctoral title would be put in one's identity card. In this sense the university status of the theology faculty shut out of the old Pázmány University was not lost. When we got to the Theological Academy, more than a decade after the great expulsions of 1959, it had a slightly strange reputation: it was said that it was not so good spiritually. So after I heard that I might be sent there, I went to visit the prefect, Vilmos Dékány, and asked him whether I shouldn't resist this. Whether I would do better politely to ask not to be sent up there, because I am worried it is not good spiritually. But the later Bishop Dékány gave me a key piece of advice, which I have followed ever since, and have done well to do so: do not ask for anything, and do not reject anything. In other words, I did not ask for it, I did not say I wanted it, but I did not say I was not willing, either. So I was sent up. I went. I took the document stating I was accepted, looked for the prefect there, eventually found him, and they told me when I could move in. Of course I asked Bishop Dékány, for the second time now, as to whom I could trust here. He named an older ordinand first of all, who had previously been a doctor: 'Doc' Kovács, who had been in the year above us as a trainee priest. Later it transpired that we were very distantly related, from the area of Nagyvárad (today Oradea, Romania). We were very happy to meet there, and later I would get to know a lot of other good people. Whatever anyone might say in retrospect, at that time the theology faculty, that is the Academy, had a good teaching staff. We had good professors, primarily older ones, but there were younger ones, too. For example, I wasn't taught by Pál Kecskés by that stage, but he looked in on some theological recollection classes.

József Félegyházy was very good as a historian; we learned a lot from him. And whatever anyone might say in retrospect about Imre Timkó, there is no question that he was a genius. My father remembered him from the 1930's. And this was no accident: he gave the welcome speech at the Eucharistic Congress in front of Cardinal Pacelli in the name of the whole of Hungarian youth. He was an exceptionally talented man. At the beginning of the 1970's, for example, simply on the basis of the principles of intellectual history, he predicted what mood of irrationality and relativism would prevail around 2000, and that one task of Christianity would be to preserve objective truth, objective understanding and an objective, critical historical attitude. When Pope John Paul II published *Fides et ratio*, we said that Professor Timkó had been right! And there were others, like Tamás Nyíri, who was an excellent lecturer. We were very fond of him. He spoke clearly, in an interesting way, and he brought many new things to his classes.

PLK: Nyíri became well-known and well-respected. But there was also Imre Timkó and his excellent book on Eastern Christianity. Was he known back then?

PE: Yes, *Eastern Christianity, Eastern Churches*. We knew it, as that was when it was first published. It is not so often seen today, but it would be worth getting people to read it. Timkó himself would teach the patrology of Altaner (Berthold Altaner: Patrology. English edition: Herder and Herder, New York, 1958). I cannot say that this is what he said at each class, because he was rather rhapsodic about it, but he instructed us to study it, and a translation of Altaner's book was published in 1947 by the Saint Stephen Association. It was possible to find a copy of it here and there. We used it to prepare for our exam. After this I took my exam with great enthusiasm and, I thought, very well, only then to see in my record book that I only got a 'good' grade (4 out of 5). My heart almost sank! I asked: Why? The Greek Catholics said that was what Timkó was like. He didn't want everyone to get a 5 out of 5, so he would give one student a 5, and the other a 4, irrespective of how they actually did. It transpired that that really was how he did it. Then I calmed down: it had not been my lack of knowledge, it had been my lack of luck. This was not a typical experience; the typical experience was that the teachers marked the exams objectively and fairly, perhaps more so than what I see in today's university world. Ferenc Gál was an excellent teacher both as a dogmatist and as an exegete. He was not a Bible specialist. But in the church samizdat literature Ferenc Gál's Biblical exegeses, which he wrote for the priesthood, and which were somehow reproduced by stencil, perhaps not even illegally, were very precious. The more assertive ordinands would collect them, so they would have the whole Gál exegesis by the time they were ordained, and be able properly to discuss any section of the Scriptures. Even beyond his printed publications, and his conference speeches, Ferenc Gál did the life of the church an extraordinary service.

PLK: As both of my conversation partners studied at universities abroad, let me ask whether 'domestic produce' was up to the grade.

PE: Absolutely! The Budapest Theological Academy's undergraduate course. The undergraduate course, I stress. Not the doctoral one, because the library lacked new journals and the latest monographs, and some of the lecturers did not quite have the energy and ambition or aptitude for research, that is, the research attitude was missing. And the circumstances at that time did not even really make this entirely possible. But the undergraduate course was much more detailed, more stable and more balanced that the Western average. The teaching was churchy, but churchy in a normal way; neither Tamás Nyíri nor András Szennay could have been accused of not teaching us about the Second Vatican Council.

PLK: Nyíri did not reject modernity, or the teaching of other types of philosophy…

PE: That's right! He had characteristics which were a rarity in those days. He was willing to deal with students personally. If there was someone whom I could visit in their home, and who was willing to talk to me about something for an hour and a half, to recommend specialist literature, it was Tamás Nyíri, may his memory be blessed. And István Kosztolányi, about whom people do not talk much today, but who was also a great teacher figure. Father Kosztolányi taught us the New Testament, and during the war a number of his books were published, for example on the explanation of the Revelations, and he was a very erudite priest in any case.

SS: He was the priest of the Regnum Marianum…

PE: When I translated Nicolas of Cusa's work *De docta ignorantia* into Hungarian, which I had to attach to my dissertation as an appendix, there was never any doubt as to whom I should ask to have a glance at it to see if my translation from the Latin was good or not. István Kodolányi was happy to look at it. May his memory be blessed. Where could we find a professor like that nowadays? Today most university lecturers teach in five places at once, and take on three public jobs on the side. Even the most highly-qualified of them don't have time to deal with their students personally.

SS: Were you taught by György Zemplén?

PE: Oh, yes! Bishop György Zemplén was a fine mind, and in point of fact he taught well, too; we only experienced the last years or months of his professorial career. I have to say that he was a very versatile man with broad cultural interests, with very fine scholastic theological knowledge. He taught moral theology as it was once meant to be taught: he explained the *Secunda Secundae* from the Summa Theologica almost like an exegete. He taught us the *Secunda Secundae*, if not in Latin form – that was in the library. If we begged him, he would occasionally give us his summaries and explanations of individual sections of this, as typed notes. And in addition to teaching and exegizing the *Secunda Secundae*, in every second class he would talk about the characterology of Léopold Szondi, and the issues the subject raised.

SS: He was Szondi's student.

PE: So you have to imagine the Zemplén notes as including one big chapter on Saint Thomas Aquinas and another on Léopold Szondi. And this is how it went. We cannot say that Zemplén's classes were not up-to-date, and sometimes they were distinctly amusing. He loved music, and literature.

PLK: How did you decide whether to be a theologian or a practising priest?

PE: That's not how it worked. We knew precisely that we don't decide about that, because we go where we are directed. The church has a disposition system, and even being sent to the Central Seminary did not mean that we would only work on theology; what seemed natural was that one would complete his studies, be ordained as a priest, and be sent out to the parishes. One did think one might be asked to do some teaching in addition to this; I did think I might once teach at the seminary in Esztergom, but that was the *non plus ultra*, and I was not even sure I would want it. Deadlines always played a big role in my life; I completed everything in the shortest time possible. When the time came, I got my baccalaureate. I received my licentiate at the earliest possible moment, that is at the end of the fifth year. The dissertation for my licentiate, which many liked, was entitled 'The Roots of Catholic Natural Law in the Philosophy of Aristotle and the Stoics'. I very much enjoyed writing it. This also proves how much of an influence my philosophy teacher, Tamás Nyíri, had on me, because I was excited by the philosophical background. In general I was the positivist, which I inherited from my father, who was a student of great jurist and Academy president Gyula Moór. In retrospect I would say that it is all a question of how you name things: it is important whether a legal regulation is a norm that is obliged to be consistent with other regulations, or whether a legislator can act freely. It is a different question what we refer to as the law. In any case, at the end of my fifth year I received my licentiate and started to write my doctoral dissertation in ecclesiastical law. This meant that even though I was sent out to be a chaplain immediately after my ordination – they didn't leave me there for a sixth year to write my dissertation, which would also have been one solution – I was sent by my bishop to Dorog, just outside Esztergom. He said this was pretty close to Budapest. If I needed to go to the library or consult with my professor, then I could do so, and get my doctorate. So I was a chaplain at the parish church in Dorog, the direct successor to Miklós Blanckenstein.

PLK: Is that when the famous encounter with Cardinal Lékai took place?

PE: After a year I took my doctorate in Budapest, as a chaplain. The teachers must have told Cardinal Lékai about this. At that time he had the opportunity and intention to try to train young priests. In this vein, one day he telephoned me out of the blue, after I got my doctorate, asking me to go out to the edge of the motorway. This was at the start of 1977, in rainy, wintry weather. He arrived in his Peugeot, wound down the window, and asked me if I would be willing to go to Rome to study law. I said that if the Cardinal were to send me, then I would be happy to go. Very well, he said, then don't tell anyone about this, but start learning Italian. It was quite clear why I should not say anything to anyone, because they would offer to help me... I did not ask for this help. I kept to Vilmos Dékány's advice: don't ask for anything. If my bishop sends me, I will undertake to study abroad, but I won't ask for it. This was all that happened – and then during the summer it became official.

PLK: What was your personal relationship with Cardinal Lékai like later on?

PE: He was a very good person. He liked his priests. He liked us, as young priests, and he liked the congregation. For example what he would do at Easter, distributing lambs for the children ... So these were very human things, which many people are still happy to remember to this day. When I conduct the anniversary mass for Cardinal Lékai, because there is always one like this in Esztergom for the last bishop to pass away, his relatives still congregate, as do many people who loved him. We knew his brother. Lékai had a large group of supporters who loved and respected him for his human qualities.

PLK: He didn't have a lot of room for manoeuvre.

PE: Indeed he didn't, but in those days everyone knew that. It is another question whether from a different world and a different situation we can say what he should have done. I think he did what he was able to do.

PLK: I am very glad to hear you say that, Cardinal Erdő.

PE: I can say more: 'A cut-down tree turns green'. The programme that the TV did with him, which then become a book, too. This was his motto as a bishop: *succisa virescit*. In this volume he makes a confession about his life, his thoughts about being a pastor, about how he sees the church, his faith, and what he would like things to be. If we ignore the eight lines where he supports the peace movement, the volume could have been written by József Mindszenty himself. With the difference that the attitude is more modern by a few decades. The book is worth reading, to see how much love and love of the church is in it! László Lékai was the type who as a student of the Collegium Germanicum would hear the great Jesuit moral theologian Professor Arthur Vermeersch's lecture at the Gregoriana, then listen to Felice Cappello on law, and the other great classics of the age. Meanwhile at the Collegium Germanico-Hungaricum there in Rome, the obligatory rule was that people would read out a book during the main meal. And what did they read out? Over seven years, in instalments, the twenty-two volumes of Ludwig von Pastor's book *Geschichte der Päpste*. So there was a history behind Cardinal

Lékai starting to quote historical anecdotes. We were very fond of him. At the same time he had a rustic humour to him, and the combination of the two was very interesting.

SS: Can we hear a little about your studies in Rome?

PE: Yes, Rome. This László Lékai, who spent seven years studying in Rome, thought that young priests should be sent there to study and come back home with degrees; he also thought that Roman professors, more precisely Jesuits, and from the Gregoriana, where he himself studied, should be invited to Hungary to lecture. But how? Such that training courses had to be held for ecclesiastical judges. As everyone knows and understands, the law progresses. He arranged for a training course to be held every summer in Esztergom. More or less the whole leadership of the Gregoriana would come over for this, spread over a number of weeks, and others would come, too. Meanwhile there was a diplomatic issue about how the non-existent Jesuit order had been entrusted with the leadership of the priestly retreat in Leányfalu, north of Budapest, that had come into being thanks to Cardinal Lékai's efforts and a benefaction from the church in Germany. Not only was it entrusted to the non-existent Jesuits, it was even mentioned in print. It was in the *Új Ember* ('New Man') magazine, I do not know which year, maybe 1986, that the change had been announced in the position of the provincial leader of the Hungarian Jesuits. But the Jesuit order did not even officially exist in Hungary! These things were connected to his past in Rome, to his personal connections. Cardinal Lékai wanted to present the intellectual life of the church to Hungarian Catholics in the stage it was then – that is, of the 1970s and 1980s – not as it was before the war. One way to this was studying abroad, while another was to bring professors to Hungary. Later this would be the main reason for my invitation to teach; when I taught in Esztergom, I had to simultaneously interpret the lectures on ecclesiastical law from Latin into Hungarian, and meanwhile I was able to become acquainted with the lecturers.

SS: What happened to the new female monastic order, the Society of Our Lady of Hungary?

PE: What happened was they negotiated its establishment. And the Society of Our Lady of Hungary was the only monastic institution that had not existed before to be allowed to operate. It still exists today.

PLK: Did the situation of the church in Hungary look different from the perspective of Rome?

PE: It was not the Hungarian but rather the global church which looked different. In Hungary, if one read the magazines *Vigília*, *Új Ember* or *Teológia*, then these were more or less in line with the progressivist German-Austrian attitude of the time. In the global church we found quite different things. This went as far as Cardinal Ciappi, who at the time was personal theologian to the Pope, giving a talk for us to start the year at the celebratory opening of the Pontifical Lateran University, which is a very papal university. Let's not forget we are talking about autumn of 1977! He said that Pope John XXIII and the Second Vatican Council had ruined everything, and that poor Pope Paul VI had hardly been able to clear up the mess. Well, that's not how we remembered it from home. That's just one picturesque detail. One could sense that there are many sides to the church, that it should not be seen as one single scheme. It is not just the progressive-conservative paradigm that determines faith and church life, but a host of other things. There is Latin America, there are the spiritual movements, and with much greater weight than we could sense from back home. The different schools of thought there are in theology. From Rome it was possible to sense these things, and to this day Rome is the richest palette from this point of view, and the most tolerant place in the whole world. In the city of Rome there are so many theological institutions, and so many different things are represented within the Catholic Church itself, that it is without any compare. Also without compare is its stock of libraries, because in the aleph system alone, which was new at the time I started teaching there, and in which they have processed the catalogues of most of the libraries of the Roman religious universities to make it possible to search them virtually, in this system alone there were fifteen million volumes the last time I used it. Where else in the world is there a specialist theological library of fifteen million volumes? Secondly, this is not fifteen million volumes as if I might buy them today, on the market, according to today's needs, but rather every individual library is a historical source in itself with the way its books are selected. There is the Angelicum library, for example, which is a tangible document of the educational tradition and intellectual horizon of the Dominican order as operating in Rome from the Middle Ages onwards. The Biblioteca Casanatense, which has since been nationalized, shows the intellectual foundations on which the Jesuit Collegio Romano operated, and at what level, as reflected in its books. There is new development too, of course, with completely new libraries. So as an opportunity, as a horizon, it is very, very broad. Teachers and students come from every corner of the globe, and it is without compare both as a religious experience and as a theological one.

PLK: How does the state of faith change in a whole society? We know how it changes in individual people.

PE: In which society? That's a key question. For example, if I have walked down the street in my clergyman in Hungary, to this day I have never been spat at, even though nowadays who knows what kinds of things are happening. In Rome I have been spat at many a time. The world varies a lot. I have thought of the woman who once spat at me at a tram stop, that if she had known how I had got there and want I wanted there, perhaps she would not have done it. At the time of Aldo Moro's assassination, the whole of Rome was in uproar, there was often tear gas, and roads would be closed. On one occasion there was a really tough left-wing demonstration on the Piazza di San Giovanni in Laterano, the square in front of the basilica of the same name, and we needed to cut through the crowd in our clergyman to get to the Pontifical Lateran University. There was nothing else to do but to buy a copy of *L'Unità*, then the newspaper of the Italian Communist Party, its front page showing outwards, and try to fight my way through the crowd, shouting '*permesso, permesso!*'. They let us through.

PLK: What can we say about Hungarian society today?

PE: My sense is that the state of faith in today's Hungary has changed somewhat since the 1980's. The starting point, the point of reference, is the middle of the 1980's. I do not think that society was less or more religious than today. We talk a great deal, organize many institutions, have reorganized many others, we publish, we argue, but I do not think that a fundamental change has taken place. Something has changed in the methods, the signs, and this change had to happen, as under the conditions of greater freedom we have to show our presence much more actively and with greater institutional energy to stay alive at the same level as in the previous system of coordinates. If, for example, I look at the statistics for baptism or ordination, then they have got worse rather than got better; at the same time interest in religion has increased among young intellectuals. For society as a whole, I wouldn't be bold enough to say that church attendance is greater than it was in 1985. Perhaps we have become a more urbane religion than we were twenty or twenty-five years ago. I can say that our institutional structures are much larger. The priesthood has contracted rather than grown, though, and there are fewer monks, and there are fewer civilians with professional skills working for us at non-market rates. We live our lives with higher expenses, with such external, material and bureaucratic burdens, because that is how we have to, how we can, right now.

PLK: A German theologian once asked me why the Hungarian churches did not make better use of the neophyte enthusiasm observed at the end of the 1980's and the beginning of the 1990's.

PE: Nowhere was it made use of. In the early 1990's there was a narrow, very uninformed class who thought that they would now have to become Christians as they had been Marxists before. In a panic, they signed their children up for religion classes, because they thought this was the way to go. It was just because of their ignorance. Anyone who knew how things really were in the West knew that this would not be expected, obligatory or necessary say for someone to keep their job. But society needed four or five years to realize this. One could easily sense, when it was said that the traffic was heavy on the road to Damascus, that for a great many people this enthusiasm was not heartfelt.

There were people who under the previous pressure had kept their distance from the church, and of these some returned to religious life or the community of believers, to the church, in genuine fashion. Others, who did so only superficially or formally, would then see that there was no need, and very soon break off. This was a wave, which passed above our heads, and I think that in this particular regard the experience was the same in all the countries of this region.

What is special in religion or in the function of religion since the change of régime in 1989 is connected to a kind of vacuum issue. To the disappearance of the official Marxist ideology in the Central- Eastern European region. In Hungary's case, this had of course quietly started to disappear well before that, just no one said so. So, even in the 1980s, there were rather few real believing Marxists to debate with, but then it all came to an end. From then on, in the souls of many people, a kind of vacuum remained; they did not know how to explain history, became receptive to all kinds of silly ideology, or else they returned to their own religious roots as grandmothers might. In those days many people would identify themselves as of Catholic cultural roots or of Reformed Church cultural roots. That is, if someone without personal religious belief found it necessary to find some kind of cultural identity, in part for ideological reasons, they would think back to their ancestors and try to look at their family background as a starting point or reference point. Of course, it is true that as a Christian religion we are indeed a factor in preserving culture. This can equally be said in this society of the other historical churches and religious groups. So in this sense, a number of people did find their roots. I am sure that Professor Schweitzer would confirm this. It was part of the era after the change of régime that people started to express this kind of cultural identity. There was a sort of change in this, too, and essentially it, too, was rooted in this vacuum. It is not only that it is no longer prohibited, but many tried to return to this as the only remaining retainer of values to which to turn from the cultural and moral vacuum. This is more drastically visible in the post-Soviet countries and the Balkan states, where politicians with little personal faith throw their weight behind their historical national churches, because they think this is where people will mostly look for their national cultural or moral heritage. Over the last sixteen years the unreligious Western ideological movements and trends have not succeeded in having any real, deep influence on this society or on the societies of this region – it is a very interesting question as to why not, but they haven't. On this subject I again have to tell a story of one of my experiences in Rome. When I got to Rome in 1977, I became aware not just of the theological literature one could see in the bookshops there, not just the ancient classics, but also the works of the modern philosophers, sociologists and psychologists. From Montesquieu to Max Weber, if you wanted some important works like these, they were there; in Hungary they were usually missing, or only available in abridged, partial form. So, I encountered a continuity in ideology or world-view which is there in the Western world, and which from the Enlightenment onwards was at variance with the Christian tradition, but nevertheless never fully broke with it.

Here in this region this continuity was broken, and the newer parts of the Western cultural tradition not carried by religious communities were not able to achieve such a great and lively influence as to present a genuine supplementary or alternative world-view alongside the religious one. And so there were many cultural and moral reasons, alongside other factors, why these societies became so strongly criminalized. Criminalization does not just depend on the institutions of law and order, but also on the community. But because of the weakness of the positive alternative, the not adequately popular and constructive nature of what was on offer – and perhaps because alternative attitudes are only really alive even in the West in narrow, intellectual circles – they were not able to achieve a broad influence. Their attempts remained instinctive.

It was a great experience to see, say in the 1990s in Romania, the bookshops full of translations of the best Western and American works of humanities scholarship. There censorship under Ceausescu was even stronger than in Hungary, and so the transformation was more obvious, too. This literature in translation appeared in Hungary, as well, thanks to the activity of many publishers, and included many very interesting things. So no one can say that nothing happened in terms of the arrival of intellectual and cultural products that could connect to or offer an alternative to the historical religions, but that this had little real effect on the ethical behaviour of society, there is no doubt. It is to this that I ascribe the manifestations of anti-religious feeling, much more brutal and much less justified than in Western Europe, which occur in this region. Particularly here. This includes many things, from the provocation of religious communities, through to hate speech, and includes genuine cultural disinformation as well as slander relating to religious communities. This often repeats itself with exactly the same scenario, almost to the point of boredom, and perhaps in a tougher and more primitive form than is usual in the West, though even in the West there are sometimes very dissonant phenomena inconsistent with democracy. One sometimes thinks back to what happened during World War II with the operation of the German army. It is not as if they treated the local populations on the Western front with kid gloves, and yet they treated the occupied countries there in a much more civilized fashion than those on the eastern front. My feeling is that in intellectual terms we have rather slipped to the eastern front; we receive many unexpected, incomprehensible and unjustified insults, which we think are not at all deserved, and it is our clear conviction that they are not in any causal relationship with our lives and our rejuvenation.

There can essentially be human errors, blunders of all kinds, but in the end what we are talking about is a persecuted religious group, as a result of external influence – it did not fight for it itself, as it did not even think such a thing would be possible – being given a certain opportunity and incentive by the government of the day to perform certain public service tasks. It was to do this way beyond its capacity, and as a result come under fire from unexpected attacks, which, I repeat, were, in addition to their inequity, simply an enormous surprise. From this perspective, the attitude of those politicians and intellectuals who continued to perform their duties in the strongly anti-religious period is one worthy of respect, one that is closer to the religious people who lived through older eras of repression. For they can remember how things were, and one can sense a kind of understanding on their part.

Despite this, some people, who may not even be able to remember, because they were part of such a privileged part of society that they would not have had a clue what was happening to the lives of believers, are now starting to say all kinds of wild things. This is something one observes with sadness, but of course without particular outrage. After all this story is not really about us, but about these societies, and how they will learn to operate in a more or less balanced way in line with general human needs. How they will learn the order and system of bearable operation. It seems this has not stabilized yet. And a lack of stability is the most destructive thing everywhere in the world, in the field of culture as in that of the economy. Our world can often evoke the era of the border fortress battles with the Turks of the principality of Transylvania, and we know that Transylvania was grateful if a ruler like Gábor Bethlen or György Rákóczi I. was able to ensure that the country be peaceful for twenty years. I think that if for once the rule of law was allowed to prevail and the circumstances affecting our daily lives were left in peace, whatever the conditions were, whether good or less good, then people would think that a great thing.

It seems that there is little chance of this, as every single year, indeed more than once a year, such categories of things change again, as if to ensure that neither the economy nor culture can operate normally. You could almost say that a large part of the energies of creative people are tied down by having to make administrative adjustments to changes coming from outside, changes that are not always necessary.

Back then, in Rome, we heard from Pio Ciprotti, the great comparative civil jurist, the theory that a legislator should be economical. That is, if they do not have to, they should not make laws, should not adjust legislation, only if this were socially genuinely necessary. Of course the change of régime brought about the need for legislation and the system to change, but this did not take the form of 'it was like this until now, and will be like that from now on'; instead, it seems we will never find a way out of the mess! It was not that one system gave way to another, but rather that a third system, that of uncertainty, seems to prevail. This is the negative side of this period, but it does have positive aspects, too. Even amidst the conditions of uncertainty there are some opportunities, like those I just mentioned, and many values are brought to the fore which are needed for us to adequately satisfy our calling in society, just as we did in the 1980's.

PLK: And a few things have proved fertile, such as the schools…

PE: Perhaps you are right. Measuring results is always hard, as the result is not just the number of children who have obtained a certificate from a Catholic school, but also the degree to which the Catholic attitude and Catholic identity are able to emerge. It is also important to know what effect this has on the professional culture, humanity and later the religious disposition of our colleagues. It is not easy to tell. At our Piarist year group's five-year reunion, only five of us attended the holy mass, but the whole class came for the dinner. At the reunion after thirty-five years, everyone was there at the holy mass, and most of them took communion, too.

SS: Studies in Rome, years in Esztergom, Budapest, how teaching in Rome started, the importance of academic education, the change of régime in 1989, Papal nuncio Archbishop Angelo Acerbi, and the establishment of the Catholic university. We would like to hear about all of these, if we could.

PE: The idea of a Catholic university in Hungary was always present. In the 19th century there had already been talk of how Catholic the University of Budapest was, and how it wasn't. There were plans to establish a Catholic university in Eger or in Esztergom, but the war put paid to these. When in 1950 the theological faculty was separated from what was now already called Loránd Eötvös University (ELTE), they did not do to it what they did in Czechoslovakia, where they moved it out of the city, but kept it as a state institution, and thereby, citing student application limits, applied a *numerus clausus* policy with regard to seminarists; instead, with a rather fortunate idea, in 1950 the state came to regard denominational theology as so anathema that they handed over this separated institution to the Hungarian Catholic Bishops' Conference. This faculty was now officially part of the church, and it was named the Theological Academy.

But in canonical law the Academy was a direct legal successor to the theological faculty of Péter Pázmány University, and degrees awarded were recognized even by the state. At the moment of the change of régime this was the only higher education institution of the Catholic Church in Hungary. When Act IV of 1990 (on freedom of conscience and religion, and on the churches) was being drawn up, it was clear that the legislative intention was that there be a system of division in which denominational theology would not really have any place within the state institutions. And by then, on the basis of Western experiences, the Holy See did not see this as desirable anyway. The idea was self-evident that theology thus needed to be liberated from its intellectual isolation, and a dialogue needed to be begun again between faith and academe and between faith and culture, in such a way that, by establishing other faculties alongside the theological one, a Catholic university would be created. Meanwhile there were external initiatives for the reinstatement of theology at ELTE University. Most of the theological faculty at the time were very alarmed by this, and not without reason, as the spirit of ELTE was quite different, and the school operated with huge student numbers. If ELTE had a hundred Marxist philosophers, then we had twelve teachers, and this was in itself a heterogeneous group. From the perspective of an intellectual dialogue, we would not have had equal conditions if attached to such a large state institution. Completely independently of this, the constitutional reform meant that this was not the opportunity open to us; what was open to us was establishing an independent body. In 1990 the education act – there was not yet any higher education act or public education act – was reformed such that it clearly recognized the right of the established churches to operate universities. In fact, the university-level theological institutions with just one faculty were listed in an official record, and so they were recognized as universities, too. At that time there was no accreditation yet, and it was not prescribed how many faculties a university has to have; they received this recognition as a result of their old, continuous status.

And it was in this casual set of circumstances that the opportunity arose, if it was going to be a university, to establish new faculties. This is how this work began. We know very well that the encouragement was from Bishop Francesco Colasuonno, who travelled the region as an internuncio. I am still talking of the period before diplomatic relations were restored. Then the encouragement we received was continuous. Of course Nuncio Acerbi was a supporter, as were others. I think that all those who noticed that this was the only way to restart the intellectual dialogue after many decades were very supportive. There were those who did not notice this, and who said that we should return to the bosom of the state university as the safest option. True indeed, but in 1990 or 1991 there was an experiment in Veszprém. What back then was the Chemical University wanted to broaden its profile, and tried to include the theological college department of the newly reopened Veszprém Seminary as a theological faculty. It turned out that the educational politicians of the time – I am talking about the period of József Antall in 1990-93 – reached the conclusion that Hungarian law did not allow for this. Cooperation was possible, but nationalization or turning the faculty into a state institution was not. With this experience in mind, and in the light of the Reformed Church taking over the teacher training college in Nagykőrös, south of Budapest, that is it maintained an institution with a secular subject, it became clear that we had to follow this same path. At first we established a foundation. Father Szabolcs Sajgó and a number of others were also involved in it. We even had hopes that perhaps the Jesuits would again help establish the Catholic university, if not as its administrator, at least as an intellectual patron, as in the era of Pázmány. We wrote to the Jesuit general, whose relevant assistant was Giuseppe Pittau SJ, later an archbishop, and secretary of the Congregation for Catholic Education, until he retired to Japan. Father Pittau stated quite clearly that the order did not sense the opportunity to take on a formal obligation for university-level work in Hungary. Our first thought was that it was historically apt but it seems less realistic to expect the Jesuit order to help us. Then the foundation began to request the old military barracks, even though there was no law on church properties at that time, and the former church properties still belonged to others.

PLK: Sorry for interrupting with a question, but at that time were the Russians still there in the building of the seminary in Esztergom?

PE: The Grand Seminary was among the first for the Russians to leave, but left it in such a state that there were also educational buildings in military areas in much better condition. Furthermore, the Catholic University Foundation did not want to be in conflict with any former owner of church property. In order for the organization of the university not to encounter strong opposition from the church side, it was important that no should sense that we intended to build a university at the expense of their property.

PLK: The grand seminary in Esztergom very much belonged to the diocese before.

PE: That's right. But given its condition we could not even think of actually using it, and Act XXXII of 1991 had not been passed yet, so we did not know whether some church properties would be returned. The Esztergom Seminary was an exception, because it was not nationalized, just occupied. They forgot to nationalize it, but the state took on all the other things. The opportunity we had left was to ask for property in a barracks. We saw a number of them, but it was a pretty uneven story, and finally we were able to acquire the property in Piliscsaba.

SS: And at one stage it was offered in exchange for the Manréza spiritual house in Dobogókő.

PE: I would never have accepted it in exchange for the Manréza! But in fact we had nothing! The university foundation had no rights or claims against the state, but with the support of local government we had the right to make requests from the treasury for educational and cultural purposes.

PLK: Were you allowed to choose from what was on offer?

PE: The choice from what was on offer was such that it was not possible to know what would happen with the Russians' potential demands on some of the barracks properties. For they said that they had undertaken various investments that increased the value of the properties, like installing boilers or central heating, new buildings, and Kiev-style houses which should not even have been permitted for use in Hungary. Indeed the Russians complained that certain local governments were, precisely on this pretext, not willing to recognize the increase in value, and the retreating Russians said this was the local governments' fault, because they had not informed them at the time that it was not permitted to build such things. And for some properties the Russians' demands were significant. We could not apply for properties with claims for hundreds of millions of Forints against them, as we had very little money. Only those came into consideration where the value-increasing investment had been smaller and the burden of such claims was thus also lower. Piliscsaba was one such property. In other respects, it is a beautiful place, and, to be honest, the reason I was not worried by it was that we had gone to that area on holiday when I was at high school, I knew it well, and thought it a wonderful place.

PLK: Is the university going to move to Esztergom one day?

PE: The situation with Esztergom is that the renovation of the grand seminary made it possible to establish significant educational, cultural and conference capacity there, and for us to integrate our higher education institutions maintained by the diocese there into Pázmány University as a college faculty. This has already been initiated, the procedure is still in progress, and there is interest from both sides. The Bologna Process has again applied new conditions to do this within, and it is never possible to know, at an administrative level, what, right now, it is possible to resolve and what, right now, it is possible to maintain. Unfortunately, this changes so often that it is very hard to plan ahead.

PLK: Finally, I would like to ask how you see the path that faith in Hungary will follow in the years to come, Cardinal.

PE: Different people have very different gifts. I do not know if I have the gift of prophecy, but I rather fear I do not. At best one can have human premonitions, but these are feeble, because on the past record there should not have been anything here for years, if we just think straight. There were so many obstacles, so many problems, education had such different priorities, that we have to see it as a miracle that in the census of 2001 the majority of the anonymous and voluntary respondents referred to themselves as Catholics. It would not be fair for someone to judge who is Catholic and who is not on the basis of some other consideration, for example whether someone is always there in church on Sundays or not. So the identity of those who call themselves Catholic, and who are Catholics according to the rules of our church, is not something that others really have the jurisdiction to question. The question of being 'religious in one's own way' can be a sociological concept, but it is not a concept that affects religious affiliation. It is a different question whether someone is a perfect follower of their own ideals or not, or how much they know about a religious system which they accept as the basis for their identity.

There is and has been enormous fluctuation on this over Hungarian history, ever since the age of Saint Stephen. What do the names of the festivals that have remained in our language prove? Those Hungarians whose only understanding of the festival of Easter – the Hungarian word for which is *Húsvét*, meaning 'taking meat', referring to the end of the fast – was that they could not eat meat before, and then could eat it again, clearly did not think in lofty theological categories, and yet they were still members of the church! Today there is also a broad section of society which basically feels attached to our church on an emotional basis, was baptised, and so counts as a member of our church, and there might always be a moment in their lives when they turn to their faith with greater interest or love. So in one sense this thing is very dynamic, and in another sense it is not merely a sociological question, while thirdly it is not certain that outsiders are able fairly to measure the realization of inner religious ideals on the basis of percentages. Even in the light of all these considerations, I do of course think it a significant problem that we need to communicate the content of our faith to people, including religious people. And in this mass media aids us greatly. But sometimes we have to use the most elementary methods; indeed, I feel an ever greater temptation and obligation to do so. This is why I stood in the middle of Saint Stephen's Basilica in Budapest on Sunday evenings in Advent and Lent, and told people in ten instalments what I believe in, which amounted to a compendium of the catechism of the Catholic church. (Péter Erdő: Misszió a városért. Katekézis a Szent István Bazilikában [Mission on the City. Catechism in Saint Stephen's Basilica], Új Ember Kiadó, Budapest 2006.)

It is a great joy that one's Catholic faith is community-related and a common heritage. After all, often there remains little more than for one to say, with empty hands and no resources, what they believe in. This is why it is so important for priests to prepare for this. They should feel the obligation this brings, and the ability for it within themselves. Bureaucracy and specialization are very great burdens. Specialization in the sense that we train many lay teachers of religion, who may possibly not be aware of the depths of faith. Many of them do excellent work, but most have only pedagogical knowledge and perhaps a bit of theological awareness, which they are very careful to pass on. Then part of the priesthood does not really think they should be personally involved in religious teaching, as there are all those religion teachers. So it is not certain that the passing on of our faith is better than it was twenty years ago; indeed, the opposite is probably true.

My view is that we have to concentrate on the content of our faith with all our energies, and, as far as the methodology is concerned, all the other things should be dealt with in their own right. And then there is not only the institutional form of this methodology. We have known since at least the time of Pope John Paul II that modern mass media makes a direct connection possible. The Roman Pope can speak to a billion people, and is not limited to giving instructions to the cardinals or the authorities of the Curia as to what guidelines to give to bishops, who then direct the organizations inside the diocese, though this is also important. But we live in a different world now, and we need to sense these opportunities and to make use of them. We also need to sense that we are thinking in terms of a global church. The cultural and linguistic experiences of the passing on of faith are something of international value.

What works in Vienna will often work equally in Budapest! What works in Paris can work for us too. It is a great treasure that people can move about freely, that the flow of ideas within the church also works with a pretty good degree of freedom, and that pastoral activity can again take place freely – we could say, freely as it once did. A foreign monk, or priest, or layman, can come here and bear witness to their own faith on the basis of their own experiences.

III.

PÉTER ERDŐ: ON THE PATH OF TRUTH AND LOVE MOST REVEREND RECTOR,

Honourable Ladies and Gentlemen!

This year we have come together for a special inaugural address. If we look around us, we can see that the primary reason for this is our new location, the renovated Grand Seminary building. The blessing of this building, just now, on the 2nd of September, was a moment of particular pleasure and awe for all of us. We were repeatedly reminded of the beautiful quotation from the prophet Habakkuk: '[…] the flock shall be cut off from the fold, and there shall be no herd in the stalls: Yet I will rejoice in the LORD, I will joy in the God of my salvation' (Hab 3:17-18). We live amidst many difficulties and problems, and yet we have reason in countless smaller and greater situations for joy. The rejuvenation of this building is a sign of joy, a sign that the Divine Providence has not left us to fend for ourselves. But this renewed building is also a call to action. It invites us to cooperate with Divine Providence, as we still have our resources at our disposal. Even if the population of the country is older than it was a few decades ago, and even if the number of Hungarians has – alas – declined, even if we often struggle with economical problems, we do still have resources. What resources? Resources in our hearts, in our selflessness, resources in our solidarity, in the solidarity which connects Catholic with Catholic, Hungarian with Hungarian, human being with human being. And this house, the renewing of this house, bears witness to just such solidarity. At least half of the costs were contributed by the various dioceses and bishops' conferences of the World Church as well as other benefactors. So we are not alone. But it is not just in terms of financial resources that we are not alone, but in terms of thoughts, ideas, and plans.

Before we started the relocation of the Chapter's Archive and the library of the Theological College or Seminary, we had to lay down plans for how we would do so in a professional manner, and to find space for all this valuable material without the system collapsing, without having to start cataloguing again from scratch, and in such a way that an environment be established in which researchers are really able to access these treasures easily and in a modern fashion. For the planning of this we requested specialists from the Catholic University of the Sacred Heart in Milan, who came a year and a half ago to study the question together with us, and reported on the results and their experiences in a conversation before their departure. They said that in Italy no one knows that such precious collections exist in this part of Central-Eastern Europe. I told them that it would soon be open to researchers; that they could come and acquaint themselves with the content in due course. It also struck me that when these collections were first established, or when at the end of the Middle Ages this great construction work here in Esztergom was first implemented, then specialists also came from Italy, just as they did to the court of King Matthias. Yes, Europe is open to us at the moment, we are of interest to others, and we do have treasures which we can proudly show to others.

The perspective and source of our own selflessness is also very important. So it is important how we approach a job, whether as the one who commissions it, or as a colleague, as a designer or contractor, how we approach it from a human angle, because there are great resources here. And it is also important that we should have a readiness for sacrifice in ourselves, which does not spare our time, our energy, even our own little private financial resources, but, for a beautiful common goal, is willing to sacrifice all this, mobilize it and put it at others' disposal.

I think that the spiritual renewal of which our Bishops' Conference spoke at the beginning of this year is a highly needed resource for us, but nevertheless a realistic one. So this is realizable not just as a dream, but at the level of actions, too.

This start to the academic year is the annual opening of the János Vitéz Roman Catholic Teacher Training College. There will be various changes here this academic year. The first, which is obvious to all, is that part of this institution will begin operation in this building. So this is not just the usual ceremony to start the year, but the opening of this college, here and now. Of this college, which bears the word 'Catholic' in its name, which, from the church's point of view, is thus immediately placed upon a footing similar to those of other Catholic universities. So its calling is to be a place for dialogue between faith and science, its calling is to show how human reason enlightened by our faith gives a broader picture of the whole of reality. It makes it possible for us to see a more complete picture of the whole world, and for this view of the whole to awake in us a feeling of responsibility. For how can someone who knows only particular corners of reality feel responsible for the whole of it? But someone who has a clearer view, has a broad perspective of the whole, will also feel responsible. Responsible for themselves, for others, for the future, for our homeland, for our environment, our region, and for the whole of humanity. So we may be small, we may appear to have no material resources, and yet so very much can and does depend on us. This particular college here, in Esztergom, is not just one of the provincial colleges in Hungary; rather, it operates in the city that was originally the capital of Hungary. In the city in which Saint Stephen was born. In the city which to this day is still the centre of the Catholic Church of Hungary. In the city which is home to one of the most significant historical and artistic collections in the whole of the Central European region. We have not just one but a number of precious public collections here in the city. Not only the Christian Museum, not only the treasury of the Basilica, not only the Primatical Archive, not only the Simor Library, not just the Bibliotheque, but even in this building now the Main Chapter's Archive of Esztergom and the old College Library. What college and what library? That of the Ancient Seminary of Esztergom as founded by Archbishop Miklós

Oláh in 1566, which began in the city of Nagyszombat (today Trnava, Slovakia) – for this city was ruled by the Turks at the time. In 1566, directly after the Council of Trent, and according to the Council's provisions, Miklós Oláh created the Seminary. The education and guidance of the priests had to be undertaken by specialists. And so the Jesuit Order had been at home in Nagyszombat since ancient times. The Library of the Jesuit College was later transferred partly to the University that was to be set up by Péter Pázmány, and in part to the Seminary. So the same ancient material, half of which today forms the oldest part of the collection of the University Library of Budapest, is also still alive here in this building, in the Library of the Theological College. Such priceless works as, for example, the printer's manuscript of the first complete printed Hungarian Catholic translation of the Bible, by György Káldi, which was stuck together into inlays to make it into cardboard. Twenty-five years ago I became aware of this, as a teacher at the seminary, when the treasured library was still in the convent building, and when I had it restored by specialists. Twenty-four letters spilled out of it, in which Viennese printer Máté Formika, who oversaw the first edition in 1624, had marked where the line-break should be at the end of each line with a red pencil. And, really, in the first printed edition, there are the line-breaks where they were marked with red pencil lines. But we have pages from medieval codices which would have been used, let's say, in the bookbinding workshop, and which prove what valuable and high-quality works were in use here in Esztergom and its vicinity, in medieval Hungary, that is before the Turkish era. I think it is a rare privilege to be able to study and work in this city, especially in the humanities, as this is the only central collection which has survived from medieval Hungary through to the present day – in its essence, if not entirely intact. So it represents a treasure which is held in great regard by researchers coming from far and wide.

The unique calling of this college, this college in particular, is to prepare students for teaching work, teaching service, teaching challenges. And today, especially here in Hungary, we know that education and nurturing are in an extraordinary crisis. And here the mistake is again a little bit with where the responsibility lies! Often we do not see the world as a whole, and so we do not measure up properly what the main job of the teacher is. Some think it is to organize outings, some that it is to arrange some event or competition, which will make them popular, but their key task is nevertheless to teach the material and to carve adults out of the children who study with us. So the dependable teaching of the curriculum, the particular, objective, curriculum, and the human and Christian nurturing of our students. This nurturing is of course primarily the family's obligation and right, but parents entrust the school with their children in order for them to be raised in line with their parental intentions. So it is not the job of the state to determine, for example, the ideological direction of this nurturing. This is the right of the parent, who is obliged, in fact, to pass on their own values to their children. The school does its job as commissioned by the parent. For this precise reason, the atmosphere of our school will, thankfully – or perhaps unfortunately – reflect the wishes of the parents. But it is in this that educators have a special role, because it is not certain that parents have stopped to think about the big questions of life. In an indirect fashion, the teacher can often nurture the parents, too. But for this it is necessary for society to value teachers not according to their meagre wages, but instead to recognize in them and in their work the exceptional and irreplaceable value they represent in nurturing the next generation. So I think that this will also be a common task, over the years, out of nothing, from our own, individual, personal, limited financial potential, with the force of simple solidarity, to establish – at least in our own religious schools – a better appreciation of teachers. I also trust that this building will be a solid location for further training of the teachers at our religious schools.

A very important question, of course, is that of communication, and social service, which also has to contain human values. It does not merely focus on instant successes or on economic results, but on people. We have to communicate not only the truth, but also love. So, for example, it is possible that incitement to hatred is sometimes very fashionable, but it can never be the subject or method of communication that is Christian in attitude. Often what needs more bravery is to be polite and patient. The opposite of this can succeed almost automatically. Human nature tends to the bad, so real bravery, real rigour, is if we are able to stay on the path of love and truth in all circumstances.

This city is a city of bridges. It looks across the Danube. This building itself looks across the Danube. For all of us who work here, who teach here or study here, research or pray here, our job is to look across the Danube. We should ponder the reality of our own history, how the various peoples have lived here, in the Carpathian basin, since the beginnings of Christianity. Let us accept that which is reality as a natural and valuable heritage. We need not invent another in its stead; it is quite beautiful and honourable a thing if, on the basis of our real history, we regard each other with esteem. I think that this is the process of conciliation which the Slovak and the Hungarian Conferences of Bishops' began here in Esztergom on 29th July this year; this is very much a relevant issue, and if it is at odds with certain trends, this only makes it all the more relevant. Day-to-day events show that Slovak Catholics and our Slovak bishop brothers are loyal to their statement made here, in Esztergom, and that they keep to their words as said here: 'we forgive, and we ask for forgiveness'.

May this building be a place for the common research of history, as all the source materials which are to be found here bear witness to the common history of this whole region.

It is particularly important that in this building, on this day, I can bless a chapel, as well. This, as well as the spiritual and further training centre, belongs to the character of our educational institutions. The Catholic University has a chapel in every faculty. Here, the chapel of the Seminary was once the largest room to look over the Danube. Now this has become the library's reading room. For the simple reason that this was the only way to arrange the location of the various institutions in the building. But we are dedicating this new chapel – as we did the old one – to Saint Stephen the King and to the Blessed Virgin. It will be down here in the basement, as part of the further training centre. We have furnished it, and had the old chapel altar saved by the parishes restored and brought back here after fifty-three years. It is an altar with a difficult history that reflects our own difficult history, but also shows our resilience in always starting what is truly important and what truly gives us hope all over again. The presence of the Eucharist in the house is, I believe, a real force that emanates, and which can produce peace, harmony and loftiness between one person and another.

May God bless this holy place, the whole community of this college, and all those who will work in this building.

Thank you for your kind attention!

(Delivered at the start-of-year ceremony at the János Vitéz Roman Catholic Teacher Training College)

IV.

SCIENCE AND MAN NATURE AND SOCIETY

SS: What is human science really?

ESV: Science and academe try to discover the secrets, characteristics and nature of nature and society to make these accessible to all and to deduce general truths from these secrets. A key part of academic activity is a belief in something that exists, and this is important when selecting a subject of research. Scientists must believe that something exists, as simply describing nature is not enough. The exploration of the secrets of nature and the uncovering of its operation, function and its particularities and connections are great challenges for the scientist. In his book *The Art of Scientific Investigation*, Beveridge writes that scientific discovery is, in fact, an art. This is true because it is a creative activity that demands intuition and an enormous body of knowledge. Experimental facts are always accompanied by further concepts and theories, which we make accessible to others in academic journals, so they become the subject of debate and thereby win further affirmation or rejection. This is how we protect ourselves against lunatics, charlatans and dilettantes. However, we also protect ourselves so that the truth of science is judged by its political utility. It would be a terrible mistake if decisions on academic and artistic matters were made by those without competence, particularly if they had power. Some Soviet scholars had to accept Lysenko's erroneous theories because they bore out the teachings of the party. It is only a slight exaggeration to say that the Soviet rejection of information technology as a vestige of cosmopolitanism ultimately led to the collapse of the system. In his work *The Novum Organum*, Bacon, whom we could call the father of modern science, stated very clearly that man must make use of nature for his own ends. Descartes, the philosopher, doctor and mathematician, was already talking of redesigning nature. He thought that with the help of mathematics, we would be able to transform our environment. Science and scholarship have always played an important role in the history of humanity, especially in the 20th and 21st centuries, as science has developed exponentially and man has, so to speak, conquered the Earth, conquered the world. All this has made man so confident of himself that it is uncertain whether he is aware of what he is playing at. But why did science and scholarship develop mostly, almost exclusively, in Europe? I would separate philosophy because this was to a large extent developed in the Far East and the Arab world, which, in a sense, remains true today. In my opinion, the explanation for this lies in the unique nature of the Ten Commandments of Judeo-Christian culture, in answers of a yes-or-no variety.

In fact, this is the method of the scientist. Scientists are faced with a dilemma when encountering a problem, and they must decide, on the basis of experiments and concepts, whether to continue down that path. This yes-or-no choice is inside the mentality of Judeo-Christian culture. How can I prove this? Take a look at Indian, Far East or Sanskrit thinking and philosophy, which, when it encounters a problem, looks for consensus and avoids a yes-or-no response. This is the unique quality of the Far East way of thinking. European thinking and philosophy is not like this; rather, it objectifies, it expropriates. I quote Saint Thomas Aquinas, who said: *nihil est in intellectu, quod non prius in sensu* (nothing is in the intellect that was not first in the senses).

This way of thinking lifted Europe above the world's other continents, from the time of Galileo to the 20th century. With time speeding up and the world being shrunk to a dwarf, the modern means of mass communication, which now make everything available to almost everyone, have made the societies of the world the best-informed they have ever been. However, the compression of time makes people forget to think about the world and about themselves. I would like to put the question to the two clerics as to what they think is the explanation for the atheism, which is increasingly gaining ground in the modern world. Science, which by now has become the foundation for society and for the economy, develops exponentially, whereas morality has, at best, developed linearly since the Greeks. The gap is widening. And here is humanity's great problem. Science enables humankind to destroy its own civilization. But what is the reason for this gap to have widened so far? And why has the church not done something to counter this? I pose the question as a scientist. We do what we have to do; I agree with the nuclear physicist Oppenheimer, who said that scientists should uncover the world's secrets, should publish everything they have discovered, but how this is then used is a moral question, and its restriction is the task of legislators.

There are other opinions; this is the point of the Pugwash Conference, that scientists should first give a warning that a finding might destroy the world and that they are not sure whether they should publish. So, there are two schools of thought in science. I am on the side of those who say we have to speak. I objected to the application of genetic technology to humans from the outset; I support its restriction, let Aldous Huxley's *Brave New World* be created, in which humans are bred to work as slaves to satisfy certain needs. Thus, science bears great responsibility, as overly quick development, with morality lagging behind, has caused a huge global problem.

SS: Human beings are what they are, and humankind's science is likewise. So the question is whether completely objective science can even exist.

ESV: Scientists and scholars look for truth, but they can never know the full truth. I would again turn to Albert Einstein's previously mentioned book. In it, he writes that it is the partial knowledge of the perfection of the world that makes people religious. If we interpret the theory of relativity, then creation in Genesis, the creation of the world is equivalent to time itself. This is indeed Albert Einstein's basic premise. One of the cornerstones of relativity theory is that time cannot be seen independently. Here, we are also discussing how it is possible to reach faith in God. As I see it – and this may not necessarily reflect the views of the others here – there are three possible routes, of which one is through natural scientific discoveries, namely, the route of the great scientists. As Einstein writes, infinite perfection and the increasing amount of the unknowable is what drives the scientist to faith, to a 'cosmic' God, even if he doubted the personal reality of this. The great Hungarian poet Attila József experienced this in a different way in his poem entitled 'God': 'By now I know him in any case, / I caught Him in the act in all his doings / And I also know, why he loves me, / I found Him appearing in my heart' (trans. Zsuzsa Tomory).

PLK: Does this mean that the scientist is by necessity someone looking for God?

ESV: No. The scientist does not begin by looking for God; he bumps into God. He bumps into the perfection of the world. Into the perfection of the microcosm at the level of nanotechnology. Into the macrocosm, the incomprehensibility of the expanding universe. At these times, the scientist bumps into something that he might not call God, but it is a fact that he finds himself in this situation. The Hungarian Benedictine monk Gellért Békés wrote a book entitled 'Searching for God' (*Istenkeresés*). I think that a scientist can reach God by searching for the secrets of the world. This is rather different!

SS: When someone tries to explain the way things are arranged relevant to each other in a room, it is not the same as in a whole apartment. And the apartment is different from a house, from a city, from a country, and so on. Depending on where I draw the boundaries within which I look for truths, secrets – this dictates how I will find theories for arranging them. My earlier question was about how objective science is. Where I place my focus, my main emphasis, depends on the variety of scientific fields. The colour of science; how much the personality of individual scientists determines the direction of particular sciences. One has to be aware oneself that one's whole branch of science is hanging from a nail that one oneself banged into one's own imagined and experienced wall of reality.

ESV: Science always tries to be objective; if it did not, it would not find the right answers to the yes-or-no questions. In my work, I must address yes-or-no questions. It is very similar, in fact, to the working of a computer. Yes-or-no and subjectivity can be excluded. Michael Polanyi brilliantly proved in his book how science and religion are interdependent, and the Holy Father spoke of the same subject at the Academy during his visit to Hungary. This is also the subject of Pope John Paul II's encyclical *Fides et ratio*.

PLK: Let's return to the definition of the concept of science and scholarship.

PE: In defining science and scholarship we tend to put things differently, more simply and more in elemental terms, than we just heard from Professor Vizi. We often talk, for example, of a system of verified knowledge. We do not specify whether it refers to nature and to society; with this we note that we can have verified knowledge about God himself, depending on whether we have a method by which to acquire such knowledge. But at this point, as regards the mode of cognizance, I would like to return in full to what Professor Vizi said, that is to nature and society. Hungarian writer Mihály Vörösmarty writes: 'never stop turning the never-ending book of nature, as in it the description of God is treasure'. We can become acquainted with the image of the Creator through the created world; on the other hand, we receive the message of a revelatory God – for Judaism and Christianity are religions based on revelation – through the mediation of society. This is what tradition is for. Nature and society, even if they are not for us exclusive subjects for science, are certainly direct subjects, the examination of which can take us, to a certain degree, beyond the created world. As regards science's demand for objectivity, I completely agree that a real scientific question always wants to find an objective truth. And to put the concept of truth behind it a little is of course a scholastic concept: the correspondence of reason to the thing. So we would like to acquire reasoned content which corresponds to or suits objective reality: *adaequatio inter rem et intellectum* (Cf. pl. St. Thomas Aquinas, Summa contra gentiles Lib. I cap. 59 no. 2: '...*veritas intellectus sit adaequatio intellectus et rei*"). It is this correspondence which one tries to learn, and from this it follows that we presume that there is an objective reality, relative to which our awareness can be correct or incorrect, and so an assumption, a hypothesis can be true or false, and we assume that we have the capacity with which to glean adequate knowledge about this objective reality. This is optimism, and the assumption that the world is knowable, as it was created by primeval love, is, I think, one that is typical of our cultural world.

Alongside all of this, perhaps the greatest problem for the modern world is a hermeneutical one. Namely that reality answers those questions we put to it. This is the methodology of questioning, so to speak. When we direct doctoral research, the first thing we have to teach our students is how they should choose a topic, how to phrase it, so that it will be possible to respond to it with reliable methods. At the same time not just Hans-Georg Gadamer (Hans-Georg Gadamer, Truth and Method, 1960), but many others, including historians like Henri Marrou (Henri I. Marrou, De la connaissance historique, Éd. Seuil, Paris 1975), drew our attention to the fact that naturally every answer which the world gives us, as we investigate nature and society, has our question inside it. And our question is socially conditioned, reflecting the conceptual and intellectual workings of its given milieu. And so this kind of relativity is there in the nature of the answers received. And yet, and this is what we are prone to forget nowadays, the awareness of the relativity, social interdependence and cultural conditioning of our question is not equivalent to the freedom to falsify history, or a licence to forge knowledge. So it is not that all scientific results are subjective and can be altered in line with whatever interests happen to appeal; rather, it is that we are self-critical even with regard to our own questions, but it seems that there are modes of questioning and there are categories which have proved their worth over many hundreds of years. When we were talking about the method of yes-or-no, I was reminded of Abélard's work Sic et non (Petrus Abaelardus, Sic et non: PL 178, 1329–1610); that is, scholastics, which made this technique a general scientific method, and which then made a significant contribution to the development of the natural sciences. The Abélard dialectic method can be recognized in the Pilpul debate of the Talmudists, and in medieval university literature in the whole Catholic world, that is in theology, canon law, and so on. I think that everything we have heard here about objectivity and the search for truth is well-grounded, although as regards the social influenceability of the question raised, a certain modesty would seem justified. This does not however exclude or parenthesize the possibility of objective knowledge, even if – and this is again in part a question of ideological attitude – we are convinced that we cannot become acquainted with every detail of the universe, because it is beyond us.

PLK: Cardinal Erdő, what would your opinion be about the relationship between knowledge and revelation?

PE: Revelation is God's freely-made personal statement to humanity, which one first recognizes personally, or in a socially determined way, and then passes on as tradition. This is the unique quality of revelatory religions, that we do not merely philosophize about the world, but we live in the conviction that God himself wanted to tell us something about the world, and that we can capture the fact and content of this statement with a kind of historical method. This is why I say that nature and society are genuinely the subject of science, at least as a direct object of examination, but from a distance we believe and claim that we can reach certain truths of knowledge about God through learning about these two sectors.

ESV: Dogma can never be the subject for an academic, as it cannot be researched. I think that dogma is a cultural product of humanity, and this is why theology is not an operational area for the Hungarian Academy of Sciences.

PE: I do not agree. In the old foundation documents of the Academy we find no doubt cast on the academic nature of theology; we merely find that the Academy will deal with all scholarly subjects with the exception of theology. In a sense the Academy is not in a position to deal with the question of theology. Our conviction is that theology is a genuine academic subject, is about real knowledge, and it tries to organize these in a certifiable way; according to our faith, however, we can glean various knowledge about God, and so we acknowledge the path that Professor Vizi mentioned, namely that even a natural scientist can progress, from the reality they investigate, to a state of awe or respect which is close to faith, or which is not at odds with religious faith. Further developing this concept, we, on the basis of historical continuity, put this in a kind of system, and, according to our sources, we can, for example, determine whether an approach or a notion is consistent with the faith of the Catholic church, historically. In this examination I think we are able to use techniques which are just as precise as in any other form of research into intellectual history.

SS: All scholarly subjects have axioms. All branches of scholarship start with assumptions they can't prove.

PE: And each branch of science has its own method measured to fit its subject. Pope John Paul II says of Catholic theology that it has a methodological obligation of loyalty to the Magisterium of the Catholic Church. This is not an obstacle to the freedom of scientific research; rather, it is a methodological prerequisite for a given discipline to be undertaken as Catholic theology (Cf. Congregation for the Doctrine of the Faith, Instr. Donum veritatis, 1990. V, 24. AAS, 1990, 1552–1568, no. 12 [=Denzinger-Hünermann no. 4873]; Pope John Paul II, Enc. Veritatis splendor, 1993. VIII. 6 no. 27–29). Of course this process of intellectual history can be seen from a different perspective, but if we do not keep ourselves to the intentions of the Magisterium, if we do not regard this as our guiding source of knowledge, then that will not be Catholic theology but rather religious history or some other discipline.

ESV: To question the basic subject of the revelation and, as such, to make it the subject of research is not acceptable.

PE: Clearly there is no place for a rejection of revelation within Catholic theology. Of course we know that the text of the Bible itself is the result of a certain development, that certain literary historical categories are the key to understanding the theological message of certain texts, not to mention the problems of textual history; then, from the 1st century onwards, a sort of compositional or dogmatizing process began within the Christian Church Since Cardinal

Newman, the problem of dogmatic history is a genuine and serious theological problem – that of how much the faith teaching of the Catholic Church develops. Clearly it was in the modernism debate, when it became clear that we accept that the teaching of our faith historically evolves as the result of confronting various objections and new concepts, and yet we nevertheless have to expound the answers to these phenomena from the heritage of tradition.

SS: If someone steps into the academic world, then there are the very important results produced over centuries, which we essentially accept. These are not dogmas, in the sense that it can be shown quite precisely how it fits together, why this formula is the right one that helps if I am working on a given, certified theory, to let me move forward. Dogmas are no different. Each dogma was preceded by incredible intellectual results which went back to the axiomatic foundations of the revelation and built and still build upon them. Through excruciating debates a consensus was forged that yes, indeed, this formula, going back to our foundations, expresses some truly important element of our truth or our knowledge. From this point on I will not follow the same intellectual journey of decades or centuries, together with its various tests, criticisms, in order again to reach the same point; rather, I accept all this, and use my good sense, just like one might in another branch of study with its equations or other tools.

PE: Let me add a few words. We both studied dogmatics with Professor Ferenc Gál. In Professor Gál's three-year dogmatics course we did not have to learn a single dogma by heart, and they were not even quoted as texts in his books. He presented the faith of the church with the method of the history of salvation, very strictly taking the Bible as his starting point. Later we would ask him whether he could list the texts of the dogmas. He said that he could if needed, and later in the entry for 'dogma' in the Hungarian Catholic Lexicon (Gál, Ferenc, Dogma, in MKL II, Budapest, 1993, 650–657) he listed some 280. In the dogmatics handbooks written with traditional methods, for example Antal Schütz (Antal Schütz, Dogmatika I–II. 3rd edn., Budapest, 1944) or Ludwig Ott (Ludwig Ott, Grundriss der katholischen Dogmatik, 2nd edn.,

Bonn, 2005), to mention two of those still often used today, there are articles printed in bold type, which we usually refer to as dogmas. True enough, but there behind every article, in thin type and in parentheses, is a dogmatic classification. These articles are not all at the same level; there are classifications such as *de fide*, which means that anyone not believing it is not Catholic. So these statements have different rankings, depending on how we get to the formulation and from what source texts. For example, if the author has just abstracted from the works of church leaders, or if something is mentioned in papal speeches, but not in celebratory obligatory statements, etc. These dogmatic classifications are quite important, and belong to that which we refer to as dogmas. So this is not all homogenous. Also, in Old Christian usage, they spoke not of dogmas but of dogma, which referred to the Christian teaching itself. It is important that traditional Christian teaching as an organic whole was also formulated more formally and with greater authority in relation to problems and in individual articles and individual statements, but this does not mean that our faith is made up only of finalized articles to be accepted.

ESV: Regarding what Cardinal Erdő is discussing, *per analogiam*: In his day, Copernicus was at home in all fields of science and scholarship. Leonardo da Vinci had extraordinary knowledge about all fields of academic inquiry. However, because science has become more specialized, individual scholars focus on smaller fields of study, and the Renaissance Man or type of academic has disappeared. Regarding dogma, there are articles in science that we believe cannot be changed. However, people are born with genuine freedom, and it is precisely in science and scholarship that they can express this attribute. We have the right to question everything! This is what distinguishes us from scholars of theology, as they do not have the right to question everything. Science only contains partial truths. It is impossible to learn the complete truth, and we are convinced of this. This is also a difference between us. Scientists and academics are characterized by their doubting to acquire certainty (*Dubitando ad veritatem pervenimus*). This is the essence of experimenting: I must prove the hypotheses that I believe to be true.

SS: I would add one more comment. It is said that a theologian cannot question certain things. I think this is a simplification of things. In every single theologian there lies that Peter who stands before Jesus when the Master talks of the Eucharist; he doesn't understand Jesus' words, but what can he do, he doesn't go on. He questions even the most fundamental thing, doesn't understand it, but stays with him out of personal loyalty. A scholar of faith, if they really are a scholar of faith, knows perfectly well that they are, indeed, able to question. They may question every single thing, as long as they know the answer. I doubt, I question, but I know the answer, and I go on from there. So I think that the theologian, or other scholar of faith, who does not question even the most basic things, is not worthy of their title. This does not mean that they are constantly in a state of questioning, for I can ask whether the fire is hot, and put my finger in it, and learn that it is indeed hot. But I don't have to do this every day if I deal with this question, as I know what it is about and I can move on from here.

PE: Let us return to theology, the study of faith. For Catholics, the methodological principle which gives this field of study its disciplinary identity is that it is built on revelation and the sources for this as authentically explained by the Magisterium. It can be discussed differently, but that is then a different discipline. One can ask whether a statement in physics is composed in a rhythmical way and sounds good or not; it is a fair enough question, just not one that lies within the discipline of physics. This is a question of methodological identity, not one of restrictions to research freedoms.

PLK: I would like to ask a question which may not belong here, strictly speaking, but is relevant nonetheless: whether the Scriptures are just knowledge or a form of scholarship.

JS: Awareness of the Scriptures is just knowledge. Exegesis – how we interpret the words of the Scriptures – is great scholarship. Let me give an example. The consensus in Bible studies – if there are some who disagree – is that chapters 40-66 of the prophet Isaiah were not written by the same author as the first 39 chapters, and rather by another author referred to as Deutero-Isaiah. The point is that in chapters 40-66, which were obviously written while in captivity in Babylon, and which raised hopes of return and redemption for a people in captivity, there is a considerable role for an unnamed prophet who calls himself, and is known by those around him as, Eved Adonai, God's servant. The non-Jewish exegesis recognizes in Eved Adonai the precursor of Jesus. The medieval Jewish and the modern Jewish exegesis sees in him the image of suffering Israel itself. The exegesis, the scholarly examination, of which authors see him as what, of how they interpret him, when they did so, is an academic field. The Scripture itself, if we give it to a fellow believer to read with no commentary – which is a dangerous act, as so much is hard to understand – is not scholarship, but provides knowledge about what this holy volume says about God and humankind. At the basic level it is knowledge; at the higher level it is an academic field. Here the key problem was the question of coming to know God.

Professor Vizi brought up a Hungarian literary example, Attila József. We can find an example in another great Hungarian poet, Endre Ady: 'Desolate, I felt / That my soul in fragments would fly asunder, / And then God's arms enfolded me, / Quiet and sudden' (Endre Ady: The Lord's Coming, trans. Bernard Adams). We can find such a literary example in the work of great Hungarian poet Dániel Berzsenyi, too. Poets bear witness to God, in different ways from scientists and also quite unlike philosophers or theologians. As we are sat here in the Hungarian Academy of Sciences, thanks to its president, Professor Vizi, I am reminded of Samu Szemere, who was director of the Teacher Training Institute, and who at first didn't become an academician because he ran our Teacher Training Institute, then in 1945 became an academician after all, but couldn't remain one ultimately, as he was an idealistic philosopher. So his position was bad as regards the public power at the time. He held the philosophy classes in the seminary, and he said, gentlemen, philosophy begins where astonishment entered human thought. He we see the relationship between theology and philosophy, of which there will a number later, as if we look at Psalm 8, we see: 'When I consider thy heavens, the work of thy fingers, the moon and the stars, which thou hast ordained; What is man, that thou art mindful of him?' Do you even notice him? And there follows an astonishing sentence: 'For thou hast made him a little lower than the angels…' (Psalms 8:4-5). The smallness and greatness of man, that man is small but can be greater, becomes manifest here in Psalm 8. One condition for this 'can be greater' is for man to know as much of the Scriptures as possible. The Scriptures essentially deal with God, in a positive and a negative sense, because the prophets already raise the question of divine justice or injustice, as, with regard to the fate of the Jews, on the one hand they talk of how many attacks ancient Israel faced from the people living around it, and on the other hand of how much disloyalty there was in ancient Israel to monotheism. That is, the prophets ask how come the path of the evil can be successful and that of the good can be a failure. So, with regard to God, theodicy already appears in the Scriptures. This is a question that has not been resolved to this day with regard to the Auschwitz complex. Despite this, for the most part the Scriptures do not question it, which for us is crucial; rather, the Scriptures make it our obligation to get to know God better. It is knowing God better that brings us closer to our faith in God.

There were always two schools of medieval philosophy. One was *creatio ex nihilo*, creation out of nothing, while the other was *chomer kadmon*, the theory of ancient matter. It is very hard to find an answer to this in the Bible. The Bible deals with the creation of the world, one in which we can only reach a final conclusion with faith, not with reason. For one thing, the first and second chapter do not say exactly the same thing. The point as far as Jewish theology is concerned is that God creates of his own sovereign will. Of his own sovereign will, God gives the created beings moral commandments; ethics and the existence of God, at least in the Hebrew Bible, are inseparable. Here it is God's sovereign will that is decisive, just as in ethics.

The question of atheism: mention that 'He does not exist' does appear in the Psalms, but this is said by the fool, comes out of the fool's mouth. The Scriptures do not really deal with proofs of the existence of God; these will be the tasks of medieval philosophy. There was a time when we were taught that philosophy is the *ancilla theologiae*, the maidservant of theology; that is, philosophers gave theologians priority. Without wanting to get into a debate,

Judaism respects it if philosophers say something about a tenet, pro or contra, but the basic tenet is the Scripture, with regard to which the academic problem is again that of whether it is entirely from God, or written by people inspired by God. Bible studies is a very complex field. It is hard to imagine, for example, that the listing of names always involved revealed truth; it is surer to say that the important things are the prophets, the ethical laws and the other social laws. The Jewish exegesis says of this that people would over the centuries have come to realize that you are not allowed to kill, cheat, steal, but the Scriptures gave this to people as a completed outcome. So we are dealing with completed things, and the Scriptures give us knowledge about God which is equally compatible both with anthropomorphism and Anthropopathism. In contrast, philosophy more speaks of God as a bodiless intellectual creature. The Scriptures also tell of Anthropopathism, the wrath of God. Elsewhere it speaks of God's merciful nature. The only way to resolve this is what we see in the Talmud, that the reason that the Bible uses its concepts of anthropomorphism and Anthropopathism is so that there is some way for man, who is so very different from God, to understand... Religious law is not a sport of legislation just for the sake of it; rather, it is by the practice of religious law that we bear witness to the one who is the source of the law.

PLK: What is the relationship between the law and freedom?

JS: The law does not oblige us to do anything which would obstruct our basic efforts to be free...

PLK: I am thinking of how the law is a restriction of freedom.

JS: There is a very stark distinction between dictatorship and democracy, because in a democracy the law is the boundary, while in a dictatorship the limit of validity of the laws created by the dictatorship represents power. So, Jewish law is democratic, because it sets a limit to power. Let me give you an example: in Rabbinical law, there is mention of how the king can start a defensive war without asking the Sanhedrin (the highest Jewish judicial council in ancient

Jerusalem), that is the Gerusia, while for an offensive war the Sanhedrin's consent is required. The king's power was already restricted by the law in ancient times. (BT: Sanhedrin 20a).

SS: Here we have an excellent opportunity to move on as regards the law and actions. As we are sitting here in the building of the Hungarian Academy of Sciences, the question arises of what academic knowledge is, of what the relationship is between knowledge, scholarship and academe, and the relationship of all these to real life.

ESV: This also has historical precedent, as after Greek rationalism, Paul the Apostle brought faith into the foreground, whereas Saint Augustine, as Chief Rabbi Schweitzer alluded to, went so far as to say that reason, knowledge and so on are slaves to faith. Following the Renaissance, the Enlightenment would then deny faith. Philosophically, this process began with Locke. At the same time, science, with its accelerated progress, strives for objectivity and in the course of striving for objectivity always has to give answers to everyday questions, too. Cardinal Richelieu said, or at least we attribute it to him, that national academies have to be established institutions that publish scholarship to a broad audience in the national language. This is the origin of the idea of establishing national academies. So, the task of the academy is not just to disclose the laws of nature and society through the work of academics but also to publicize this body of knowledge, making it accessible for as many people as possible. The Hungarian Academy of Sciences was born of the idea of Count István Széchenyi to transmit to the wider public the scientific spirit of the age, in Hungarian, thereby nurturing the Hungarian language. At that time, this was taken to include literature, the arts, theology and also natural sciences. Our task is to ensure that such an academy exists in the 21st century. Publishing the results of academic inquiry is an obligation. I think that the Hungarian Academy of Sciences currently satisfies this obligation with the 'Universal University' (Mindentudás Egyeteme; officially 'Encompass' in English) and with its now almost serial organization of the World Science Forum. This is the job of a national academy. Whereas faith has the primary role in Christianity,

Judaism, as we have heard, instead holds a more pragmatic conception of faith at its focus; so, in academe, the acquisition and passing on of knowledge is the most important task.

JS: A great number of laws were made in relation to the Sabbath and the prohibition of activities on Saturdays. This includes what reform theology, especially in America, does not accept, but which we do, for example restrictions on travel. Why am I not allowed to get on a bus on Saturdays? In order not to be among those because of whom someone does work on that day; this is why I undertake to walk on Saturdays. Our conservative believers do this, as do all those who are functionaries in the synagogue, but we do not generally make this strict observance of the Sabbath an issue of conscience for followers of the neolog rite.

ESV: There are many health-related laws in the Scriptures that are suited to that period. Restrictions on eating were put into law, which refer to the consumption of animals and other foods that are to be avoided for public health reasons.

JS: Yes, this is the right position to take, although religious history stresses some very daring concepts, namely that among the banned animals there were once also taboo animals. This is a scientific attitude, but we stay with the position in the Scriptures, which speaks of clean and unclean animals; this is the word of the Scriptures on this question, and we do not go beyond it.

PLK: We have already talked about the forms of faith and of knowledge…

ESV: Moreover, let us again mention Pope John Paul II's encyclical *Fides et ratio*, which is very important from the point of view of the relationship between faith and science, as it is a special feature of the modern age that rejects faith. *Fides et ratio* meanwhile juxtaposes them *expressis verbis*, putting the two phenomena on the same footing.

PE: May I reflect on this a little? Medieval scholastics quite vigorously debated the relationship between faith and science. And the conclusion of these debates was, in the end, that there is no *duplex veritas*. There is no such thing as something being true according to faith, but false according to objective, correct science, or vice versa. For us it is important from a doctrinal point of view that there cannot be an unresolvable contradiction between the two, because the same God is the Creator of the whole world whose laws we investigate, and with the experiences of which we construct certain laws using certain abstractions, just like the one who revealed himself in the Bible in a well-known way. And for this reason we exclude any essential opposition; faith enlightens human reason, and so it is more than anything an aid to anyone who accepts faith to acquire knowledge more certainly, to question the world more probingly, convinced they will find an answer to their questions.

The other big question which was raised here was the relation between faith and actions. This was indeed raised in such a Rabbinical form in the books of the New Testament, too, and the end result was that faith without actions is dead (Jam 2:17). So we return to the Ten Commandments, as for us the laws of ethics are not merely sensible rules for behaviour, but are the result of a personal relationship with God. For 'I am the LORD'. At the same time the other actions are important, too; it is not enough to believe in God, one must live likewise. Specific actions live on in Catholic tradition, and are even collected in lists; so much do they live on that the *Commpendium of the Catechism of the Catholic Church*, published last year by Pope Benedict XVI, which is now available in Hungarian, too, has an appendix with a list of the corporal and spiritual works of mercy. These actions are already very familiar in their content from the world of the Old Testament.

JS: The post-Biblical tradition lists 613 commandments in the Torah of Moses, some of which are positive, to do, and others negative, to avoid doing. Another part is the broader explanation, in practical terms, applied to the life of society, of the rest of the Book of Exodus after the Ten Commandments, in point of fact of the lapidary laws of the Ten Commandments. In terms of actions, Jewish thinking goes further, logically speaking in a so-called deductive way, and from the laws of the Scriptures Rabbinical literature prescribes further rules, that is prohibitions and obligations, but these ultimately are all traced back to the Scriptures, back to faith.

PLK: Professor Schweitzer, can you clarify what is the Torah and what is the Talmud?

JS: The Torah is the five books of Moses, while the Talmud is the combined name for two great literary works, the Mishnah and the Gemara. The Mishnah was edited in around 200 CE. There are different versions of the Talmud, and the fuller one, the so-called Babylonian Talmud, includes the examination of the debates over the laws in the Mishnah, as well as a number of ethically-related Scripture explanations. Ethnographic, medical and many other not necessarily interconnected observations and statements can be found in it. The Babylonian Talmud is the collection of an enormous amount of material from about 220 CE to about 500 CE, recording the views of some two thousand scholars, ending in around 500 CE. The Palestinian Talmud is a smaller collection which starts at about the same time as the Babylonian one, and finishes between 300 CE and 400 CE (for more detail see Encyclopedia Judaica, Vol. 15, Encyclopedia Judaica, Jerusalem, s. v. Talmud, s. v. Amora). The Talmud is the debating and enlightening of the laws in the Torah; the Talmud is more academe, because it already includes debate, which is one condition for academe. I would prove this with a specific article. I am sure you know the Hanukkah festival (165 BCE, the festival of the inauguration of the sanctuary) from the Book of Maccabees, which is about the prohibition of the Jewish religion as Greek power spreads; in the 2nd century, in the Holy Land, this leads to a war of independence, in which the Maccabees fought on the side of the Jews, in partisan-like groups, and later in the regular army. The triumph in this war was to clean the Sanctuary of Jerusalem from the Zeus idols, and again to consecrate the altar for monotheism. The consecration took place with holy oil. There is a legend that the holy oil was enough for one day, but burned for eight days. The feast of consecration is eight days. Now comes the debate: on one view, if we have poured in the oil needed for one day, and this burned for eight days, then, logically, there was less oil on the seventh day than the eighth, and so on, and so every day a flame had to be quenched, as the oil was being used up. On the other view, however, if the oil for one day lasted for eight days, then we should light a candle every day, and this continues until the eighth day. So there are debates like this one and similar ones. There is consensus in the Talmud, however, or if there isn't, then in the later literature. The practical religious law is called Halakha; the road to be followed, and which always follows a logical path from some Biblical law.

PE: I think that in Professor Schweitzer's previous comment there was a reference to war, peace, even justice. When we investigate the problem of knowledge or of knowledge and morality, then we first collide into it from the side of society, while it is my conviction that there are very significant, perhaps increasingly significant moral problems on the side of natural sciences, too. I think that a new and very powerful experience we have today is the collapse of society and of culture. These phenomena are focussed around two main concepts: subjectivism and formalism. The real question, which is the key to mission and to church service, is what can we give, do, and respond in this situation, and as the mediators of Christ's truth, love and mystery? I would introduce a few examples of this intellectual situation. I don't want to say them all at once, but rather as they come; the opportunity and method for searching for the Christian answer is the goal on account of which I want to say these things. For one thing we were talking about was why the progress of the ethical response has lagged behind scientific questions.

The first such example is that of war, law and justice. The Dominican monk Francisco de Vitoria's lecture entitled *De iure belli* was delivered at the celebratory session of the University of Salamanca in 1539 (Francisco De Vitoria, De iure belli, ed. C. Galli, Roma-Bari 2005 [Universale Latera 852]). These old lectures delivered to entire universities are important. In a given historical and intellectual context they mark out the whole of humanity's struggle with a particular issue. And one of the greatest questions of life facing humanity is that of war and peace. The mainstream of Catholic tradition has always tried to judge man's behaviour from an ethical perspective, even in war. For we are responsible for our every free and conscious human act; there is no part of life which can exclude itself from the laws of ethics. De Vitoria's lecture was the result of new historical phenomena. How does ethics respond to this? The discovery of America and the experience of the first decades of Spanish colonialization forced the greatest theological thinkers of the age into ethical reflection. It was exactly the Catholic Church and Catholic theology which reacted with astonishment to Pizarro's bloody conquests in Peru and to the cruel atrocities of the Conquistadors in general. What was the ethical basis for colonialization as such? This question was already raised by the first generation. Many, with de Vitoria at their helm, established an objective set of criteria to judge whether a war was just. They also examined what is permissible in such a war against the enemy and against the innocent citizens of an enemy country. They also grappled with the difficulty that a war cannot be equally just for both parties, as this would establish an ethical as well as other basis for an endless chain of retribution and vengeance. They also had to confront the significant practical problem of how princes and leaders, or their simple subjects, could judge the justification of war in specific situations that were often complicated. This is the point where modern subjectivism and formalism's concept of law and international law, based merely on agreement, as an arbitrary system of norms, departs and deviates from the objective, moderate realism of Aristotle or Saint Thomas Aquinas. Deviates from the acceptance that the foundations of reality and within it the objectively just order of society are part of the world and of humanity as a result of the logic and goodness of creation. In short, the objective system of norms is what is usually called natural law.

SS: If you don't mind me asking, just what is natural law, exactly?

PE: Law or not – it hardly matters what term is used for it. People talk of a natural law of ethics, but my opinion is that, whatever we call it, it remains a question as to who determines the content of this natural law. Human common sense, the Catholic approach holds, and in the case of doubt the Magisterium, which authoritatively explains revelation. But aside from the abstract content of norms, we have to know the particular situation or state of affairs in order to judge it. And this is where the problem of terrible complexity begins. This was such a burden for the people of the modern era that over centuries many gradually gave up hope in the possibility of judging specific situations with objective ethical criteria. Out of this and, among other factors, out of precisely the difficulty of the question of war and politics, would emerge agnosticism, subjectivism and mere formalism, all as the abandonment of the possibility of objective knowledge. The reflections of 450 years ago became fashionable and relevant again in the 20th century.

Compared to the setup brought by modern era, the Europe-centric worldview with many players, the situation has changed in a number of respects. I think that part of this new situation has been the era of the two superpowers, then from 1989 of the single superpower. It is not clear that the average person, or even the average politician, is able to weigh up the nature and extent of the disparity between the weaponry of the superpower and the potential of the others! Is the difference as big as it was back then between the Spanish and the Incas? What does all this mean for the existence of international law, for the conditions for just, moral war? If the subjects of international life are radically unequal, then the rug has been pulled out from underneath the norms of international behaviour based on understanding between states implicitly assumed to be equal and sovereign, and on treaties both fictive and real. Then the question arises of whether there is a *dominus mundi* in a concrete, mundane sense, and most of all whether there is need for a new system of objective ethical norms which don't appeal to a consensus.

ESV: When we mention morality and the 21st century, when we judge the wars, then we cannot avoid noting that during the time of prehistoric man, there was not yet any need for laws and regulations, as there would be after humanity began to multiply and larger communities were formed. There can be no doubt that the Judeo-Christian intellectual and cultural world produced the basic laws and rules of how to live together and was able to establish the common good, the *bonum commune*. Of course, I am not thinking of Walter Lipmann's philosophy of the common good, about what the role of the state is, but rather what gives credibility to the leader of a community, whether large or small, and the ethical norms that must be observed by the individual, by small communities, large communities, by the state. Put simply: for one person vis-à-vis another. Here, the philosophy of love appears. When we fulfill this by including our enemy in the group of potential love, we then establish a philosophical basis for how we should behave. By making the development of the world economy incredibly fast, science has fundamentally altered the relationship between people. Science provides something that humanity immediately makes use of – because we live in an age, I think, in which self-interest is the engine even for friendship, rather than a more or less similar estimation of real human values. No attention is paid to the fact that self-interest means the 'common good' for only a select few people, whereas values ought to be a positive thing for everyone. Precisely for this reason, I have a rather negative opinion of the activity of the established churches, as they should have a cardinal role in warning humanity on a day-to-day basis that we have reached the point at which even existence and our relationship with other people is a basic question. Science has its own ethical obligation, too; the scientist evidently does. How and when should they speak up? How should they alert others if they see some type of danger? It is my conviction that the basic problem of our age is not an economic one, but is primarily a moral one. Again, I emphasize that churches and the state have – or should have – a very serious obligation to solve this. The decline in social capital is in large part due to the fact that Hungarian society has completely lost its trust in politicians. This loss of trust has only further strengthened the tendency of people to throw to the wind the consensuses and morals developed over the past centuries as far as relationships between people are concerned and as far as the relationship between people and their environment is concerned. In his book *The Great Disruption* (F. Fukuyama, The Great Disruption: Human Nature and the Reconstitution of Social Order, London, 1999), Francis Fukuyama was already discussing how the unravelling of worldwide social cohesion would have to be followed by a 'great realignment'. The collapse of the Roman Empire was caused by the basic moral rules disappearing from its society, rules that are indispensable for the orderly operation of society, the economy and financial matters.

The ability for cooperation is a characteristic unique to the human species – that is, humans do not just want to look after themselves but are able to and share this faculty with others. Alongside self-interest, they are capable of recognizing that there are common values that serve the interests of a smaller community and even those of a larger society. So, one of the most important tasks of modern state power is developing a community of values that serves real human and community needs.

SS: What would the everyday life of a more responsible church look like in this context?

ESV: If we look at history, we can see that the various religions have played a very important role in transforming individual societies. It can be observed that in any given period, people were driven to religion by their uncertainties and anxiety, seeking support and finding relief in the community life provided by religion. The secular world increasingly lacks community manifestations and the practice of compassion. The appearance of nationalism also proves that people have a strong need to belong to a community, to a nation, and that this can also be exploited for the wrong objectives. This is why it is important to create a healthy sense of nation. In truth, this is what is compensated for by the Olympics, world championships, international football games, and various competitions. So, churches need to be present in people's everyday lives and not just on Sundays. The churches should take on much more in dealing with social problems. They should set an example and find the structural forms that are effective. The modern world has new challenges. They should not lag behind the world's great changes. They should be ahead of them.

SS: In practice most institutions through which the church could do more have become secularized. Hospitals, schools, care homes; to maintain these needs a strong human and financial background in any case, if they are to operate properly. The current situation in Hungary also concerns the way that moral, intellectual and financial support needs to be guaranteed for these duties, because if all this is taken away from the churches, they will really struggle to complete all these tasks.

PE: I would like to go back to a tiny detail: that we should give an example. This summer, the Hungarian and Slovak bishops' conferences completed a celebratory ritual of conciliation in Esztergom. The message 'We forgive and ask for forgiveness' was expressed by both sides, and reaching this took a number of years. This action was rather ignored by the ordinary media in Hungary and Slovakia. They produced very few news items about it. And when certain nationalist phenomena started to emerge, there were two statements, which no newspaper published, either here or in Slovakia. There could at least be circumstances in which our efforts would be accepted if only for the sake of equality...

Science, society, ethics. How should Christianity perform its role? My first answer to this would be to say that it makes our situation no easier, and neither did it ever do so in the early modern period, that the consequences of truth and natural law and of objective morality have to be applied to an increasingly complex world. It is no accident that alongside politics and war it is the ethical response to the questions raised by science that is hardest for us. We feel compassion and empathy rather than anger, disappointment and disgust towards those who are disappointed and have given up hope on such moral judgments, because they think them impossible, and who think in terms of legal and moral rules that change dynamically and radically even at a societal level and which we develop and adjust according to various opinions and interests and in line with some formal criteria.

What is Christianity's response to this? For one thing, it worries for Western culture and humanity. For if coexistence has objective norms that are written into our nature, then a failure to acknowledge this and its neglect in theoretical and practical terms risks the existence of both individual and community. Similarly, there are signs that the West's breaking with its own traditional world-view and values decreases its competitiveness relative to other civilizations, even if the technical and scientific gap between them is still significant. This helps us understand Huntington's distressing vision of the conflict between civilizations (Samuel P. Huntington, The Clash of Civilizations and the Remaking of World Order, Simon & Schuster, New York, 1996). Secondly, Christianity strives to see its values implemented in the Western world.

This effort seems pretty ineffectual at present. It is enough to allude in this context to the attempts made during the preparation of the European Union's constitutional treaty, which appeared to the public to be unsuccessful, as God and Christianity were not in the end mentioned in the preamble to the document. There was, however, partial protection of the current legal status of the churches and spiritual communities, as their contribution to Europe was recognized, as was the need for regular dialogue between them and the European Union. Concepts of Judeo-Christian origin, like the freedom and dignity of the individual, were also recognized.

Meanwhile religious affairs remain in the national jurisdiction of the individual member states. At least formally and for the time being. For the Union's bodies can still take jurisdiction over principles which may influence the internal rights of individual member states. Such new criteria may undermine the principles and institutions that, according to our Christian faith, we see as objectively valuable because of the laws of our nature in the area of marriage, the family, the protection of life, and other issues. They can undermine them even in countries where society – still – broadly accepts them. They can also challenge and gradually erode the legal status and freedom of the churches and religious communities in the individual member states. If we believe in the fact that the key values we represent are truly the desires of our nature, that is the objective rules of our existence and our happiness, then we also have to assume that a deep and lasting departure from them will destroy society. Pope John Paul II spoke of the culture of death. The eminent Hungarian conservative industrialist and politician Móric Kornfeld quoted the Old Testament: 'My people are destroyed for lack of knowledge' (Hos 4:6). Dante writes in De Monarchia that law is the material and personal relationship between one man and another, the unharmed maintenance of which protects human society, while its abandonment destroys it (Dante, *De Monarchia*, Liber secundus, V, 1). Because of this, concern for people and for civilization obliges Christians to struggle for the social acceptance and protection of the values they avow.

For this, the so-called Christian politics in the West, at least as seen from here in Central-Eastern Europe, does not prove to be effective enough. Perhaps the conviction and intention is weak; perhaps the social support it needs is missing. Nevertheless, if we feel solidarity with the existence of Western civilization – and as its survival depends on the flowering of basic human values, humanity and Christian love demands this solidarity of us – we have to honour all those efforts, including civic, Christian democratic, indeed in the traditional sense even social democratic efforts, which have the goal of slowing and weakening those legislative, administrative and judicial actions with which some would aim to destroy the institutions and values desired by the law of nature.

The question can arise of whether, if civilization's self-destruction reaches a critical point, those in control of economic, political, communicational and other powers will not by necessity turn to traditional values and historical religious communities, especially given the pressure and competition coming from other civilizations. So for the Christian thinker the attitude of 'the worse it gets, the better' could be tempting, with the hope that the more quickly Western civilization destroys itself, the sooner it will be forced to return to traditional values. But this thought must be kept at a distance from Christianity, as good ends do not justify sinful means. In any case, the values professed by Christianity are not tied to civilization, but are universal. We have a calling that is towards all cultures and all peoples. The effect of globalization and mass media is evident, and brings an opportunity for the Gospels to be proclaimed to all nations. Just as during the collapse and partial transfer of the Roman Empire and its culture the church laid roots among the so-called Barbarian tribes, so, back when today's Western civilization came into being, today we feel a possibility and a calling to introduce our faith to the peoples of Africa and Asia in a realistic fashion. This process requires time. It is not helped by quick collapses and general conflicts.

JS: I wholeheartedly agree with what Cardinal Erdő says. The question is who are listening to us. We might share these beautiful thoughts in order to contribute to the improvement of people's lives, at least in ethical and emotional terms. But I am afraid that our sphere of influence and in general the potential for ethical influence is very limited. People will respond that that is all very nice, but that you are speculative people who sit in your rooms with your books, and other people are carried away by life, often meaning the easy, uninhibited and unscrupulous making of money. I know that we need money to live, and that it is everyone's obligation to provide the best possible standard of living for their family, but we can very precisely see that our ethical influence is very small relative to tremendous series of unethical actions. It seems like a rhetorical question, but just what are the methods which are able to have a broader influence? Cardinal Erdő was just saying how in this unfortunate Hungarian-Slovak question a reassuring event took place involving both councils of bishops, but I didn't hear anything about this in the newspapers or on television or radio. Such events should somehow be brought to public attention in greater measure.

ESV: I think that science and academe are in a more favorable position than the two historical churches that provide Europe's cultural foundation, as the Lisbon decision states that the society and economy of the European Union must be knowledge-based. Our responsibility in this is enormous. We must not forget that science and the economy would like to guarantee sustainable development, that is, that at least in this corner of the globe, living standards should be as high as possible. However, it is a human characteristic that we would like to get as much of something as possible, and to this end, we apply almost every minute and hour of the day to acquiring things. This is where an absence appears: the absence of realizing one's ethical obligation to others and, likewise, the absence of the state realizing its obligation to its citizens. I see this as Europe's greatest problem today. It is not possible to say that in the 21st century, there is no need for religious life, nor for science and scholarship, because they have already made so much progress. Though there are, in fact, such negative, strongly anti-academic voices.

PLK: Without bringing daily politics into it, what can the explanation be for these anti-academic opinions?

ESV: It is that some expect science to bring utility as quickly as possible. The conviction has developed, here in Hungary, too, that only profitable endeavors should be supported. The magic of money, the omnipotence of money, the idolization of money, even making a 'god' out of money: all this makes its presence known in daily politics, and these people then ask why we would address things that do not bring immediate profit – more precisely, things that do not bring immediate profit for them. This type of pragmatism, or rather this type of mercenary attitude, corrodes this basic philosophy and vocation of science and scholarship, the process of learning about the created world. Only things that bring a return are needed. This way of thinking brings grave dangers. A *bon mot*: Michael Faraday, who was a member of the Royal Society, was drinking whisky and smoking a cigar when the Chancellor of the Exchequer at the time happened to join him at his table. At approximately 9 p.m., Faraday stood up and told the gentlemen he needed to leave and return to his lab. The Chancellor of the Exchequer tried to persuade him to stay, commenting on what nice cigars there were, how good the dinner would be, and wondering why he would leave then. The Chancellor asked, 'What are you tinkering with back there, anyway?' To which Faraday replied, 'Chancellor, I can assure you that what I am tinkering with will bring your successors a great amount of income'. And he was right: he was working on electricity. This story is another illustration of how an overgrowth of the pragmatic approach can destroy the classical founding principle of science that is still valid today.

SS: Let me return to the relationship between academic knowledge, science, and everyday life. One can play in the space between two scientific heresies, and hope to bring them together: there are fields of study which have no relation to real life, there are those fields of study which concentrate merely on pragmatic results.

ESV: Linguist and Islamic scholar Ignaz Goldziher's research in the Middle East from a century ago is proving useful right now, with the Arab question coming to the fore. So, it is never possible to say that a certain academic discipline is not of any use!

JS: Goldziher's works in Hungarian are just now being translated into English…

ESV: We do not have the right to say that something is useless. When Alexander Fleming discovered penicillin in 1928, people said, so what, another medicine. Now we know just how much this new medicine has brought us. The readiness for action of the Allied divisions in World War II was greatly increased because a broad spectrum of bacterial infections had become quickly treatable, whereas the Germans only had Ultraseptil at their disposal. The consequences of any one particular discovery are incalculable. This is why one must not ruin the internal logic of science with external interference. The speed at which we get to know the world is getting faster and faster, and the number of encounters with the unknown is increasing.

SS: How might it be possible to make the obligation of the churches a bit more real, a bit more life-shaping? In the last few days I have talked a lot to a Hungarian lawyer living in the United States, László rsy, who said how in a number of larger Jesuit provinces they made great efforts to establish institutions for the various social problems encountered in everyday life, investing energy, people, and money. At the same time many problems are ones that a good law would sort out completely. Many finish their degrees at the school of law there, and enter the world of legislation. Somehow this feedback doesn't work; they could pass a good law to deal with a bad situation, and then they wouldn't need these Sisyphean struggles.

ESV: The rule of law always trails behind life. It tries to provide answers to the problems that arise in everyday life, to order disorder. We cannot expect it to produce laws that are forward-thinking, as its unique characteristic is precisely its conservatism. This is in contrast to the natural sciences or the social sciences, which address phenomena when they are still completely unfamiliar to society. This is why I mentioned the responsibility of the church and of the literate, which includes the church, too, of course. We would expect the historical churches to adapt to the challenges of modern life. And modern life has created new types of communication systems as the result of the information revolution, and the fact that the church, God's voice, cannot be heard more loudly depends on how much the church can adjust to the challenges of the modern era, and how much it makes use of the technical possibilities at its disposal. The Academy has to pay attention to all this, just as scholarship does.

JS: I would like to ask, with respect, how you think it possible, Professor Vizi, technically speaking, to reach the wider classes of society. What would this look like in practice? The use of more modern methods, I mean.

ESV: I think it should be the obligation of the state to assist the work of the literate, precisely on the basis of the philosophy of the common good – and at taxpayers' expense. Those who work for the common good should have their operation eased.

JS: Because it is just about better use of mass communication.

ESV: That is right. Those half-hour so-called religious programs and the like really amount to nothing, even though the whole point of public service broadcasting would be to broadcast programs in the interest of the common good. Consider the example of the 'Universal University' ('Encompass'). When I became president of the Academy, we had the idea of putting this into practice. Everyone warned me against it, saying no one had any need for this in today's world. And look what happened: it has been a great success, with more than one and a half million people watching each episode. There is, indeed, demand for beautiful and good things. I am convinced that there is also a demand for spiritual life, for passing on love and ethics, for art, for culture.

JS: We need to convince the media to spend more time on what Professor Vizi has listed. What would be effective would be for non-professionals to talk about it. Not priests, but scientists, scholars, writers, poets; of the priests people will say that they are just addressing their flock.

ESV: Oh, but there was that joint lecture given by Cardinal Erdő and Chief Rabbi Schweitzer together! What a success it was! A world event, we could say.

PE: Please let me join in with a self-critical comment. This in part certainly depends on the effectiveness of our participation in these communication channels, but we do have a kind of substantive problem with this, too. These modern phenomena inspire us Christians to examine how we can, today, on the basis of our faith, give responses based on objective natural laws and positive divine law to these pressing ethical questions. Subjectivism and agnosticism cannot be dealt with simply with reference to the tendency of human nature to bad. Though, in the conviction of believers, the workings of evil in the world is a real and great force, this is not an explanation for everything. It is often bitterness and disappointment that lie behind subjectivism and agnosticism, as to many questions our Christian faith offers answers that are too general and hard to apply to particular circumstances. Because of this, some say that Biblical tradition is too ancient to give adequate direction on our detailed problems. Even de Vitoria's principles did not give adequate guidance about just war; indeed, it is precisely from some of his thoughts that Grotius, Hobbes and Kant reach their deist, sensualist, formalist, in a word typically modern principles. We are nevertheless strong in our belief, as put by Pope Benedict XVI in his first public speech (Benedict XVI, Homilia, 24 April 2005), that the church lives, the church is young. Christ's teaching and his good news are always relevant. We see in them God's conclusive words to humanity. So we must not give up on the search for moral answers; we are not allowed not to comment on the moral implications of new questions. And this demands enormous strength. A constant dialogue between natural scientists, political scientists, economists, and many other professionals, with generous and in this sense humble theologians faithfully representing the church's faith and holy tradition. This is one of the best functions of the Catholic universities. And of the papal councils and local church bodies. In recent times the contemplation of a great number of discoveries and changes has made many theologians uncertain. For example, since the age of Enlightenment or from the 19th century onwards, geology, the theory of evolution, and other disciplines have seemed to be at odds with certain details of the story of Creation in the Bible if taken literally.

Meanwhile historical criticism and form criticism began to make a distinction between the essence of the theological message and the details belonging to the culture and world-view, if you like, the scientific world-view, of the era. But within the church this distinction required the assistance of newer and newer articles from the Magisterium. In fact, the fast progress and development of natural sciences and the fast alterations to the accepted positions led the theologians becoming tired of keeping up these processes of progress and of trying to dress up the teachings of their faith in specific images adjusted to these newer and newer world-views. And yet this is very important for the effectiveness of the preaching of the word and of looking for specific solutions. The works of Stanley Jaki, for example, were of interest to the Hungarian public. Indeed, sometimes reports on personal theological experiences relating to their professional lives come from the scientific community and from religious economists. Yet it is as if, as a corollary of the ideological agnosticism of the new and latest era, there is in theological circles a demand for some kind of natural scientific agnosticism or a separation based on self-defence.

So the question remains of how we could tie our faith to the uncertain, ever-changing world-view of the natural sciences, or to the ever-newer opportunities offered by technology. It is as if this awe were to characterize the theological thinking of many of us, even though, according to our faith, we can get to know God! According to the statement of the First Vatican Council, based on the New Testament, God is 'the source and end of all things, can be known with certainty from the consideration of created things, by the natural power of human reason: ever since the creation of the world, his invisible nature has been clearly perceived in the things that have been made' (First Vatican Council, Const. Dei Filius, chapter 2, part 1; Denzinger-Hünermann no. 3004. Cf. Rom 1:20). So God, to some degree, can be seen from the created world. That is, the created world is knowable with human reason, if not in its entirety and in its every detail, but with objective value. This is beautifully emphasized by Pope John Paul II in his *Fides et ratio*. Faith rushes to the aid of reason, which doubts the possibility for certain and true knowledge (Pope John Paul II, Enc. Fides et ratio, 14 Sep 1998, no. 5-6). The assumption of the knowability, rationality and logicality of the world is a typical characteristic of the optimism of the Western world, feeding in part from its Judeo-Christian religious roots.

So we are obliged, as a church, to regard human science with trust and with the curiosity that its importance and value deserve.

ESV: I would add a few thoughts about good and evil. I completely agree: progress brings bad things in its wake. The debate between Settembrini and Naphta in *The Magic Mountain* symbolizes this, as does Lucifer in Imre Madách's *The Tragedy of Man* (Az ember tragédiája): the good person, who defends ethics, defends their own truth. The church has to do the same, making use of the results of modern science and adapting to the challenges those results generate. Just as there is a need for a devil's advocate during canonization, so too is there a need in science for criticism, as we are not certain that what we claim, what a scientist claims, is true. It is all that criticism that in the end convinces you whether you are on the right track.

JS: I would just add to this a quote from earlier than the literary parallels, from the story of creation: the propensity for bad is there in everyone from their youth. We are born with a clean slate. We see that little children are cute, naïve, well-intentioned, tell the truth, don't hide anything, and later, as they become civilized, the bad things cling to them. We haven't talked about education yet, though this has a significant effect on someone. Education begins in the family and continues at school. If we have a suggestion, like how people should be understanding with each other, then we should stress the importance of education as much as that of what is ethically good.

SS: And education as a science soon proves itself useful if it is put into practice in schools.

ESV: The results of science and the study of the results of science provide an equal opportunity for everyone. The state can have a significant role in aiding this equality of opportunity. This is connected to what we have been discussing all along, the role of ethics. This is the infrastructure we have to think in terms of and that will determine Europe's future.

JS: When equality of opportunity is the greatest question. The child who through no fault of their own grows up in a house without books does not start out with the same chances as the child from a family with books. Those who begin with a disadvantage need to be supported, and this is very difficult.

ESV: One would expect the communication tools of public service broadcasting to serve the interests of Hungarian citizens better. One would also expect them to respect the rights of citizens to develop culturally as they see fit. If they are atheists, they are welcome to be that, but to raise them to become atheists is not acceptable.

PE: How does an ethical norm work? On the one hand we are talking about what an ethical norm is, what the basis for it is, how to recognize it; on the other hand we have to talk about how individual people bring their own particular ethical decisions. And an ethical decision is a value judgment. It has the form of syllogism, has a consequential nature, and has at least two premises. One is the moral principle, which a religious person gets from the source of religious knowledge, that is the Bible; the other is the existing knowledge about the specific situation. So it is obvious that the commandment 'do not steal' forbids me from taking something from someone. But if I think that a cow is just a stray, I have the right to take it as my own.

JS: In Jewish law it has to be declared to be without owner. There is a very nice literary example of this; the novel of a Polish Jewish writer begins with it being a very cold winter, and the protagonist stands by the window of his room and sees two kids sneaking into his shed where he keeps his firewood. The kids have obviously gone there to steal firewood. He opens the window and shouts out a Hebrew word: *hefker!* Which means 'no owner'. So if he states that the firewood there has no owner, then he absolves the two kids from the crime of stealing. It is beautiful both poetically and legally.

PE: It does indeed show very nicely how there is a state of affairs that we have to judge or qualify ethically. Our life today is so complicated, whether economic life, the world of natural science, or even simply secular law! People often do not even know the current state of legislation, but this does not absolve them from the consequences; yet it is knowing the state of affairs and the position of the law that is one of the premises for making an ethical decision! If my knowledge is not precise or faithful enough, then my conclusions will be weaker, and in vain is the principle I am applying a clean one if I am not adequately acquainted with reality.

JS: The weight of the power of the state often plays a role in ethical decisions. I will give a single example from my time as a rabbi in Pécs. We had one or two teachers among our congregation, who, on our greatest festival, the Day of Atonement, and the evening before it, would have liked to come along to the synagogue. We know that there was a time when if a teacher had walked into and come out of the synagogue in the middle of Kossuth Square on the evening before a festival, by the third day he would have lost his job. So one's actions are not always decided by free will, but can be influenced by more pressing external factors. In parentheses I would note that we did find a solution: they came in around the back into my room, and I went into the temple, leaving the door ajar; they could hear everything, but it was not likely that they would be caught for the great crime of entering the temple.

SS: Here I would return to Professor Vizi's earlier comment on the development of ethics as a scholarly discipline. How much can timeless ethical laws serve the life of the individual and the community in the long term, even in the context of a responsibility to one's surroundings? It is certain that this field is not given a prominent role in denominational ethical teaching and research.

ESV: If we are talking about ethics, we always need to mention the community, as ethics is about our relationship to each other, to the community, to nature. I am convinced that Europe is making a huge mistake when it pays so little attention to this. The fast development of science and technology, of course, makes it possible for us to forget about this. We are overwhelmed by the flood of innovations; small communities, the basic texture of society, have collapsed.

It is impossible to see where this will take us. Sociology has already made note of this, but the political authorities, only capable of thinking in terms of electoral cycles, ignore this, which is a great mistake. I think that the demographic crisis affecting Europe is also an ethical issue. The basic instinct for the species to survive has become secondary to the accumulation of pleasures in everyday life, and this is boosted by globalization, the powers-that-be and politics, as they will do anything under the sun to retain their power. The consequences will be inestimable. The situation is worst in Germany, Spain and Italy. In these countries, even minimal reproduction is not achieved, that is, the population is declining. The demographic crisis, which also affects Hungary, could bring inestimable consequences: by 2030-2040, the proportion between those generating the national income and those demanding support from the national income will shift dramatically in favor of the latter, which could lead to the complete disintegration of sustainable development and the economic and social equilibrium.

Moreover, the crisis of the family, the proportion of people living alone, even of people raising children alone, is rising so quickly that it is having a real effect on social capital; sociologically speaking, it will lead to an increase in the number of those at the bottom of the hierarchy, the poor, and to an increase in criminality.

At the same time, with a declining population, the average age will rise, which means that the composition of society will shift even more towards those depending on national income. The funds generated by those who are now pensioners have long since been spent, and the next generation will not be able to generate as much as will be needed for the livelihoods of this growing section of society. Thus, Europe is facing a grave demographic crisis to come by 2040-2050, especially if we look at the populations and birth rates of the Islamic peoples. Meanwhile, the cultural crisis has essentially already begun.

V.

The World of the Academy and Acts of Defiance In Conversation with Professor E. Sylvester Vizi

PLK: What was your family background?

ESV: My father was from Apostag, a village 100 km to the south of Budapest. They were smallholders, on quite a large estate, but my father had many siblings, so he moved to Budapest. That is where he met my mother, who was the daughter of a wealthy bourgeois family from Óbuda; they married for love, which my mother's parents objected to. My father played chess and wrote poems; he died very young from tuberculosis. In those days, that was a folk illness of that region between the Danube and Tisza rivers. My father was Calvinist, my mother was Catholic; I was born a Roman Catholic because my father signed a dispensation. I was enrolled in the Sophianum as my elementary school; this was the Sacred Heart on Mikszáth Kálmán Square, a girls' school run by nuns, where they needed altar boys, and so, they took on four of us boys. Every morning, the four of us served as altar boys at the school mass at 6:30 a.m., 7 a.m. and 7:30 a.m.

This all started before World War II ended. The sisters were very fond of us, as we created a different world in this all-girl school. We sat in the same class as the girls – indeed, we were something like boarders, so we studied there in the evenings, too. The language teaching, French and German, was very strong. Our priest, Father Schandl, set out the order for our days, and in the evenings, we would serve at the 7 p.m. litany. In those days, only boys could serve at mass, so we needed to be present.

SS: How many years did you spend there? Did you stay in touch with the nuns in any way?

ESV: Four years. Then, I started going to the Benedictines in Rigó Street, which later became the Fazekas High School, where Fülöp Dombos was my class teacher and Xavér Szunyogh was my literature teacher and later my spiritual father. Today, few people know who he was. He was a world-famous scholar. Inside his robust figure was a very good soul, as meek as a lamb; he was immediately lovable. I was taught by Kamill Borbély, Arisztid Kovács and Árkád Simon. Gyula Kaposy was my sports teacher. Árkád Simon was the Latin teacher, who would rap our knuckles if we could not decline our verbs properly. I would just add that there was an entrance examination to get into the Benedictine school, and Shvoy, the bishop of Székesfehérvár at the time, took me under his wing, although I did not need it. It is also part of my life story that my mother remarried, to an engineer, a good man named Menyhárt Nagy. They raised, but I retained my surname.

I belong to the generation that fled the front, that still remembers the burning bank building on the corner of Kecskeméti Street and Calvin Square in central Budapest, that hid from the Russians in the basement, together with our Jewish compatriots in hiding, and that still remembers the question asked by the Arrow Cross men and the German patrolmen: do you have any family in the countryside? I was the one they sent out to respond, as a boy with blonde hair and blue eyes who spoke excellent German. I remember the sweepings of the attic, too, because I inherited an estate from my father, and because I was a minor belonging to the Board of Guardians, it was not taken from me. I belong to the generation that had part of its family deported and imprisoned and that is still terrified of a ring of the doorbell after 10 p.m. because back then this could only be the secret police or the political services. I belong to the generation that lived through the events of the Hungarian Uprising in 1956; as a national guard, I even took part in them in Pécs, as that is where I attended medical school. I lived through the reprisals that followed, and, together with others in my generation, I lived through that relative freedom, freedom to travel, behind which, of course, lie evil principles as well. I belong to the generation as a member of which I was able to build a career, to see the world, to study in Oxford, to work in America, and eventually to become president of the Hungarian Academy of Sciences.

However, what I have not yet said is that I am a member of the generation that locked up the church, together with István Kovács, when they removed the priests from the sanctuary of the Sacred Heart of Jesus church. We were twelve years old, and we were the two altar boys. It was evening, after evensong. The father pushed the keys into our hands. So, an important stretch of Hungary's history accompanied my life.

SS: If you think back to the people who played a formative role in your youth, whom else would you mention?

ESV: In addition to Xavér Szunyogh, whom I have already mentioned, there was Károly Tihanyi, my literature teacher at the Fáy High School. He was a teacher who had returned from the front and taught in the András Fáy High School. He was also my class teacher for some time and had a strong influence on the way my personality developed. In those days, I played many sports; I was on the first team for athletics, chess and tennis.

PLK: How did this love for sport develop?

ESV: I ended up at the András Fáy High School, where Zoltán Szabó was my sports teacher. Sports were important in my family. The Olympian Márta Nagy was my first cousin – the daughter of my mother's older sister. We were in the same class at the Sacred Heart; in 1956, she competed in the Olympics in Melbourne, as a member of the gymnastics team. I remember how we accompanied her to the center of Budapest, where they travelled to Prague and then to Melbourne. I always played sports at the Kinizsi Football Club in Ferencváros, Budapest, and I have to say that sports gave me a great deal. To return to Károly Tihanyi – he gave me my love for Hungarian literature. He was also able to communicate, in coded form, the essence of human decency, which I cannot forget to this day. He died just a few days ago, at the age of 95. He was such a unique character, who apart from making one love Hungarian literature also strengthened one's Hungarian identity. This was unique back then, as it was only possible to do so in coded form. And yet many of us in the class got the message and processed it internally. Meeting him was always an experience, and remained one to remember afterwards.

PLK: In chronological order, after the Sacred Heart you went on to the Benedictine High School, which they closed down meanwhile.

ESV: I was then meant to go to Pannonhalma, but there was the problem that I would have to pay the school fees in kind with natural produce. We lived in Budapest, so this was not possible. It was no use that I was a 'landowner' through the Board of Guardians; everything had to be handed over to the state!
PLK: How big was the estate that you inherited, Professor Vizi?

ESV: It was not much, just a few hectares, as it was divided between many siblings. 300 rose peaches, 300 cherry trees and 300 sour cherry trees, that was the estate, and a few hectares of vines. It was worked by István Vizi, my Uncle Pista, as commissioned by the Board of Guardians, but, as I said, everything had to be handed over to the state. My father was one of six siblings. To return to the chronology, a few other schools came next, but I ended up at the András Fáy High School in Mester Street. It is enough if I tell you that seven of our academicians attended it. Why was it such a good high school? They soaked up a lot of children when the religious high schools were abolished, for example, from the Benedictine high school in Csepel, in the south of Budapest as well as from other schools in the vicinity. Originally, there could not have been many students here. The teaching staff was very good, and Károly Tihanyi taught all of us. I would just add that he devoted his entire life to teaching. At 7 p.m., when we went to do training, as the Ferencváros training sessions were held in our school's very well-equipped gym, he was still there! He lived to nurture the young. For example, he knew very well how to punish us. At the Benedictine school, as it so happens, I began my career by receiving a head-master's censure, at the first break. The high school's athletic field was in the courtyard of the tobacco factory – it is all built up now. This is between Baross Street, the Grand Boulevard, and Rigó Street. We were playing a strategy game with friends. The school bell rang, and I was just about to win, I wanted us to finish it, all this in the presence of Kamill Borbély! The school bell ringing was a serious matter, so I had to present myself. That is how I started my years with the Benedictines.

SS: Tihanyi's encouragement of physical education was really just him nurturing your soul.

ESV: Gyula Kaposy, who was an Olympian, was my sports teacher at the Benedictine school. My stamina that remains today, my ability to focus, can all be traced back to me being on a first-rate athletics team: I won a Budapest-wide parallel bars competition, chess had a strong influence on my way of thinking, and this is all thanks to what I learned there. In my opinion, school is incredibly important, alongside family support. Genetically, you only inherit the basic structure, the hardware. The software, which is only really installed during nurturing, is gained from role models, small events, actions and reactions. It is in this that nurturing has its importance – this is why the family environment, school and one's group of friends are so crucial. The elemental reflexes gained and the ethical and behavioral patterns learned are still in working order fifty years later. In each new situation – because exactly similar situations do not of course repeat themselves very often – these acquired patterns determine how one behaves in the given circumstances.

SS: What role did the awareness of the many generations of family have during your life, Professor Vizi?

ESV: On the one hand, on my father's side, the incredibly hard-working family from Apostag had an important effect. The diligence of every member of the family, my aunts and uncles, was one example. On the other side, my mother's very unusual form of upbringing affected me in ways I can only fully appreciate now. She always filled me with incredible confidence. If I went to take an exam, she would tell me that I would pass. If I went to participate in a competition, she would that say I would win. She always gave a positive feeling, and this was very important to me: my mother trusts me. At home with the family, with the broader family, I received the same. As far as politics is concerned, that was very mixed. The family would often come together to play bridge, which I learned pretty quickly, too. As a young boy, I would sit there, enjoy the beauty of the game's logic, and listen to the adults. So, in my childhood, I breathed in the way the adults thought as well as their political views. On the communist deportations, for example, my aunt's family, with five children, were given two hours to leave their house; they were forcibly resettled to Hortobágy. I owe a debt of gratitude to my circle of friends, too, as they gave me a great many positive impulses. István Kovács, the 'Doc', whom we have already mentioned, was my sworn friend; he finished university and then went to Sopron to be a pediatrician, as this was his parents' wish.

SS: Then he entered the seminary in Esztergom, then studied at the Central Seminary in Budapest – we were there together for three years. When I returned from Canada, I visited him; he was still well at the time, but afterwards he would eventually lose his battle with cancer.

ESV: I visited him every morning to bathe him and talk to him.

PLK: Let's continue perhaps with your years in Pécs.

ESV: It was in Pécs that I started university; there were fantastic lecturers there. Szilárd Dornhoffer, János Szentágothai, Kálmán Lissák, Jen Entz, István Környei, and László Csolnoky: we were surrounded by world-class researchers, and that is where we were during the 1956 Uprising…

PLK: We'd appreciate hearing about that in more detail.

ESV: A university national guard battalion was established in Pécs, involving students of medicine and law. We had various tasks; some of us, including me, collected food and took it up to Budapest with some 25 trucks. We were properly armed; we had rifles and grenades. We were full of hope. We were happy. We were floating above the ground. The invading Soviet tank brigade surrounded the dormitory on 1848 Square. We marched by there, with our weapons. Another part of our team went up to the Mecsek mountains. We did not give ourselves up for four days. We were surrounded; there are photographs of it. The battalion commander was name István Rozsos, and he would later become a chief surgeon in Kaposvár. At that time, I was working as a student assistant in the department of chemistry, for Professor Csolnoky, who came over and said, 'Boys, have you gone mad? Just have a look around!' And that is when we gave ourselves up, the Russians came in, gave us a bit of knocking about, took our weapons, and the whole thing ended. The real reprisals were carried out not by the Russians but by the Hungarians, the university people. A great many of us emigrated. I went to Budapest – at the suggestion of my tutor, József Tigyi – together with others who had become too conspicuous. Those of us who left were not harmed, but those who stayed were really made to pay. They were excluded from the university and sent to the camp at Kistarcsa for two years, some for four years. Countrywide the reprisals were terrible and on a massive scale: 4500 people were imprisoned, 229 were executed, some as late as 1961. For a long time, I did not dare return to Pécs. However, then the post of head of the pharmacology department at the University of Pécs became vacant, and I applied for it. It turned out that it was impossible for me to get, despite the fact that the Medicine Department of the Hungarian Academy of Sciences voted for me by a huge majority. Emil

Schultheisz – a former minister and still alive today – wanted to appoint me. However, it was blocked by the 'upper echelons'. It sounds odd, but this was the lucky stroke of my life. I did not leave Budapest to be the head of a department; instead, I stayed in the capital, and continued work alongside Academician József Knoll. Knoll gave wonderful opportunities: I could go abroad, first to Germany, then to Britain, where my career began. Later János Szentágothai took me under his wing, so I could make lightning progress.

PLK: When did you get your degree, and where did you find employment afterwards?

ESV: I received my degree in 1961, and as my political affiliations were less than ideal, Mrs. Kristóf, wife of the secretary of the Presidential Council, who was head of the appointments committee, offered me a job in Székesfehérvár, and in gynecology at that, even though I wanted to go into research. At the university in Budapest, meanwhile, they did not want to offer me a job at any price. Then, Academician Béla Issekutz, head of the department, made a phone call to the chief executive of EGYT (Unified Pharmaceutical and Foodstuffs Factory, today EGIS), Mr. Láng, or Comrade Láng – who was a very decent man – who, in turn, spoke to Mrs. István Szatmári, head of the personnel department. Szatmári brought me onto the staff of EGYT, but I was immediately transferred to the Institute, so I could remain at the university, in the department run by Béla Issekutz, just not in a university job, but rather an EGYT one. I was put next to assistant lecturer Amália Pfeiffer. When I started work, Professor Issekutz invited me in and asked me, 'My dear boy, what do you want to work on?' I replied, 'Professor Issekutz, I would like to work on digitalis, the medicine affecting the heart.' And he said, 'My dear boy, do not work on that because that is what Professor Gusztáv Fritz has been working on for 30 years, and it will take you ten years to catch up with his knowledge. Here is the brain and the medicines for the brain about which we know so little. Neither does the world. Research that.' That is how I became a brain researcher. So, luck played a large role in this, as did the circumstances of the time.

PLK: How long did the EGYT job last?

ESV: A year all told, as afterwards Béla Issekutz simply sorted it out internally. I followed the usual career ladder: assistant lecturer, lecturer, reader, then professor; I was head of department in Szabolcs Street, Budapest, that is at the Doctors' Further Training Institute; I am a professor at Semmelweis University of Medicine as my second job to this day; I become a member of the Academy of Sciences, first a corresponding member, and then…

PLK: This is too simple like this. Perhaps let's first talk about those particular synapses that led this far!

ESV: So, I began to work on the brain. I had the chance to go to Mainz, Germany, to an excellent institute, where world-famous researchers were working; then, after coming back home, I was granted a Riker scholarship to Oxford, to work alongside Sir William Paton. Sir William was a proud Scotsman and fan of Zoltán Kodály; Kodály received an honorary doctorate from the University of Oxford at the time I was there. Paton always had just the one subordinate whom he oversaw, and at that time, it was me. He had no children, so he only dealt with me. I would often accompany him home in the evenings and we would talk. He was the next personality I can trace my professional successes back to. 'Not enough that will seem but partly true: / Only a truth eternal and whole will do.' said the great Hungarian poet János Arany (prose translation of excerpt from Vojtina's Ars Poetica). This is the synthesizing attitude I got from József Knoll. Everything has to be seen in terms of connections and interdependencies. From Paton, I learned to think analytically, which is the most important, and this is what I pass on to my own students, of whom fourteen are by now university professors around the world, and all are highly respected. You do not merely have to learn the methodology, of how to do what, but also how to process results, how to look for truth. To this contributed Father Xavér Szunyogh, Károly Tihanyi, and my other teachers, who taught me the Hungarian language, Hungarian literature, and how the good, the beautiful and the true all connect, and how they assume one another. Because what is beautiful has to be true and *vice versa*. Furthermore, this is all connected to ethics and faith, which are the defining factors of our everyday lives.

In addition to all that I learned from him, I would also continue to receive Paton's support. The support of someone at Oxford means much in the academic world. My articles were published in very good journals; my citation index is more than 11,000, which is an enormous figure. In Hungary, I worked on one of the neurotransmitters, noradrenaline, which is in the brain and also the periphery. This chemical is responsible for inducing arousal. My boss there worked on the other, parasympathetic one, and so we decided to investigate the relationship between them. According to the textbooks, the relationship between the two is that one depolarizes – that is, it lessens tension – whereas the other hyperpolarizes, or increases tension. In my experiments, I discovered that the release of one blocks that of the other, not allowing it to have its effect, and as such this is a very economical form of interaction, of inhibition. I called this presynaptic inhibition, inhibition prior to synapsis. At the time, this was an absolutely new discovery. However, when I submitted my article, it received a very bad review, as they asked what I was thinking because there could not be any synaptic connection between two nerve types where I had written that there was one. All right, then the connection is not a synaptic one, and the chemical overcomes the distance between the two nerves by 'swimming across'. This is how the non-synaptic theory developed, from an act of defiance. I had to convince everyone; I had to fight my way through the objectors.

SS: But Paton supported you…

ESV: But of course, and he understood! The younger ones said this was a real discovery that no one else would believe. Meanwhile, my family was back in Hungary, in 'captivity'; they were not allowed to leave.

SS: How long did you live abroad?

ESV: Almost three years. My wife could have joined me, but our child could not, so she stayed behind, too. Like a hostage. That is what it was like for everyone. If not, that was for some other reason…

SS: How long did it take for your theory to be accepted?

ESV: It took more than two decades for it to be accepted. In 1984, I published a monograph about this, and in 2000, I also described how the majority of medicines affect those protein receptors which are not located on the synapses. The synapse is an exceptionally narrow gap in which endogenous materials are present in incredibly high concentrations, the effect of which, according to the law of mass action, is almost impossible to counterbalance. This can be calculated with simple mathematics.

PLK: Did this research bring any recognition?

ESV: It did. I received the Széchenyi prize, from József Antall, Hungary's first post-communist premier. I was awarded a high civic honor in 2000.

PLK: And back in the old system?

ESV: I achieved the rank of professor. I was able to make professional progress. It is a great mistake when some people say they did not become Nobel Prize winners because they were held back. The great, exceptional personalities, whose work was accompanied by a particular character type, were able to get by. In the period before the change in 1990, we were able to travel; scientists were able to travel to all ends of the Earth, together with their families; Hungary was by then a relatively liberalized country. It was a meeting place where conferences were hosted, and in the 1970s and 1980s scientists and academics from the socialist and from the Western countries could come together here.

SS: Do you get adequate international recognition?

ESV: The greatest recognition was that an incredible number of people cited my works and in a positive way, and I received a huge number of invitations. I was awarded the Galileo Galilei Prize in Italy, the Pro Meritis Prize from the European Academy of Sciences and Arts in Salzburg, and I am a member or doctor *honoris causa* of eight foreign academies.

PLK: Professor Vizi, I have heard from a number of scientists active in your field that you have been nominated more than once for the Nobel Prize. Are you aware of this, and if so, how do you feel about it?

ESV: I think there is no doubt that the Nobel Prize is the greatest recognition that a scientist can receive. However, one should also know that this is really the result of work by a great number of people. There are rumors like that. Of course, the scientists in question, the ones nominated, have the least information about this. I cannot say anything either to confirm or deny this gossip. My original discovery, that at the end of nerve cells, there are sensing, receptor proteins capable of sensing the chemical message coming from a different nerve cell, and of responding to it, has brought a decisive change to the world's pharmaceutical industry. By now, many medicines have come into circulation, which bring billions of dollars of profit to pharmaceutical companies and were developed on the basis of my discovery. Another discovery I made also evoked a considerable response. I proved that alongside the synaptic connection, that is, when two nerve cells are linked very tightly together, there is also a non-synaptic system of connection. In this instance, a single nerve cell is able to send messages to many million nerve cells far away from it, as the chemical neurotransmitter material released from the terminal of a single nerve cell diffuses far into the distance. However, there are receptors that are much more sensitive than this, perhaps a thousand or ten thousand times more sensitive than those located inside the synapse. I have stated in a number of publications that the lion's share of our medicines affect these receptors. This provided a further opportunity to the pharmaceutical companies and medicinal research to develop new types of medicines that block or stimulate these receptors. Thanks to this discovery, it is now possible to find a partial explanation for a many illnesses of the nervous system, such depression or Parkinson's disease. It is already a great recognition that there is a positive response to this in the international literature, and today, there are hundreds of internationally recognized laboratories working on these subjects.

SS: If I could ask an entirely different type of question. Everyone has an image of what we call God, and has an internal experience about the source of our existence, which is usually called a secret or mystery. In someone who turns very strongly outwards, to the material world, like research into material, the two must surely come together, the material world and its source, and they reach that secret. In fortunate cases personal faith can connect to this.

ESV: I think the greatest thing that humankind has been given is the chance of free choice, to decide when and where and how to act. The last of these, really, is ethics. What has stayed with me since my childhood is that if I can give something to someone, for example, love, if I can help someone, if I can make a sacrifice for a good cause, then the rewards for these things are far greater than if I were only taking care of myself. And love is the only human attribute where the more of it one gives, the more one retains. This was a secret because it was only after many, many ordeals and many, many failures, but also successes, that I realized it. And this is closely connected to the possibility of human freedom. It is the same when one talks about faith. I have already said that there are those who reach faith with blind faith, through the catechism. There are those who do so because of their emotional make-up, in response to an inner fear, to clutch at someone, and that someone is God. And there is a third path, too, at the end of which is something which I might not describe as God, but rather it is the wonders experienced while getting to know the world and the incredible complexity, organization and ultimately unknowable nature of its material that bring one to one's knees. This is how a scientist can reach the point at which they are in awe of the perfection in the created world, of the Creator. Let me say here what popular Hungarian writer Frigyes Karinthy wrote in his notebook: 'The discovery of God. I sense that I will sooner find my way to him through doubting him that in blind faith in him.

Religion puts him in Heaven – science is looking for him all over the world.' And doubt is the most important characteristic of the researcher. The point, then, is that human beings gaze at the created world and its perfection in awe. An order of which it is unimaginable that it might have developed by accident or of its own accord. Perhaps only a scientist can reach this feeling. I think this is the inevitability of the coexistence of faith and learning, and I think the greatest opportunity is for someone to be a believer. I followed this route to faith myself, following the upbringing the catechism can provide. If I am here as a scientist confessing his faith, let me say that the dichotomy is not between knowledge and faith, but between atheism and theism.

PLK: I think that the great masters were all believers.

ESV: Of course they were! As was Sir William Paton, along with everyone else I have mentioned.

SS: There was talk of your time in Britain. Would you say something about your time in Germany, too, Professor Vizi?

ESV: I was there for six months; I was at the pharmacology institute at the University of Mainz. I worked and studied alongside Professors Lindmar, Muscholl and Kuschinsky, in addition to getting to know a new world. It was also an exciting experience to be able to buy a used Ford Taunus car from my monthly scholarship grant, which I then took home. In Hungary, there were a total of 12,000 cars at the time – and one of them was mine.

PLK: Professor Vizi, did you spend time in the United States, too?

ESV: Yes, at the Albert Einstein College of Medicine at Yeshiva University. This is a very rich university, where I ended up thanks to Sir William Paton's recommendation, and I was a visiting professor from 1984 to 2002. I worked with Francis Ferenc Foldes, a professor of Hungarian extraction. Every year for a few months, I would work there and live there with my family; I was very well paid, I published a lot – it was a different world. I felt I was much-loved there, and I felt good about it, too. It was a very different world from conservative Oxford, where Sir William invited me to apply for a university chair. I also worked at the Catholic University of Leuven, and on my way home I had a professorial invitation in Mainz. I should add to the story that I was in the car with my family and asked them whether I should turn off the road. They said no, so we came home. I never emigrated, though I had many good job offers. Abroad, people said that our system would never change itself, that only we could change it, from the inside.

SS: This was still the opinion even in the late 1980s.

ESV: In New York, visiting famous émigré Hungarian publisher Sándor Püski, whose wife Ilona would cook such nice things for us, I met Béla Király, a famous military commander turned historian after fleeing to the United States from the communist regime, whose books I would carry home to Hungary. We also met émigré Hungarian politicians Béla Varga and László Varga there. I brought back to Hungary the underground book by Miklós Duray, *Kutyaszorító* ('Trap'), and Béla Király's book *The First War between Socialist States*.

PLK: And running the Academy is a whole new challenge, very different from a laboratory.

ESV: There is no greater honor for a Hungarian scholar than to become president of the Hungarian Academy of Sciences. My predecessors include József Eötvös and Loránd Eötvös, Ágoston Trefort, Zoltán Kodály, János Szentágothai, Iván T. Berend, Domokos Kosáry, to name a few of the seventeen who have filled this role. We are able to work amidst such reliquaries as poet János Arany's chair, István Széchenyi's furniture, great poet Mihály Vörösmarty's bookshelf, and on the walls are the great and good of the Hungarian nation's scholars and artists, all witness to the Hungarian nation's best most glorious days. The Hungarian Academy was always a believer in progress and reform. The survival of the Hungarian nation and the Hungarian language – these are questions in which the Academy always played a key role. There were times when it was muzzled, but it was never put out of action! It has been constantly active since 1825, and in Hungary, there was always a need for it to exist. The academy in Austria was only established twenty years later! The Hungarian Academy of Sciences has played – and, I think, continues to play – a special role in forming Hungarian national identity. In the academy, you can find Hungary's national past, unique treasures that we preserve, as this is part of establishing a healthy, decent national identity. The nation should indeed be proud of what it has from the past to be proud of.

PLK: How did it work out in official terms?

ESV: I was the vice-president of the Academy for six years, and afterwards I was elected president. The post of vice-president was an unpaid one, and that was quite different. Currently, as the president of the Academy, I have to defend its independence, its autonomy, and the freedom of research. We live in times in which there is a need for this, as they are trying to erode the foundations of the national institution thinking and working in terms of values – times in which, to use the words of our great poet József Attila, 'Wily fear governs us', in which money and profit override everything. Eugene Paul Wigner, the Hungarian Nobel Prize-winning physicist, wrote of Michael Polanyi's experiences in Russia as a cautionary tale: 'he heard Nicolai Bukharin arguing that science under socialism must cease to be carried out for its own sake and must be firmly harnessed to the needs of the Five Year Plan' (The Collected Works of Eugene Paul Wigner, Springer, 2001). Polanyi also wrote about this in his book *The Contempt of Freedom*. This politics of science seems to be coming to bear here, too. All this just when the European Union, in the light of the Lisbon Treaty, wants to build Europe's future on research, principally on primary research. It is not hard to imagine that in such an age the existence of an academy based on values and displaying values is a problem for some. Nevertheless, it remains one of the country's most popular institutions. People accept its values.

PLK: What do you think the future holds for the Academy?

ESV: It will continue to have an important role in the 21st century. We face new challenges to which we must adapt, but not by rejecting our existing principles, but by finding other, efficient methods, such as the Universal University ('Encompass') or the World Science Forum. Where participants can explain just how grave a crisis can emerge from the exponentially speed-up progress of science without the settling and progress of the question of morality. Just what terrible danger lies in the existence of that red button there at the hands of various warlords, who can use rockets to set in motion our ultimate demise? The world has shrunk to a village, in which all six and a half billion of us live, and there will be ever more of us, full of vexing economic and social problems, the North-South divide, and a million local issues – not to mention the clash of civilizations! In such a situation, there is great need for all institutions that protect and create values – and this is no less true of the Academy.

PLK: If we could perhaps ask about your family life, too.

ESV: I have a wonderful wife, Dr. Veronika Ádám, who supports me in everything. She is also an academic researcher, a doctor, and academic vice-rector at Semmelweis University of Budapest. I have two beautiful children, Veronika and Attila, and three grandchildren, Daniella, Dániel and Dorottya. Most importantly, the atmosphere at home makes it an island of peace to return to and wind down in, where the wrinkles on one's brow are smoothed out, where one gets words of encouragement with which to start the daily battle again the next morning, only to return home again for compassion and understanding.

VI.

E. Sylvester Vizi: Conscience and Science

> *Spectabilis et magnifice, nobis honorande!*
> **Ladies and gentlemen!**
> *Willst du immer weiter schweifen?*
> *Sieh, das Gute liegt so nah.*
> ('Do you wish to roam farther and farther?
> See the good that lies so near.')
> (Goethe: Erinnerung)

Goethe asked this question in the 18th century. Times have changed since then – science and scholarship have become part of humanity's cultural heritage. In the last century, science has been the engine of social progress, has in the main served the good of humanity, and its results – unlike in the past – have been accessible to an increasing number of people. It is the intention of the European Union to create the 'society of knowledge'. Europe must do so if it is to keep pace with the United States and Japan; otherwise, it will become stagnant and not develop.

However, in public forums, the question often arises of why so much money has to be spent on basic research. As there are millions of people so poor that they cannot even afford the medicines and therapies that are effective at the moment. Why do we have to invest in space research, and why do we have to invest in research fields from which we cannot expect advantages and results for humanity in the short term? Why does the human genome need to be mapped? A whole list of similar questions could be raised, but this is a short-sighted way of thinking. I would like to discuss these questions in my lecture and to emphasize the importance of ethical questions and conscientiousness in the use of scientific results.

In his encyclical *Fides et ratio* ('Faith and Reason'), Pope John Paul II stressed that a meeting of faith and reason is a significant step forward, and that the act of recognizing the truth plays an important role. He emphasized that faith and reason can be mutually beneficial to one another.

Most people do not even stop to think how much our everyday lives are dominated by scientific and technological results developed and established by scientists: electricity, radio, mobile phones, synthetic materials, fax machines, televisions, computers, airplanes, satellites and antibiotics, to mention just a few examples.

Science and technology have increasingly become a key basic ingredient in our everyday lives. They make life easier for all of us. They give us the feeling that the world is small, as we can travel 10,000 kilometers in a single day, and we can send a news bulletin in a few milliseconds.

In large part, we have scientists to thank for our 21st-century lives. As a result of their work, events all over the world are closely connected to each other. The world has shrunk. Television and the World Wide Web have made us into the best-informed society ever – and, let us be honest, the most manipulated society. At the same time, this technology has supported the rise of mass media, which some see as a threat to cultural diversity and values.

Genetics is a field of enquiry that enjoys particularly great public interest, with people asking: what is happening in these scientists' laboratories, in point of fact? The public is increasingly anxious that in these labs genetic engineering will transform nature forever, creating supermen or supermonsters.

On 25 June 2000, US President Bill Clinton and UK Prime Minister Tony Blair announced at a press conference at the White House that the international Human Genome Project and the Celera Genomics Corporation had completed their mapping of the human genome, the design plan of the way humans are made.

The decoding of the human genome was a landmark in medical science, ushering in a new era. An era that would bring new possibilities for preventing, treating and healing diseases. 'With this opportunity, we have crossed the Rubicon of nature,' announced Johannes Huber, president of the Austrian government's committee on bioethics. He was right. The changes occurring in our genes are responsible for several thousand inherited illnesses, for example, Huntington's disease, Down syndrome and cell fibrosis. In addition, genes affect the development of many thousands of other illnesses. A number of very widespread illnesses, such as diabetes and heart failure, can be caused – so they think – by a number of changing genes acting together. As every change to these genes only makes a slight contribution to the development of the illness, thus far, it has been very difficult to identify these genes and their effects.

They are decoding the entirely of the secret of the human body, all 3.2 billion molecular letters of the DNA that appears in almost every human cell. By understanding these 'letters' and being able to read these 'books', we will be able to predict how likely a particular individual is to contract which illness. We hope this will contribute to us being able to develop medical therapies designed for particular individuals and that by correcting the genetic defects of patients, we might be able to fight against diseases and to prevent them from taking root.

If these letters can be read, and it looks like they can, then various questions can be raised. For example, which woman would not like to look into the crystal ball and learn whether she has the gene that will cause breast cancer? What does this mean for Insurance Companies, for example? Can they find out the results of such tests, and bring this information to the attention of others? Can they raise insurance premiums on the basis of the results of the tests? Or for example: what happens with employers? Can the employee refuse the test when applying for a job because they know that on the basis of their genetic structure they may represent a risk for the employer in the future? Who can have the right to know what the crystal ball reveals?

Just us, or our spouses and our children, too? Perhaps everyone? What will happen to our private sphere?

We need to give answers to these questions as soon as possible. Not just from the perspective of medical science, but from the point of view of the development of society as a whole. If we make it possible to read the 'letters' of this 'book', every gene, good and bad, then law-makers have to restrict access to this. Otherwise, we will be exposed to a variety of dangerous possibilities and will have to say goodbye to our private spheres.

Genetically, people are 99.9% identical whatever their ethnic background, but there are nevertheless certain differences. These could lead to discrimination and intolerant worldviews. Or are we perhaps able to use our knowledge to serve the good of humanity?

The private sphere of the individual must be defended, and the information gleaned must not be used to discriminate against individuals or against groups. The United States has taken the first step: the US Congress has passed a law seeking to prevent knowledge about the genetic map leading to the infringement of private life. We Europeans must also take the necessary steps if we want to build a knowledge society with humanity in Europe, and if we want to prevent ourselves heading towards 'custom-made babies' and an era of high-technology eugenics.

Without doubt, we have seen that in this regard, we are dealing not with science fiction but with real opportunities of science. The 'made-to-measure human' is no longer a figment of the imagination. Cloning is one step in the breeding of people. The word 'cloning' refers to the preparation of a genetically identical living creature on the basis of a living sample, and in this case, the creature is a human. A news story went around the globe: on the second day of Christmas, so they say, an American woman brought the first cloned baby into the world. If this really did happen at all, then what did happen exactly? Ladies and gentlemen, please allow me to shed light on this with my own words. We can assume that in this instance, they removed the sperm from one of the mother's egg cells. The DNA necessary for cloning would have been taken from one of the mother's skin cells. And this DNA was planted into the empty egg. The egg capable of reproduction was placed in the uterus. And the mother, as announced, brought a baby into the world nine months later. Her daughter was genetically identical to her. This means that the girl she brought into the world is her own identical twin. This was the technology used to create Dolly, the cloned sheep. There is no evidence of human cloning yet, but it is said that further experiments are to come. Since then, according to media reports, a few more clone babies have supposedly been born, but there is no proof of the cloning. We hope there never will be. This type of reproduction, this type of technology could, *ad absurdum*, lead to a purely female society, without men. (Of course, it would also be possible to take the genetic material from a man's skin cell, and in this case, the boy coming into the world would be his father's identical twin. Meanwhile, for the woman, the boy she had given birth to would be her husband's twin brother.) At the very least, this technology would lead to the proportion between the sexes changing.

The Commission of the European Union demands a worldwide ban on human cloning. Human cloning is illegal in exactly thirty countries, including Hungary. However, countries such as China, Israel and the United Kingdom thus far have rejected a ban on cloning for therapeutic purposes. Cloning for therapeutic purposes would mean creating embryos to breed replacement tissues or replacement organs, and after using these, they would destroy the embryos. They use embryos, as it happens, to glean stem cells capable of creating various tissues. In my opinion, the cloning of embryos to obtain stem cells should be banned across the world with universal authority, as an embryo is already a living organism biologically speaking, but not yet a legal individual. It is capable of life and can develop into a human being. Two weeks ago, the German Bundestag debated the question of the cloning of human descendants. The German parliament asked the federal government not only to ban cloning for reproductive purposes but also to ban it for the duplication of embryos exclusively for medical and academic purposes. The US Senate has also submitted a bill seeking to guarantee a complete ban on human cloning. They even want to ban the import of embryos and their use for scientific purposes.

With reproductive cloning, the breeding of people, we have reached the boundary in science that we must not cross! France is planning to order the punishment of the reproductive cloning of human beings as a 'crime against human dignity'. This carries a prison sentence of twenty years. In my opinion, there is a need for a worldwide ban on cloning! This does not just have to be stopped for ethical reasons. There is a sect whose members believe in immortality, more precisely, that cloning makes eternal life possible. However, this – and as a brain researcher, I can be sure – is a misconception. One person is more than just a collection of their genes. To be a human being means we are special, that we all think in our own way, we all feel, we all love. Everything depends on the activity of the brain, on the way we were brought up, on our experiences, and these are characteristics which became ours after our genetic make-up was developed.

The public is right to be worried that the experiments just mentioned, this technology, will lead to Aldous Huxley's *Brave New World*. In this world, accidental selection is replaced by a planned and technologically managed breeding and upbringing of human descendants. Today's society must be convinced that experiments of this type need to be brought under control. Were there to be cloning, there would be problems with people's unrepeatability, uniqueness and identity: 'Who am I? Who is my father? Where am I from?' These are the questions to which everyone must find answers to be themselves. However, in the instance of a cloned human being, there are no answers to these questions, and so, in addition to physical progress in a bad direction, there might also be emotional problems.

This is why there can be no doubt that we need very strict guidelines on medicine's developmental tendencies like this. We must address the ethics and legal possibilities of modern medical science. And scientists have to listen to their conscience. The current situation is very similar to that in which the Hungarian physicist Leo Szilard and Albert Einstein wrote to the president of the United States to try to prevent the dropping of the atomic bomb. They knew what the effects of such an atomic bomb could be. This was a sign of the scientists' conscience. We have to state quite unequivocally what European governments have so far done on this question. Has what they have done been sufficient, or has it not? The answer is that it has not. Have we done everything that is needed? The answer is that we have not. European governments have not sorted out these ethical questions in time, and what they have done is not enough. Alas, there are still very many European countries that have no legislation on this issue at all.

The development of the sciences cannot be stopped, just as history itself cannot be stopped. The current problem is that the development of the sciences is progressing very quickly, such that legislation, the elaboration of new laws and regulations, can hardly keep pace with this progress.

And what is the situation with us, scientists? What should our role in this be? What, in fact, does society expect of us when we discuss these ethical questions? I think we need to draw the attention of parliamentary deputies to the danger of misuse. Their job is to make decisions on how to solve these ethical questions so that scientists can continue to do their work.

Nature has to be researched – this is, of course, our task. We need freedom, to study everything we want to. Art, education and academic work have to be free; otherwise, the history of humanity will not make progress. And yet, this freedom must not be used for irresponsible and unethical research. The experimentation on embryos is a boundary we must not transgress.

Do we have to turn all our knowledge into action? Do we have to introduce everything we have discovered into everyday life? Should we freely put into practice everything that can be achieved in science? My answer is no. Only those results that can have a good effect on humanity should be applied. This means that members of parliaments, the members of the political elite, must work closely together with us, scientists and scholars, to implement our common goals in line with the best of our knowledge and with our conscience, in the interests of society as a whole.

Today, ethics is humanity's greatest problem. Perhaps T.S. Eliot put it best:

> 'Where is the Life we have lost in living?
> Where is the wisdom we have lost in knowledge?
> Where is the knowledge we have lost in information?'
> (Chorus from *The Rock* stage play)

(Delivered at the annual ceremonial meeting of the European Academy of Sciences and Arts in Salzburg, when E. Sylvester Vizi, president of the

Hungarian Academy of Sciences, and member of the European Academy of Sciences and Arts, was awarded the *Pro Meritis* Prize.

The laudation was given by Prince Nikolaus Lobkowicz. The meeting's ceremonial lecture was delivered by E. Sylvester Vizi in German.)

VII.

ETHICS, ERAS SINS AND FORGIVENESS

ESV: My starting point would be that modern thought, which is essentially the result of the development of science, has eroded fundamental things such as how the source of all intellectual and moral value is God, who created the world. This process began with Copernicus and Galileo, and in parallel with this was the church's attitude to science at the time, a tragic example of which was Giordano Bruno being burned at the stake, or the Galileo trial. Then, came Nietzsche, who stated that God was dead, and later Camus, one of the fathers of modern existentialism, who raised essentially the same question. Earlier Marx had argued that religion and a way of life stemming from religion was the deceiver, or opium, of the people. And all this shook European morality to its foundations, in particular the fundamental morality of Europe based on Greek and Judeo-Christian culture. This situation also eroded the social, economic and other interpretation of the Ten Commandments as something unique and primary. So, on the one hand, we see a turning away from religion, and on the other hand, the Nietzschean concept of the *Übermensch*, which holds that man is the depository of all of this, that he thought up God, that, in fact, God appeared in human thinking as an emotional or psychological crutch, and so it is really man who is called on to decide everything.

All this is accompanied by the Industrial Revolution, establishing the use of cheap labor, the development of the economy, which would then later be followed by the information revolution, which makes possible the cheap use of humanity's intellectual resources. So, the first lighting of the fire is physical strength, the Industrial Revolution, the second lighting of the fire is the use of atomic energy, and the third is the information revolution. Thanks to this, the world economy develops even more rapidly, and this is when mankind lays a claim to determine morality for itself and to do the same with ethical laws, as by now, it regards economic interests as the primary engine of progress. This is, in fact, how the world has been transformed, that the role of values and of morality in social life has declined, even in small communities. And the institution of the family collapses, and with it crumble the human values that were characteristic until now, which is what brings us to the 21st century. It is a different question, I think, how humanity beats a retreat to religion, to faith in God, or however I put it, because it has a need to clutch at something. Paradoxically, this is precisely because, as a result of the very fast development of the world, people can no longer understand what is going on around them. In the twenty-first century, everything is motivated by financial interest, even friendships are made on this basis, and any view of real human values as being on a par with these has become almost insignificant. In short, the world is losing its values and is in a moral crisis. I think that the crisis in Hungarian society is primarily not economic but moral. And this moral crisis is actually a global phenomenon, which has sneaked its way here, too, as a necessary accompaniment to globalization. One should heed Hungarian poet Dániel Berzsenyi: 'the firm foundation of every land / must be morality untarnished / which, if destroyed, Rome will fall and founder' ('To the Hungarians', trans. Ádám Makkai). The big question is: Will Europe share Rome's fate?

PE: If we talk about ethics, we are talking about a system of social norms, which we traditionally distinguish from other systems of social norms, like the law, convention, or manners, by its subject and its sanction. We are talking about norms of behaviour which are intersubjective, and which – according to our faith – can have sanctions in two dimensions. First, at a social level, the sanction for immoral behaviour is others' censure or condemnation, as opposed to obligatory physical sanctions provisioned for illegal acts or to the rejection of those breaking codes of conduct. Followers of Biblical religions believe that this system of social norms is not autonomous in the sense that humanity can just create it for itself, entirely freely and independently of its existing nature; that is, we are not in a position to invent the norms of ethics for ourselves. For if it is a system of norms, then it involves rules, rules which are universal; rules always bear in mind a certain state of affairs which is characterized by a certain generality, and this is what they have to connect to a certain judgment: it is from the state of affairs that the sanction is concluded. True, but the general rule has always to be applied to the individual case. In order to reach the content of norms, some kind of knowledge is needed of humanity itself, of society, the world around us, and – according to our faith – this world is a created world, a world which in part reflects the will of the Creator, and so it is not for us to determine the requirements and desires of this world, including our own humanity – we have to discover these for ourselves. So far I could say that we are on the plane of natural ethics; I am not yet talking about a merely human and merely autonomous system. But over and above this we also know what we might call a supernatural ethics based on revelation, that is, God tells us his will, and this message we inherit in the form of normative traditions. So this is even more than the mere human discovery of the created world. For precisely this reason the sanctions corresponding to ethics do not just appear in this mundane world, but, rather, we believe that they do so after death, too; that is, in our relationship with God, ethics also has a sanction.

The problem of sin is one of the cardinal questions of ethics. If we quiz the Bible for what it tells us, why there are all kinds of bad things in the world, illnesses, wars, death, then we find that it points to sin as the cause of all of these. It does not regard sin as a malfunction, a simple system disorder to be rectified with the right equipment. Neither does it regard it as something which can simply be denied and then the problem is gone; rather, it relates it to the personal relationship between God and man. So ethics does not just concern relations between members of society; it also embodies the relationship between man and God. For this precise reason, the positive motivation for preserving it and its system of sanctions goes beyond mere social behaviour and judgment. If this is how things are, and furthermore God has expressed his wish not just through nature but with his revelatory word, then we see that faith, our faith based on Biblical revelation, and our most scientific knowledge and personal conviction of nature and of humanity, or our will, which affects our actions, all form one unified whole. According to our convictions, ethics as a phenomenon operates like this from the outset. It is in this system of norms that individual actions are played out, which we then have to judge.

ESV: However, there is no denying that during the development of history, the results of science – natural and social science – and the forms of consensus present among people and in society have influenced the opinion of actions between one person and another and between man and his environment. And this is an ethical approach, which is, in part, the right approach.

PE: Ethical judgment depends directly on one's view of the world, that is, what we know of the world. In other words, science is always a challenge to ethics, because it provides better and more precise knowledge of the world around us, and so it can give a new picture of the consequences of our actions.

SS: It makes this better and more precise, but also more uncertain, as it is always changing.

PE: And more complicated, which also makes ethical judgment more difficult. I think this is one of the greatest difficulties for believers' ethical reflection today, that the image we have created of the world is ever more complex, as we know more and more of the details.

ESV: What I wanted to outline was the way in which we have become distant from divine revelation and the ethical system of norms based on religion, and the way humanity found the courage to acquire and monopolize the right to say what ethics is.

PE: In a certain sense we feel we are becoming distant from it, but I am not convinced we are actually doing so. We can approach this question in a number of ways. One is a knowledge of norms or values and following principles as a way of behaviour. If we see it from this angle, then the history of ethics very nicely shows that the difference between the marriage relations among people in the Middle Ages and the family relations widespread in the world today is not so great. That is, I saw for myself as a chaplain while researching family records that in the 1700s it was not rare in Catholic villages for the majority of children to be registered as illegitimate. The fact that there is an awareness of values in society does not necessarily mean that the actual behaviour of the majority adapts to them. And yet it is significant whether or not there is such a notional ideal.

To return to the other matter of autonomy and heteronomy: someone can of course reach a point when they say that they themselves want to define the rules for their own behaviour and for society's behaviour, to define these in a sovereign way. Very well, but from a scientific point of view this is impossible: the fact is that human beings exist, and a world exists around human beings. This means that everyone has certain elements around them that they cannot disregard. They can determine rules for themselves irrespective of this, but this will not work. The world itself will be what puts things in their place, perhaps slowly; we know from biology of the broader distribution and then containment of species, even to the point of their extinction; many things could happen to the human species during its history, including something that comes from its own behaviour. On the positive side, we can say that if we recognize a connection between one and the other, then from then on it belongs to our objective imperative. If the pathogen of an infectious disease is recognized, and we realize how it spreads, then we clearly have an ethical obligation to take care not to infect others. Before we understood the mechanism, this ethical norm was obviously not present. So I think that complete autonomy is more of an illusion, let's say the illusion of a narrow intellectual élite, but this does not change the fact that community behaviour which differs significantly from the objective circumstances of existence, particularly if it differs from them in a normative way, not just in individual cases, will be counterproductive and lead to the destruction of the community's values and its operation.

ESV: I think that it is precisely the rapid development of science and the economy that makes people, the individual, uncertain, and this sense of insecurity is what I think will grow in the decades to come and lead to society increasingly yearning for 'order' – in quotation marks, of course. Order in people's heads, in relationships between people, and so too in morality. Cardinal Erdő says that recognizing the law and obeying it are two separate things. This is true and characteristic of society, but it is precisely this uncertainty that will lead to more and more people demanding the compulsory adherence to some type of ethical norms. Let me give an example: the North-South gap, the enormous difference between rich and poor countries, and a difference between enormous incomes and utter poverty within individual countries that – for the vast majority of people – is unacceptable, which seems to be a harbinger of revolution, that this is unacceptable because it is unethical. Just as, back then, there was a motif in Calvin's and Luther's revolt against various pleasures, so too will this appear in the 21ˢᵗ century. I was just reading that in Germany, they want to raise the pay of leaders of big multinational companies by thirty percent, but society objects to this because the difference will be too great. Why does one person get infinitely much, and the other person infinitely little, out of what they put on the table together? My feeling is that as people become weaker, as their sense of security declines, this will sooner or later lead to society demanding greater morality.

PLK: Will this lead to a new model or new ideals?

PE: If I may say so, this subject is very familiar from traditional Catholic moral theology, namely the subject of the virtue of justice. I think that justice is one of the central categories of the moral teaching for social and economic life; not in vain does Saint Augustine quote the Bible, that *Iustitia est regnorum fundamentum*, 'the solid foundation for any state is justice' (Cf. Psa 89:14; 97:2). Our theology of ethics traditionally divides this justice between distributive justice, commutative justice, social justice, and so on.

ESV: Let me refer to the *bonum commune*, the common good, which, according to Saint Augustine, is a fundamental criterion for salvation, which put in modern terms means that the real objective is not merely personal success, personal wealth, or even intellectual richness but also serving the interests of other people, of society (cf. Walter Lippmann: The Public Philosophy, New York, 1955).

PE: Here again is a fundamental question of world-view. For if we say that justice is *suum cuique tribuendi voluntas* (For the Christian elaboration of the ancient principle, see Saint Thomas Aquinas, Summa Theologica 2 II q. 58 a. 1), that is, that everyone is allowed their will, then we are always talking about some kind of goods. But what is good for people, and what are the goods that people need? The recognition of this depends to a huge degree on science, on how we see the world, whether in terms of health, or the pollution of the environment. I think – if as an outsider I am permitted to allow myself prophecies – that this might be the point at which a moral consensus becomes necessary and some kind of objective ethics is globally applied. This is where we can most sense that activities occurring at some points of the globe can have a strong and direct effect on the very possibility for human existence elsewhere in the world. But the responsibility to the environment only becomes conscious when science reaches the point at which it can show what relationships there are.

ESV: It says in the Old Testament to subdue the earth, but later it also says to take care of it because it is yours.

JS: Already in Genesis we read *le-ovda u-le-'shomra*: work it and protect it. The notions of truth and justice have come up a lot in what was just discussed. There is a sentence in the fifth book of Moses: *tzedek, tzedek, tirdof*, translated precisely as 'justice, justice, thou shalt pursue'. But this is the point at which James may have understood the Masoretic text better than the Masoretes did, because in the Vulgate one instance of *tzedek* is translated as an adverb: *iuste, quod iustum quereris*, that is, 'what you think as just, you should justly pursue'. It is clear that the Hebrew Bible – we prefer to call it this, rather than the Old Testament – adjusts itself to the world-view of Antiquity, and so already in the Ten Commandments it adjusts the concept of the just mode to the ancient view of the world when it prescribes the obligation of work for six days a week ('Six days shalt thou labour') and extends the right to rest on the seventh day to everyone. The Sabbath is a later development.

I would mention the problem of loan interest and ethics, which is a significant question, as in point of fact the Hebrew Bible prohibits the taking of interest, but later economic progress in Jewish law led to a transformation which within the given circumstances made commerce and related financial dealings possible.

Basic ethical norms have not changed since the revelation, as one must not kill, steal, etc., and this is held up by any mundane legal system. So the basic norms are there. There is also the norm of love, which also caused a problem in the past, as in the famous words in Leviticus chapter 19 ('thou shalt love thy neighbour as thyself'). This includes the Hebrew word *recha*, translated by the Vulgate as 'proximus', from which it was easy to infer that the prohibition of love only referred to proximus. But later they realized, from letters sent to the Pope, that the noun *recha* had been around back when they demanded gold and silver items from the Egyptians in lieu of wages they had not paid. And it could not be said of the Egyptians that they were proximus, people who were close. According to this, the *recha* is equivalent to the universal expression of love for thy neighbour. If we continue this, prophetic literature is full of ethical axioms, primarily the condemnation of unacceptable acts by the Jewish subjects of the ancient Jewish state. Typical of this is the first chapter of the book of Isaiah, from which it transpires that the enemy is almost at the gate of Jerusalem, but you have not yet come to your senses. Your New Moons – which were very important days at the time – and your Saturdays evoke the hatred of my soul, said the prophet, in God's name. For there is no ethical truth, wash your hands, which are full of blood. So the prophet provides ethical norms, and makes our lives easier by so doing, as he gives us a way by which to live. It is a different question as to why people don't keep to them – selfishness, hunger for power, a desire to thieve, or because of society.

ESV: No, people have been given freedom and make their own choices.

JS: They have been given freedom; the notion of freedom is there in the fifth book of Moses: 'See, I have set before thee this day life and good, and death and evil; In that I command thee this day to love the LORD thy God' (Deut 30:15-16). Try managing that under a communist dictatorship. So, the point here is that there are ethical norms, which we know, but social circumstances have not made it possible for everyone to emphasize the ethical norms they know. I'll end on a funny note: when I taught homiletics, Israel was the sworn enemy of the Soviet Union. It was crazy; more people lived in a single street in Moscow than the whole of Israel, but Israel was the sworn enemy. A boy asked me, and not just in jest, whether it was allowed to talk of Zionism from the pulpit. Sure you can, I replied – but you can say the 'amen' in the camp at Kistarcsa. So there are certain pressurizing social conditions in which some prophetic souls, who were not born to be heroes, say what the Bible says, that there is 'a time to keep silence, and a time to speak' (Ecc 3:7).

ESV: To stay with the example of blood being spilled, during the Holocaust, people understandably cried out asking where God was.

JS: The Holocaust is a problem to which there is no answer. I myself dealt with this issue with an article entitled 'Faith in God after Auschwitz', in the Hungarian Catholic journal Teológia. There is no answer to this, because alas we saw very little of the God who lets truth triumph and who cares for and defends his people. Those who escaped could say that God saved them. But if such a person asks me why God didn't save his father, I have no answer to give them. A professor said about this that there is no theological answer, but if we were not to continue Jewish life, then even that would be destroyed which Hitler left.

The Bible shows us ethical behaviour, but it is society's role and responsibility to ensure that this is ultimately achieved without danger to life.

ESV: Chief Rabbi Schweitzer, you just said that the task of society, that is, of small communities and of the people of a nation, is to enforce these minimal ethical foundations, which are needed.

JS: Professor Vizi, that is the task of the powerful.

ESV: But who chooses the powerful?

JS: In a republic, in principle it is the people, in practice the people's representatives, but in a royal system this is not the case. After the defeat of the Revolution of 1848-49, for example, Austrian emperor Franz Joseph, who came to the throne at the age of eighteen, executed a great number of Hungarian patriots. The populace played no role in this decision; in point of fact it was just his mother, Princess Sophie of Bavaria, who was whispering in his ear. It is not only the ordinary people who are to be held to account; in the shadow of the powers-that-be, they have the least responsibility, as they are silent. Of those who shout today, take a look at how many of them were standing there on Budapest's great Andrássy Boulevard cheering communist premier János Kádár as he passed by. The job of those in power is to generate moral opportunities for life.

ESV: They should generate the conditions for it. If they are not there, then it is the responsibility of the literate to speak out, irrespective of whether they assisted or objected to the rise to power of the government or party in question. The literate should be independent even at times like these.

JS: Yes, this is there in the Talmud: the wise should watch their words.

ESV: It is also there in the great Hungarian Saint Stephen's admonitions to his son Saint Emeric: my son, listen to the wise – to the old, as he puts it – and never pay attention to the words of those who are bogus. As he put it: 'do not consult with those less wise'.

JS: But, for the sake of example, if he had not succeeded in executing some of the pagans, and if the pagans had won, then what would they have said? Few things take one or seduce one to sin as power does. I was always surprised when in Germany, as I have found few gentlemen as kind, erudite and refined as the German theologians were.

ESV: Because you encountered the literate... Every nation has its rabble.

JS: And yet this nation gave the worst of rabbles. Here one can only speak of individuals. For I can look to the German Gentile priests I have met with the greatest respect, and yet it was Germans who murdered my father. We should never generalize, but rather we should break ethical behaviour down to the level of the individual.

ESV: I have just come from Apostag, where there is a synagogue that has been awarded the Europa Nostra award for its restoration. The façade is classical, the interior baroque. In the 1670s and 1680s the Jews chased out of Moravia and the Czech lands settled in this little village between the Danube and Tisza rivers, on the banks of the Danube, which is a thousand years old and is famous as the place that the bishop of Kalocsa gathered his troops and supporters against Charles Robert. The village got its name from the rotunda depicting the twelve apostles. 150-160 Jews settled in a village that had 800 inhabitants at the time, and they lived together in complete tranquility until the Holocaust. Then, the Jews were deported; a total of six of them survived. This little village might have been a bit larger by then, but it was powerless against the regime. This is why I would like to return to the point that those who are able to think in terms of the past, the present and the future are obliged to speak out if something develops in a very dangerous way. Perhaps this is uncomfortable or unpleasant, but the responsibility is infinitely great. Thomas Mann was able to speak out. One must speak out and not stand idly by; as our great poet Mihály Babits put it, 'among criminals, he who stays silent is a collaborator'.

JS: Especially in Switzerland. This is a tough issue; I'll give an example closer to home. Bishop Vilmos Apor was able to speak out in Győr in the west of Hungary, but not everyone is Vilmos Apor. There were those who spoke out less; there were those who objected, but kept quiet out of fear. Sorry for referring to myself, but in the first days after the Nazi Arrow Cross took power in Hungary, I felt perfectly fine in the house for deportees; the policemen were not exactly top-notch gentlemen, but still behaved much more sophisticatedly than the Arrow Cross thugs on the street. Fear is a terrible thing, and for a life without fear we had to establish democracy.

ESV: This is the basis for the thinking of Hungarian liberal political philosopher István Bibó.

JS: Democracy should provide a guarantee. I don't want to get into daily politics, but yesterday my wife was having tea with a girlfriend who lives in the building behind the statue of Lajos Kossuth on Budapest's Kossuth Square, and so she had to cross the square in front of the Hungarian parliament building; she said it was better I didn't know what kind of things are graffitied on the columns. I'm not afraid, not after the Germans and the Russians, after *was passiert*, you can't think of anything worse happening, but still, this is terrible. This is incompatible with democracy.

What I want to get out of this is that anyone whose life has been under threat knows that they have to be heroic. Before he was hanged, Hungarian revolutionary general János Damjanich said to the young hangman: 'Careful, don't ruffle my beard!' Just yesterday we had a guest who told us they had visited the birthplace of Károly Leiningen-Westerburg, a German general in the Hungarian army, somewhere near Frankfurt. He was hanged as a defender of Hungarian freedom, but didn't speak a word of Hungarian. These are rare people, worthy of respect; but the average person is afraid.

ESV: This is a basic human characteristic...

JS: That's right, and so they cannot be scorned for it.

ESV: There is another essential human characteristic: that in a group, in a crowd, a person loses that minimal ethical sense they would otherwise have because instead of remaining sovereign, they follow the others. And following bad is easier than expressing good on an individual basis, as this would involve breaking away from the group.

SS: A crowd bears a great responsibility; we know what a great blessing a crowd can be, for example when the Jewish people came together when Moses read out the Ten Commandments.

JS: Yes, and when Korah rebelled against him, it meant trouble. I would like to return to the question of sin: at the beginning the Bible is saying that death is the consequence of sin. When in the Scriptures there is mention of the right of female descendants to inherit, the daughters of Zelophehad say: because we are daughters, and not sons, are we not to inherit from our father? Then Moses makes it legal for daughters to inherit, but Zelophehad dies, and his daughters ask: why did he die, when he did not even take part in Korah's rebellion? This part reflects the notion that death is the consequence of sin. (The Flood also happens because of humanity's sin.) But this train of thought is not completed everywhere in the Scriptures. The book of Ecclesiastes raises a series of problems about the question of man, God, sin, and so on. At the end it says: 'Then shall the dust return to the earth as it was: and the spirit shall return unto God who gave it' (Ecc 12:7). So, according to this description, death is not a punishment, but rather something natural, the end of a life.

There is much mention in the Bible of the fact that sin exists. Part of the third book of Moses, regarding sacrifices, mentions sacrifices for sin. When Judaism replaced the ritual of sacrifice with prayer – which was a lengthy process, and largely took place during captivity in Babylon, as there was no Sanctuary where sacrifices could be presented – then absolution, atonement took on a very important role. To this day the position of Jewish theology on this is that, as a result of introspection, we should first expiate with an apology our sins against our fellow human beings, as sins against the Almighty, failures to obey the law, can only be expiated once we have appeased God for our sins against our fellow human beings. We can again return to how we have obligations to God, for example the Ten Commandments.

ESV: The modern world also demands a certain level and 'type' of morality, basic norms, otherwise the economy could not function. And yet people break certain rules of the game, even though they recognize that the rules and their observance are necessary. The rapid progress of academe demands the same thing – progress in jurisprudence and social science as much as progress in the laws of physics and biology. I will also give you an example of how ethics changes in my field. In Roman times, a doctor's oath established certain norms, but, for example, it was prohibited to treat and waste time and medicine on an incurable patient. Then, with the appearance of Jesus and influenced by the miracles he performed, which were described in detail by Luke, the physician from Antioch, the motif of compassion entered medical treatment, and became ennobled as an ethical norm. This is a beautiful moment in the history of medical practice. To this day it remains the key task for a doctor – and here I am again alluding to the Hungarian-born psychoanalyst Michael Balint – to relate to a patient as one human to another, following the example of Jesus' actions.

JS: One of the deputy ambassadors from Israel, Dr. Gordon, was a doctor. There was a time when this Dr. Gordon and I gave a lecture to a small group at the faculty of medicine on the history of medieval Jewish medicine. After the lecture he told me that before he became a diplomat he had been head doctor in a large hospital department, where an unfortunate patient had been lying, whose brain was no longer alive, but whose body was being kept alive. The family had already said that it was a shame to leave the poor thing to suffer like this, but Dr. Gordon replied that he could not take responsibility for taking the patient off the life support machine and thereby be the direct cause of a person, albeit a being leading a vegetative life, not a full human being, being destroyed. They sued him for it…

ESV: Chief Rabbi Schweitzer was a member of the ethics committee established in 1989, which included, among others, Tamás Nyíri, László Sólyom, János Szentágothai, and of which I was president. We talked about suicide, euthanasia – both active and passive euthanasia – as ethical problems and published opinions on them. We received very critical responses from many parts of the press, but here we are nevertheless, we can stomach it, and the fact that the phrasing in Hungarian medical law is quite different, say, from that in the Netherlands is thanks to us.

JS: ...So Dr. Gordon said that he would not take the patient off the machines. The case went to trial; the court brought the family's lawyer as a witness, who stated that there was no point to leaving the machines on, as the family do love the patient, but the negatives are so many... Dr. Gordon replied to the lawyer that he was welcome to do it himself – it would be just one simple motion. The lawyer wouldn't do it.

ESV: Of course he would not; only a doctor can perform euthanasia.

JS: Dr. Gordon had asked him to do it and showed him how.

ESV: That would have been murder.

SS: This is like when Jesus said to the accusers of the woman taken in adultery, 'He that is without sin among you, let him first cast a stone at her' (John 8:7).

PE: What Chief Rabbi Schweitzer said about the communist régime started a very interesting train of thought. There was mention of an ethical crisis, of ethical transformation...

JS: All of us who lived here then were in many senses in an ethical crisis, but at the risk of being pretentious, I would say that we had to weigh up whether we should have something or have nothing at all. On the other hand, I would add that I had a very decent office deputy who asked me, 'Your excellency, they are always asking me what is happening here in the office.' To which I replied, 'Tell them they are invited to any of our meetings; nothing special happens here.'

PE: In the various different parts of the world the main problems of social ethics vary, in part because of the history of the last decades. These differences are interestingly revealed in the social teaching of the Catholic Church. I could almost say that in the last decades it was primarily the problems of Latin America which inspired these statements. The question of structural sin, in-justice, exploitation and the ignorance of the dignity of the human individual

– these were the main themes, and through these came the theology of liberation. The teaching of the Holy See on this was worthy of note, as it published two instructions, one after the next; the current pope, Pope Benedict XVI, played an important role in both. These two instructions effectively put the theology of liberation in its place, because it clarified that the Christian religion does not promise people paradise on Earth, and that the salvation we proclaim is not complete earthly happiness, but principally liberation from sin: this is liberation in a theological sense. It is a different question that we have obligations to society, moral obligations, but this does not mean that we are able to create paradise in this world.

This train of thought accumulated a great list of experiences, especially relating to the problem of poverty and injustice. I think that now, almost everywhere in the former communist countries, there are such typical situations which characterize our current ethical state; one of these is obviously that at the start of the communist period private property was confiscated, and so ordinary people, too, had their land, shops and workshops taken from them. In many countries this property was never returned; rather, there was a more or less nominal compensation process, but this was not comprehensive, and the former small property owners were not in a position to compete on equal terms with big international companies. They remained in a more difficult and less favourable economic position, even though they used to own property which was taken from them without compensation. Also, and most importantly, for at least forty years it had been not only the ideology but in part also the law in these countries that an employee would not receive full compensation for their work in the form of payment, that only a small part of the value added would be given to them in financial form, but they would be given the right to free services in their retirement or when ill, that their children would be educated for free, and that they would receive social welfare, if they needed it. Some elements of this, like the right as a citizen to free medical treatment, which in the 1970s was transferred to the Hungarian constitution from the Stalinist one in the Soviet Union, was no mere moral encouragement, but an article of constitutional law. And then, when the change of régime came, society managed to forget about these promises or acquired rights, the part of employees' wages which had not been paid, but which justice demanded still be theirs, amidst the glee of freedom. Since then this has only further accumulated, and it is clear that there are difficulties paying for this and providing for it in future. Which presents a major structural problem, the reorganization of health provision, the transformation of education, and so on; at the same time we are facing a really serious moral debt, and this, as I said, is the same for all former socialist countries. A debt in a moral or perhaps even legal sense, which is an organic part of the state's national debt, except that this is not a debt to foreign countries, in dollars, but to the country's citizens who worked during this period. The honest and just treatment of this problem is, I think, the key question for our current society. This does not mean that we should be angry with anyone about this; rather it means that the solutions have to be found to this reality by keeping an open mind and weighing things up carefully. There was mentioned how a doctor should love their patients; I would say of the powers-that-be, those with power, in slightly old-fashioned and folk terms, that the ruler should love their people. People should be loved, and this then makes us more inventive in finding fair solutions.

ESV: It is very difficult for society to accept this situation, including this moral debt, because society is starting to forget how things were before and instead waits to see what it will get in the future. In the last decades, pension contributions have not been capitalized. On the basis of so-called Swiss indexation, the pay as you go system, we paid out pensions from the contributions that had been paid in. Then, we changed everything, introduced the system characteristic of capitalism, but we forgot to take into account the particularities of the last forty years. For the future, this means that the Hungarian population will not get what it expects to get, that which the populations of developed, Western, EU countries get, and thus will be dissatisfied. This will lead to a conflict that I think will be hard to manage, for example, because honesty would have been fantastically valuable at the outset and will continue to be so. In the instance in which the population does not know what is happening and why, and it merely senses that prices are rising, that it cannot satisfy its elementary needs, the minimal things which are required for the relatively secure life they are used to, then existential insecurity takes hold. This can drive crowds out to protest in the street. And if economic reforms and reforms of the welfare system are absolutely necessary – and I, for one, think they are, even if this will be very painful – then it will still not be possible to soften or compensate for the severe errors of recent years. So, serious social conflict could develop, precisely because of the lack of fairness and equality – the average Hungarian feels, rightly, that they have been done an injustice.

VIII.

RABA EMUNAT ELKHA

(IN YOU THE FAITH IS STRONG)

IN CONVERSATION WITH JÓZSEF SCHWEITZER

JS: After I was born a great family tragedy occurred, as my mother died, at the age of twenty-three, when I was one. My father never remarried. All this took place in Veszprém in central Hungary, where my late mother's father was the chief rabbi. My grandmother was still a young lady. They had four daughters, one of whom died, and they were left with three: all past school-leaving age. They raised me after that, together with my father, as we lived opposite each other. My father, a lawyer, could not be described as religious, but when he had time, he would be there at the temple on a Friday evening, and at big festivals; he was a conscious Jew. But in the end I was brought up in a rabbi's house, my grandfather's house; my grandfather was a very conservative theological and rite-observing man, and so in our house the whole of life took place in the spirit and practice of Judaism; this is what I was born into, this is what was natural. My grandfather's house was primarily characterized by the housekeeping being strictly in line with ritual requirements. This means that not only can dairy and meat dishes not be mixed, but neither could the cutlery:

there is a knife for butter, for cheese, for dairy, and one for meat items. This is how I learned to eat: one had to take care not to mix them up. I didn't even have to take care myself, but I knew that there was a different-coloured table-cloth and different plates for dairy meals than for meat ones. Meat meals usually meant a white tablecloth and porcelain plates, while a coloured table-cloth and coloured plates would be used for dairy meals. There was nothing special about this for me; neither was the fact that my grandfather would be at the service in the synagogue in the morning and in the evening.

In Veszprém in those days there were more than 300 Jewish families – around 1000 souls altogether. On Miklós Horthy Street – I think that's what it was called at the time – there was a large plot, and if you looked at it from the street there was a two-storey house on one side, with the cantor's apart-ment on the ground floor, and the rabbi's apartment on the first floor. On the other side there was a three-storey house, also with a cantor's apartment on the ground floor, and a school on the upper two floors. It was a grammar school for a while, while there were enough children, and an elementary school all the way until 1944. One of the older teachers, the director, also lived there. These two buildings on each side were connected with a decorated iron railing; through this one entered the temple courtyard, and at the end of the plot was the synagogue itself, with three storeys, galleries on the upper two floors, and a nice big organ. So on one side ran Miklós Horthy Street, and on the other the wheat market. The temple courtyard was a natural playground for me. There was one more building on the plot – a smaller temple which could be heated. It was not possible to heat the big synagogue back then, and in winter it was very cold; Veszprém, near the Bakony Mountains, is a windy city in any case, and this is why the winter temple was built. Part of my childhood was spent there; there was also an avenue named after Plosser, some city bigwig, which led from our house out to the park and to the playground. In my first year at elementary school we moved up to Budapest; until then, this part of Veszprém was where my life took place.

SS: Can you remember any tradition which was unique back then to Veszprém and which no longer exists today?

JS: I can't remember anything like that, but so few people survived after the deportations that the regular, traditional religious life that was everywhere in Veszprém and taken for granted is no longer.

It is important to note that there are two shades to our denomination: the Orthodox, which follows rites and practices strictly, and completely prohibits work on Saturdays, and the neolog. Veszprém was a neolog community, which means that most of the shops were open on Saturdays. They were there in the synagogue on a Friday evening, if business hours had finished. On Saturday mornings, as for the majority of the members of the community Saturday was not a leisure day, there were fewer people. But the big festivals, of course, like New Year or the Day of Atonement, were sacrosanct: every shop was closed and no one went into their office. In fact, in all Jewish families Friday evening was celebrated as the arrival of the Sabbath: the table was laid in white, and candles were lit. Housewives would light at least two candles, but my grandmother lit four, as she would always put a candle into the holder which had belonged to my late mother just as she would in their own holders. On Friday evening there was dinner, sometimes big, sometimes small, in the small dining room; there were two pieces of challah bread there – two, to remind us of the two days' worth of manna that fell for the people of Israel on Fridays (as they could not gather it on Saturdays). There was wine on the table, in a chalice, at the part of the table where the host sat, and across from him, at the end of the table, the candles. There was usually a freshly-cooked dinner on Fridays; in Veszprém, in the winter months, an essential part of this was fish from nearby Lake Balaton, bass or perch, with sweet walnut sauce. When I arrived in Pécs, in the south-west corner of Hungary, to take up my position as a rabbi, I was still unmarried, and I would be invited to dinner on Friday evening; I would start talking about this fish with walnut, and the housewives would be taken aback, as they had never heard of it. This was a specialty of Transdanubia; I was an old hand as a rabbi when I got to Győr, in the north-west, where there was also fish with walnut. In general we would eat meat soup and carp with paprika on Fridays; in winter we had the meat cooked with the soup, in our case usually with chestnut sauce. So everything was sweet, and the challah bread was very tasty, which back then was produced not by a baker, but at home. There was a big kitchen, with two staff members permanently there, and on Fridays my grandmother would always be fudding about in the kitchen, too. The very nice thing I remember from before I started school was how they made *lángos* (Hungarian savoury fried dough) from the edge of the challah bread on Fridays, for my grandfather, who would still be in the office on Fridays, and for me, who would be playing there in his office, the first room to be properly warmed each morning; they would bring the *lángos* as a 10am snack.

SS: How fixed were everyone's places in the temple?

JS: The men sat on the ground floor, the women on the gallery on the first floor, and the girls on the second-floor gallery. The organist was L rinc Ritter, who I still see in front of my eyes as a tall old gentleman dressed in dark grey; next to him there were two cantors, occasionally three, and there was my grandfather, the rabbi. At elementary school the general teachers taught religion classes, and at the grammar school it was the teacher who was head of the elementary; these men had generally graduated from the Jewish teacher training college, which also trained them to teach religion classes. And at the high school and the upper school, the trade school, my grandfather was the teacher. Dr. Andor Steiner, a member of one of the big Veszprém families, who was a doctor in Budapest at the time, told me, by then rabbi of Pécs, a story about this when we happened to meet while on holiday in Balatonfüred. The Steiners were traders in spirits and *pálinka*; they had a big shop and warehouse. When I was living in Pest with my grandparents, but my father still lived in Veszprém, for two summers I went and lived with him, and on Saturdays we would always be invited to the Steiners' for lunch. Andor Steiner told me that he went to a Piarist school where one of his teachers asked him: 'Tell me, Andor, you enter every school competition and you always receive a commendation, whether for this, or for that, and yet none of you ever come to us with a question about Latin, about Hungarian, about German, or asking us to provide literature, even though this is allowed for your submissions, and we would be allowed to help.' And he replied: 'Well, for us the situation is that we can go to the much-respected rabbi at a certain time in the afternoon, when he welcomes all his students, and as he has a doctorate in literature, Latin, and all the other things, he can provide all the help we need.' For my grandfather's students it was worth more than ten sermons that they could go and visit him, and he was quite at home in these high school subjects. At the Rabbinical seminary, which in those days lasted ten years, five in the lower class, five in the upper class, Latin and Greek played a highly important role. The seminary began at the fifth year of high school, at the age of fourteen. You had to take an entrance exam made up of Latin and Hebrew grammar, translation of the Pentateuch and the first Prophets, and of ten-fifteen pages of so-called Talmudic literature.

SS: Did you begin the seminary at the age of fifteen, Professor Schweitzer?

JS: No. There were two options. It was possible to begin after graduating with a baccalaureate from high school, but in that case you had to know the Hebrew material from the first five years and take a baccalaureate in it. I was very happy at the Jewish high school, where we did quite a lot of Bible studies and Hebrew; my grandfather helped me with my studies, and there was a teacher from the upper class at the seminary who dealt with me. As much as was possible, my grandfather wanted to avoid a member of the family attending the school at which he taught, when they could go somewhere else, lest it appear that there could be any special family treatment; so I stayed at the Jewish high school if for this reason alone. I took my baccalaureate exams in Hebrew with the seminary students of my age, and we joined the upper class together. As after the deportations there were not many applicants, especially with the destruction of the Jewry in the provinces, only the upper class remained. The directors of the seminary added a year or two of zero-year introductory studies, depending on a child's previous knowledge. When I was director, there were two years like this, so the rabbinical seminary in fact lasted for seven years. The rules of the seminary stated that if possible it should be required that students also acquire a university qualification, and get a doctorate – this they could do at the faculty of humanities at the university. In a few rare cases, I don't know why, they made an exception. When the *numerus clausus* laws were introduced, restricting the numbers of Jews at education institutions, an exceptional solution was found in order for the previously established rights of the seminary not to be affected: at the faculty of humanities at the university they said that anyone with a certificate from the seminary that they were a full student there would be accepted as a full student with restricted rights. Their record books were a different shape and colour, and they could not take courses leading to examinations qualifying them to be teachers. The permitted subjects were thus the 'pure academic disciplines': philosophy, psychology, education, Oriental languages. These are what we were allowed to take at the university, and it was from these that we could choose a subject for our doctorates, too. They took care to see that we couldn't take courses which might have brought lucrative opportunities.

SS: Was it easy for you to get used to Budapest, after Veszprém?

JS: Of course. I had already done the second half of my first year of elementary school here, but even before that I had visited Budapest many times with my father, who had siblings living here. His sister lived at 49 F Street in Buda, where we would stay if we were in Budapest. Important memories for me included seeing a tram for the first time, before I started school, and when I was first in the market hall on Batthyány Square, as both represented something new relative to Veszprém. There was a cinema there in Veszprém, and also here in Budapest; as a child, I didn't go to the theatre either here or there; I had family in both cities, but I still remember with wonder seeing that mass of yellow glide towards me, and that great market, the likes of which one didn't see in Veszprém.

In the building next to where we are now, on the second floor, was the rabbinical seminary; the teacher training college was on the first floor, and the teaching school that belonged to it was on the ground floor. And as we lived here, in what at the time was Archduke Sándor Street, I started my first year of elementary school in this building, in this teaching school. But then we moved to the Danube embankment, to what today is Balassi Bálint Street, which at the time was called Személynök Street. Then this school wasn't right for me, because we don't travel on Saturdays. Now, my grandfather taught here, and was rabbi at the synagogue in Csáky Street, now called Heged s Gyula Street, close to the Vígszínház theatre. So on Saturdays we had to walk from here to there, but this did not work, as they learned after a year, and so we moved over there to the Danube embankment. I would say something about the summers. Every summer we would go to Balatonalmádi, as this was the closest Lake Balaton resort to Veszprém. And when it was not yet warm enough for bathing, but it was ideal for walks and for sitting somewhere for a bite to eat, then we would visit Balatonfüred, a few kilometres away. In spring and autumn we would head to Balatonfüred, on a Sunday afternoon, or whenever my father managed to break away from his office for a free afternoon. But to get to Balatonalmádi, we had to change trains, so it was a bit complicated. Once a friend of my father's from the nearby city of Székesfehérvár, who had an automobile, came across on some business or other to Veszprém. He took us to Almádi in his automobile: that, at the age of four or five, was the first time I had ever been in one. I had not sat in an automobile, but I had sat in a carriage, which is something my children have not sat in. Veszprém had two spots popular for Sunday outings, where people drank beer, and the children drank raspberry soda; one was the Kiskúti Inn, the other the Betekints Inn. Sometimes, on an autumn afternoon when we went out to one of these with my father, we went by carriage, which was a special experience for a child.

PLK: Can you recall what your relationship to your surroundings was like as a child?

JS: I was very fond of tennis; at that time only as a spectator. There in the park there was a tennis court, and my father I were watching when a gentleman called out from the court, recognizing my father and telling us not to stand outside but inviting us to come inside and take a seat. My father politely refused, saying thank you, but that we needed to get going. He told me that he hadn't accepted the invitation because the tennis court belonged to MOVE (Hungarian National Defence Association). MOVE was an anti-Semitic, radical right-wing organization.

But between colleagues, especially in personal relations, this did not turn ugly, as evidenced by the young lawyer playing tennis at MOVE inviting my father onto the court. There was, I think, polite or collegial contact within a certain bourgeois class with a certain similar attitude, but I don't think there was a deeper friendship, at least not on my father's part. In Veszprém there was a café called the Elit, which seemed a very elegant place in my eyes, and had an outside terrace; a great many of the Jewish lawyers and traders frequented it. My father had a regulars' table together with Móric Spitzer, a lawyer, and president of the Jewish congregation, and his brother, Józsi Spitzer, as well as a lawyer called Miklós Fischer. After leaving the office they would sit and talk there for an hour. And there was another restaurant, the Korona, which was more the meeting place for the right-wing community – something, interestingly enough, I only learned later. As a high school student I had foraged amidst my father's belongings, and found a notebook detailing a duel. The story behind this was that my father and his group were eating at the Korona, only for another group to sit at a nearby table and to make taunting remarks about their Jewishness; at this, my father, who was a reserve army officer, stood up to defend his honour and that of his company. The gentlemanly custom at the time was that if someone was insulted, then a duel would ensue.

I also know that when in the 1920s the infantrymen marched past the synagogue and the rabbi's house, they sang a song: 'We'll knock the walnut off the tree, and knock dead every Jew we see'. My father and other Jewish reserve officers requested an interview with the city commander, and officially registered their objection, which the city commander accepted. My aunts told me this story – afterwards the song was no longer sung.

I'd add the following story about the pestilence of anti-Semitism: I was a little boy when one of the maids taught me a song that was fashionable at the time. It went: 'Erger, Berger, Schlossberger, every Jew's a swindler'. I didn't understand what it was about. The family came home in the evening, and I starting to sing. They asked me where I learned this. I said from Mári the maid. Mári was dismissed the following day – my dear girl, this tune isn't popular around here, have a good day.

Anti-Semitism cannot have been that great, as my father was ultimately a deputy notary public; his boss, Péter Nagy, was a government counsellor, so officially called 'honourable gentleman', but I called him 'uncle honourable gentleman'. Every day at noon, during lunch hour, my father escorted his boss home to his house towards the park, and then came to collect me from the park. This Péter Nagy must have been a democrat, because come afternoon he would not go into the office, but sit in the Elit café and play chess. And there was a master barber, who was very good at chess, who would play with him. In those days for a royal notary public to play chess with a master barber – men of different social significance – was unusual.

One of the trainee lawyers, whom I heard my father referring to as Ferenc Siberna, turned out to be a member of the Hungarian Nazi Arrow Cross, and was the Arrow Cross mayor of Veszprém in 1944. I don't know much about this, as I didn't have a close connection to Veszprém by this time: in 1944 my father had been deported from Újpest, and the Veszprém members of the family from Veszprém. I didn't have many contacts in Veszprém, but we did hear that Ferenc Siberna, whom I had never heard a bad word about as a child, had become the Arrow Cross mayor. He even attacked Cardinal József Mindszenty.

As I see it from my own modest perspective, people lived very well until higher political circles started to force anti-Semitic policies on people. My grandfather had a pleasant official relationship with the bishop, Nándor Rott. My father was on informal terms with Pál Wéber, Nándor Rott's secretary. My father once told me of how the grandparents were understandably hugely distressed when my mother died. A Catholic canon called Strauss was at my grandfather's side a great deal in the days that followed, trying to keep his spirits up; my father would continue to mention this with gratitude many years later.

PLK: How were you pointed towards faith as a child?

JS: This is what was natural for us. It was natural that we ate kosher food; it was natural that if we went out to eat, we went to Steiner's shop. Steiner had a part that was a tavern, and at the back, opening onto the courtyard, was a restaurant with white tablecloths. There was no need to explain this; it was as natural as the fact that we are sitting here drinking something.

PLK: Who taught you to pray, for example?

JS: My grandfather taught me to read in Hebrew, while my grandmother taught me the prayers which a child has to know how to pray. The whole of education is best if a family provides it so naturally as for one not to imagine it could be otherwise.

A person changes if they have grandchildren: they fall in love with these little children. We have twin grandchildren, two boys of six. The children were having lunch here, and my grandson Péter asked his grandmother, 'Ágnes, do you eat kosher? Because we are only allowed kosher.' So it is best, it is beautiful, if it is natural, if it comes naturally.

I have always kept myself to this. When we were students in the 1940s, we didn't, on account of the very sad public circumstances, go to the social spots where young people would go on a Saturday or Sunday afternoon for tea or for dancing. We visited families, ones who lived in bigger homes, for what bourgeois families called a festive gathering. I don't know whether they have them anymore, because by the time my son and daughter were that age, afternoon festivities had become evening parties. But in my day we had these festivities, at which they always knew that there were one or two boys who observed the ritual laws, and they gave the others sandwiches of one kind or another, while they gave us cheese or egg ones, whatever was available and allowed.

SS: How did it work in practice when your grandmother taught you how to pray?

JS: She asked me to say the prayers with her, because a small child should know them. This should all take place in Jewish kindergarten, as it does today, but in Veszprém in those days there was no Jewish kindergarten. She would get up, wash her hands, rinse her mouth, and say, in Hebrew: 'I give thanks to you, eternal King, that in your mercy you have given me my life back'. For they believed that when someone is asleep they are not alive. *Rabo emonos elho* – we have great faith in you. This is the first prayer that a young child has to learn: a morning prayer.

PLK: There is another important stage in a boy's life: preparing for the *bar mitzvah*. How did this happen in those days?

JS: This happens when boys are thirteen years of age. In Budapest, where there were many boys, there were classes, or one could prepare for it privately. The classes were usually held by the religion teacher, or if someone prepared by private means, the parents hired someone, usually someone studying in the upper class at the rabbinical seminary. I personally was prepared by my grandfather. When I was a rabbi in Pécs, there weren't many boys, but there were a couple, and I prepared them myself.

The *bar mitzvah* is a celebratory ritual held in the temple on the occasion of reaching the age of religious responsibility.

SS: How deep a memory is that of your own *bar mitzvah*, and how much can you remember of it?

JS: I was greeted by two rabbis, as my grandfather was there, and there was also a young rabbi, my grandfather's junior rabbi, József Berkovits, who initiated me separately as a child of the rabbi's family. Then I was given a nice wristwatch, as was the custom, and I was given new, dark blue clothes, and in the afternoon there was a light afternoon meal for the adults, given by my grandfather, and a meal on the following afternoon for my classmates. I have to say that, quite honestly, the event did not evoke great emotions in me, as every Saturday one boy or other would have his *bar mitzvah*. In those days, when we were in third and fourth grade at high school, a great many Saturdays and Sundays were spent as guests of meals for *bar mitzvah* ceremonies.

SS: You mentioned the morning prayers and the blessing of wine and bread. Were there other important prayers, like evening prayers, for example?

JS: We were also taught prayers to say before going to bed. 'Let the Eternal One be blessed, who covers us with sleep, who protects us, and allows us to wake up well.'

An observant religious Jew always has his head covered, and we had this custom at home, too; we ate with our heads covered. And in general, if there was someone from the family with us at my grandparents' house for lunch or dinner who was less religious, they would also sit there with their head covered, to comply with my grandfather. We always prayed after eating, too. Sorry for the comparison, but it was like brushing your teeth or washing yourself – this is how life went.

SS: What other prayers does an observant religious Jewish young man say?

JS: There aren't any separate psalm songs or anything like that, but there is a regular weekday, Saturday and feast day liturgy.

For Saturday, tradition prescribes three meals: one on Friday evening, one during the day on Saturday, and one on Saturday afternoon. On these Saturday occasions the prayer after the meal is introduced by Psalm 126: 'When the LORD turned again the captivity of Zion, we were like them that dream. Then was our mouth filled with laughter, and our tongue with singing.' For weekdays there is Psalm 137: 'By the rivers of Babylon, there we sat down, yea, we wept, when we remembered Zion. We hanged our harps upon the willows in the midst thereof. For there they that carried us away captive required of us a song; and they that wasted us required of us mirth, saying, Sing us one of the songs of Zion. How shall we sing the LORD's song in a strange land?' This was the psalm sung before weekday meals, and Psalm 126, which is optimistic, was for Friday evenings and for Saturdays.

Every aspect of life was connected to some kind of religious experience, from waking up in the morning and going to bed through to food.

PLK: How did you prepare yourself for a career as a rabbi?

JS: The job itself appealed to me; I liked the sermons, the studying. Just as a doctor's child can find medicine appealing, so for me it was this calling that left a deep impression.

I was interested in sermons, which I paid attention to, as well. When I accompanied my grandfather from Személynök Street to the synagogue in Csáky Street on weekdays, always on foot, as it was not far, and then we came back, I asked him questions, to which he replied. I learned a great deal in the meantime, while we walked, particularly if he would encounter a colleague he would walk along with a bit, and I would follow on alongside them, and listen, and I soaked up a great deal from these conversations.

PLK: It was already a very difficult time when you entered the rabbinical seminary...

JS: I entered in 1941. It was a difficult period, but those studying at the seminary were given an educational exemption from forced labour service. The question was how well-intentioned the commander of the conscription service was. If he was well-intentioned, he would say, here's the exemption from the ministry, that's fine. If he was ill-intentioned, he would say they would investigate its authenticity, but they would never do so, and the person in question would be stuck there. There wasn't much they could do.

PLK: So it must only have been after the war that you graduated.

JS: Yes, it was after the war that we got our doctorates. That was in 1946, the time of the tax peng currency used to deal with hyperinflation, and I paid the doctoral fees in tax peng . At that time what most kept us going was the great interest in Palestine and the demands for a state of Israel. The Israeli newspapers wrote a great deal, and these made their way to Budapest. For the Budapest newspapers to publish authentic news from Israel, such articles had to be translated from Hebrew into Hungarian. There were those of us who made a living out of this. I had lost my father, and we got some kind of scholarship in tax peng , but this didn't go far. These translations, on the other hand, were well paid.

PLK: When was it possible to sense, as war drew close, that something would happen, that something was wrong?

JS: It was possible partly with the Jewish laws which began in 1938, which robbed ever more people of the chance to make a living, and partly with the *Anschluss*. When the Germans entered Vienna in 1938 we had direct news of what the Germans were doing, as many people escaped to Budapest. And then came Prime Minister Kálmán Darányi with the Jewish laws as part of the Programme of Győr. Take a look at the newspapers of the time: a great number of column inches were taken up with the debates in the Upper and Lower Houses of Parliament, and with political statements both pro and contra, with both supportive and critical arguments. In practice, as it was put at the time, truthfully if a little romantically, we were excluded outside the fortifications of the constitution. We did not have the rights that another Hungarian citizen had. Not to mention that if we go back in time we see that this anti-Semitic movement truly began with the *numerus clausus* in 1920, constraining access to education for certain groups, and which 'diplomatically' referred not to religion but to the proportion of the national minorities living in Hungary; that is, they would accept this many of say Serbian nationality, and this many Jews. This was illegal from the outset, as the emancipation of the Jews in 1868 meant that citizens of Jewish faith were in all respects identical to citizens not of Jewish faith, while the Law of Reception in 1895 ensured that the Jewish faith was fully accepted. Now all at once it was made clear that there was no talk of religion here: Jews were regarded not as a religion but as a race. They wanted to give the impression that they were not out to harm religion, but the whole thing was *de facto* targeting the Jews. This had the consequence that eminent figures like Eugene Wigner, Leo Szilard and Edward Teller, whom I had the good fortune to meet personally in Israel, and other great alumni of the famous Fasori Gimnázium, left Hungary, either during the *numerus clausus* or following it, as they could not find positions worthy of their talents and interests. So it would later happen that at conferences on atomic science, if they wanted to speak amongst themselves in confidence, they would do so in Hungarian.

I just received a book about the life of wartime Hungarian prime minister Pál Teleki; he was a complex figure. On the one hand he was a great scholar of geography, and on the other he was very unstable, repeatedly overcome by a desperate mood. The book writes about Teleki's anti-Semitism, which he was very inconsistent about. His starting point was that Béla Kun and the others behind the short-lived Hungarian Soviet Republic of 1919 were Jews, which is true, and that the whole of Communism was nothing else than an attempt at Jewish control of the world under the name of Bolshevism. And once the Jews had achieved global power, their next step would be financial control of the world, see the Rothschilds, etc. Later, however, when the Hungarian government was in need of money, Teleki was part of the negotiations with Adolf Ullmann, the director of the Hungarian General Credit Bank, to allow the government the credit it needed to get on with things. The book also covers Count Bethlen's negotiations with the Rothschilds, while Teleki was still politically active, for Hungary to receive loan funds before it became impossible to support the state. There is no mention here of the Jewish world order or Jewish control of the world financial system, but this very scholarly man viewed this issue in an extraordinarily biased way. I think that similar reasoning on his part was behind the *numerus clausus* laws.

So, after *numerus clausus*, it could be felt that the universities were not the right places for Jews to make progress, and in 1938, when Darányi submitted the First Jewish Law, they first wanted to limit Jewish participation in certain professions to twenty per cent, then to six per cent. This was a very unambiguous step, and Béla Imrédy *et al.* were effectively encouraging Jews to emigrate, with which they would be given assistance, and Jews could even take some of their worldly goods with them. Samu Stern, who at the time was the president of the Hungarian Jewish Council, wrote a book of his memoirs, in which he relates a conversation with one of the prime ministers to introduce a Jewish law. The prime minister encouraged them to emigrate, while they pointed out two difficulties with this: one, that it cost a great deal of money, which people who have lost their jobs don't have, and two, that there is nowhere to emigrate to, as here are the Germans, Austrians and Poles in a much tougher situation than we are, and if there is a country that welcomes Jews, then they will accept ones from those countries first. As he tells in his memoirs, Samu Stern, together with community elder Károly Wilhelm, who was an authority on legal matters, explained this to the prime minister, who just ignored these arguments, and told them that hitherto they had followed a policy of assimilation, but that they should take note that the government's policy had now become one of dissimilation, and the key issue was emigration. And to this they said all right, but many people don't have the money for this, and even if they do, where can they go? Because individual countries only give visiting visas to those depositing great amounts of money, or in a country like Switzerland, for example, twelve years of residency were required for someone to acquire citizenship.

The mood of the time was desperate, and everyone lived in the hope that perhaps they wouldn't be able to implement these plans after all, and that Hitler would fall before they did.

PLK: Were stories going around of what would happen to people?

JS: Not definite ones. I remember seeing a photograph in a right-wing magazine showing what a good life Jews in the Warsaw Ghetto had. The photograph was taken in a bar where people were dancing – a ghetto with a bar. It was possible to produce photos like that. The average person didn't know much about the deportations or the events in Poland, but we did know that something bad was going on; we thought that if things in Hungary didn't get worse, this much we could put up with. When my father, who had previously lived in Újpest, was already in the ghetto, he told me over the telephone that if this is as bad as it gets, we'd survive. But we couldn't know.

On 19th March 1944 the Germans entered Hungary. We were in the school building in Wesselényi Street, Budapest, where Béla Vihar, who was a poet and a teacher, was giving an example lesson in religious studies, in which he was using drawings and the spoken word to tell of how Moses smashes the stone tablets because of the golden calf. And the school inspector, Dr. Zoltán Kohn, was also there. All of a sudden a junior officer came in and whispered something to Dr. Kohn, who replied, 'Good God, we're done for!' He turned to Béla Vihar: 'Mr. Vihar, please be so kind as to cut the lesson short. I've just received the news that the Germans have entered Hungary. We must stop and everyone must go home.' The following day it turned out that the Germans had gone into the rabbinical seminary and taken charge of it, turning it into a temporary house of confinement for deportees. The women were crowded into the first floor; the men onto the second.

SS: Was it the Gestapo which commandeered it?

JS: The Hungarian Gestapo, led by infamous inspector Péter Hain, and in such a way that they had the beds brought from the boarding house – where I was living at the time – and put into the classrooms on the first and second floors, from which they had the benches removed. And on that Monday they began the arrests, taking significant representatives of Jewish business and intellectual life to the seminary as the official temporary house of confinement, including Regent Horthy's in-house surgeon, Professor Jen Ádám, though he was released upon the regent's intervention. They took Leó Buday-Goldberger and Jen Vida in there, who were both members of the upper house of parliament, that is, who were untouchable in this sense, but this didn't interest the Germans. Those dragged in here were then taken to Kistarcsa, an internment camp outside Budapest, and from there to Auschwitz. Under the military government of Géza Lakatos things eased, and the seminary was turned from an internment facility to a barracks for gendarmes; it functioned as a facility for deportees only under the government of Döme Sztójay.

To return to the 19th of March, 1944, I went up to Újpest to visit my father, who lived in a house with a garden, where he did not feel comfortable; he did not leave the house, did not listen to the radio, and it was from me that he learned what had happened. He said, 'All right, let's go out into the town and have a look.' And we did go out for a look; German tanks stood in front of Újpest town hall. And I said to my father that these people were going to kill us. To which he replied: 'My dear boy, you've been too much in touch with these unfortunate Jews from Poland and Slovakia.' And this was true, for my father didn't want me to eat the canteen food, and so he paid for me to eat at a private cafeteria which really was frequented by a great many Polish and Slovak Jews staying in Hungary under assumed names. I learned about many things from talking to them, but I didn't tell my family, or my father, as I didn't see why I should upset them. And my father now said to me, 'How can you imagine such things happening in Hungary? This is a state with the rule of law, a cultured nation! These things which the Slovaks and Poles do could not happen here in Hungary! There will be bad things, but not like that.' And then what happened happened.

SS: How did the story at the rabbinical seminary continue after that – your own training?

JS: When we were liberated, on 18th January 1945, the building was already empty. The director at the time, Professor Löwinger, actually lived there. We were so attached to the institute that, interestingly, all of us who were in Budapest met here on the day after the liberation. Everyone went to try to put their lives back together. Before anything else, Löwinger tried to have a look at the library together with Professor Hahn, as the Germans, at the request of the Nazis' Institute for Study of the Jewish Question, had sent people with library skills there to wrap up important books and have them sent back to the Institute in Frankfurt. The rabbis who went to look at the library saw that those sent by the Institute for Study of the Jewish Question had not really known what they were doing, as they had hardly taken away any important books. It transpired that the ones they did send had only got as far as Prague, as a result of the military situation. Many thousands of volumes remained in Prague, even under the communist dictatorship, carefully cared for by the Czechoslovak State Jewish Museum. They were reluctant to send them back, but we did get them all back in the end.

Then teaching slowly began to start again; an important part of this was the canteen reopening. We came in to eat, so we were already together; by spring teaching could resume, in a room which had received the least damage.

I remember Sándor Scheiber holding his first lecture in a dishevelled black robe, but nevertheless a black robe, and in a celebratory atmosphere accompanied by still broken windows. For on the morning of 19th March 1944 Scheiber had come up to Budapest from Dunaföldvár, 100 kilometres to the south, where he was rabbi; the dedication of the grave of Professor Heller, who we have mentioned a number of times, was set for that day. He was not able to go back, and so the clothes he had come in stayed with him. His wife was with him, and they stayed at her parents' home. He learned that Jews were not allowed to travel – I hadn't been aware of this. No one made any official statement about this, he just learned that it was the case, and did not even go to the station. I didn't know, and on the 19th I was up in Újpest at my father's house. On Monday it was possible to know about this, and I asked him what he knew, and he said he didn't know anything. I said that was fine, and that I would come up and visit him on Tuesday. As he lived in Újpest, and I lived in Pest, the way we usually met was that I went up to his office between 5 and 6 o'clock and we would leave together.

PLK: Where did your father work then, and what did he do?

JS: On the Tuesday, 21st March, I got on the tram to Újpest to visit my father. Újpest counted as a separate town back then, and at the city boundary they declared that those of the Israelite faith had to go and identify themselves. I had my university student identification in my pocket; that was more than enough. I was taken into a detention room, where there were already many Jews; it turned out that Jews were stopped en route from Pest to Újpest and from Újpest to Pest and taken into the detention room. There they said that the committee would arrive which would check our identification. I was lucky, as a functionary I knew was also travelling on the tram, and I asked him to be so kind as to go up to my father and to tell him that there was some kind of identification process, and so I would be late. My father waited, ever more distressed, and I didn't get there, and couldn't let him know, either. It was night when they let me out. They kept me there from five in the afternoon until midnight, and then a police officer came who was decent, and also not.

I imagine he had to produce numbers of how many had been detained, but he tried to assist where he could. He was impolite; he said, 'Young man, you can wait; we'll take the older ones first.' Someone said to him, 'If you please, I work at the United Lightbulbs factory in Újpest, and I live in Pest; I was on my way home.' The officer replied, 'Engineer, you either go here, or you go there; you Jews are no longer allowed to wander about.' He asked anyone wanting quickly to go to the provinces to say so. He gathered those people up. Outside we saw a prisoner transport vehicle outside; he must have taken them in that. Then it was my turn; he asked me why I wasn't doing forced labour service. I answered that I was exempted as a university student. 'What's that, and why?' he asked. 'Here you are,' I said. 'You can run a check on me. Please call Dr. Zsigmond Morvai, royal notary public, here's his number, my father's his deputy. He will confirm that around 5 o'clock I sent a message to my father at his office that I would get there late because of some identification issue.' He replied that I could either be in Újpest, or in Budapest, but I couldn't commute between the two. I chose Budapest.

PLK: Let's return, if we can, to the personal fate of your family members…

JS: My father was one of nine siblings; one of them fell in the First World War. My uncle Ferenc died on forced labour service, en route. He was an old man, and they were marching them along from Budapest towards Vienna, when he died. My father died in Auschwitz. Of his brothers, Jen and Aladár survived; they were on forced labour service, and escaped. My father's sisters also escaped; one of my aunts, Paula, was a teacher in Tatabánya, married a Christian, converted to Catholicism, and so she survived. The others, my aunts Margit, Terka and Irén, all survived in the Budapest ghetto until it was liberated. The fate of my cousins was more tragic: my cousin Bori was shot dead by the Arrow Cross, while we don't know whether my other cousin, Miklós, was shot by the Germans or by the Russians, as they were hiding in the Vérmez green space in central Buda. Miklós would have gone on to be a great mathematician; the Miklós Schweitzer Mathematics Competition is named after him to this day.

I can't remember my paternal grandparents; my paternal grandfather died before I was born. That's where my name, József, and my synagogue name, come from. I only have the vaguest memories of my paternal grandmother, as she lived in Budapest when we lived in Veszprém. I just remember that she was an old lady who sat in an armchair, who took some kind of white powder, and coughed a lot. She did say a few words to me, but it was nothing like as close a relationship as I had with my maternal grandparents there where I grew up.

So the family really did fall apart. My father's boss went after him to try to save him, but all the publicity, requests, evidence that he was ill, were all in vain – he had to be destroyed.

As for me personally, after the Arrow Cross coup I tried to hide somewhere, but I was caught. I was not wearing a yellow star. I ended up in a house of confinement for deportees, from where they took me to the great synagogue in Dohány Street, which was being used as a collection point. On a certain Thursday they let me go home; on the Friday every Jew in my building under the age of 60 was taken away. Then we had to dig trenches in the vicinity of Budapest. This was a farce: the idea was that the Russian tanks, which had managed to cross the Carpathian mountains, would then be held up because of the trenches we dug. A committee from the Ministry of Defence came out there, and dismissed many old and ill men. Those who remained were taken back to Budapest and added to a forced labour service division on Aréna Avenue (today's Dózsa György Avenue); that is where I ended up. I was placed in a forced labour unit which meandered about in Transdanubia. Then I managed to come to Budapest by saying I was coming to get winter clothes, and I didn't go back. Quite a few others asked to leave in the same way and didn't return. I went to 29 Vadász Street, the so-called Glass House, where I stayed until the liberation. This was a hovel by the end. I went in as if it were an embassy, only to find a huge hovel. There were very many of us, and together with one of my colleagues I was given a place to sleep in the attic. They had blankets there. They said we had to sleep 'canton-style', that is, on our sides. We couldn't lie back, as there wasn't enough space. But by the standards of the time it counted as a protected place, and yet it wasn't, because they fired into the cellars; Professor Scheiber's mother was shot in the head there, as were many others in various parts of the building. The Arrow Cross attacked the building on the afternoon of 31st December, and took those living in the Glass House out on to the street. By that time us younger ones were living in the house next door, which was the building of the Hungarian Football Association, the MLSZ. It was a secret safe-house; they didn't know about it. From there we heard them taking people out of 29 Vadász Street.

IX.

AT THE BEATIFICATION OF SÁRA SALKAHÁZI
JÓZSEF SCHWEITZER'S SPEECH

I have the honour, as part of today's lofty occasion, to add a few words of the Jewish community's gratitude, respect and undying remembrance to the memory of Sára Salkaházi, who died a martyr's death in the days of the rule of terror in 1944.

I myself lived through these terrible times, as did my wife, as a young student, as we both lived here in Budapest, a place of mourning, red with the blood of the innocent. I know from my own experience, as do those sharing my fate who lived here at that time, as well as every decent and human thinking person, just how dangerous and heroic an act it was at that time to help Jews, and even more so to offer refuge from the hundred deaths hanging over them.

A Transylvanian Hungarian Jewish lady writer who lived at that time wrote: 'You can always love'. Let us add that to love at that time, to act out of love and solidarity, to save Jewish lives, represented unparalleled heroism.

What can have given Sára Salkaházi strength for this life-saving, heroic act? I believe her deep faith in God can in part have come from the Psalm which reads: 'Yea, though I walk through the valley of the shadow of death, I will fear no evil: for thou art with me; thy rod and thy staff they comfort me' (Psa 23:4).

Thanks to her faith, she obeyed the commandment of love at the highest level and to her death. I also remember those who suffered the fate of death together with her in the grave of the waves of the Danube. Vilma Bernovits, religion teacher, and three Jewish ladies. We know the names of two of them, but not of the third.

One of the ladies who suffered death had a daughter who ended up in Israel, and who already in 1968 submitted Sára Salkaházi's name to be immortalized at the Jerusalem Institute of Yad Vashem, which has as one of its tasks the academic study of the Holocaust, and as another the immortalization of the names and memories of non-Jewish individuals who saved the lives of their Jewish brethren even if it endangered or cost them their own lives. And thus the people of Israel immortalized the life-saving act of Sára Salkaházi in 1972 after and as a result of an investigation into it, published a celebratory document about it, and planted a tree in Sára Salkaházi's memory along the Avenue of the Righteous Among the Nations. The Jewish community in Hungary had done this earlier, out of duty and out of conscience, marking the location of her death as a martyr in Budapest with a memorial plaque.

Let us call forth her honourable memory with the words from the Scriptures which can be read on the document immortalizing her name.

Ve natati lahem yad vashem asher yo yikaret.

I give them an enduring name and memory; this can never be destroyed.

X.

A View from the Past to the Future

JS: It is a great problem for seeing clearly in today's ethical judgments that this was not taken seriously in the past, because a great number of people would say things that they did not believe deep down in their hearts. And by saying things that they did not honestly think, the weight of the whole of justice and honour was lessened; they made it almost acceptable for one to say one thing at one's workplace and quite another while doing unofficial moonlighting at home, and for this to become people's lifeblood. Hypocrisy became easy.

SS: Let's go back to the roots of this. What is the connection between ethical laws and life? Is ethical behaviour the path to life, or where does it lead? Ethical laws are in a sense nothing other than a force for protecting, enriching and preserving life, partly on the basis of experience. There are two general kinds of approach to ethical laws. One approach sees these instructions as very much a tool for someone to develop their inner workings and become more human; they know that it is directly good for them to go in this direction – this is very typical of the attitude of Eastern ethics. This presents itself not as ethics but as laws: do this, and you will live, as we find in the Hebrew Bible. The other approach holds that these ethical laws, these systems of norms, somehow come into being, and society starts to implement them, with coercion and force, in part out of self-defence, and those who encounter these laws forget about their connection to life. It makes a big difference which mindset people apply to ethical laws. I want with this to turn back to the start of the Hebrew Bible, where it literally says, do this and thou shalt live.

JS: There is a path along which someone doesn't do something for some reason, following their religion. Contrition is an inner emotional process, and if it weren't a rather outdated notion, I would say that it is a form of self-criticism in the best sense; how I dealt with my family, how I behaved here and there, and a determination not to do it again. Judaism states clearly – to use ancient terms – that if someone says they are going to sin, but will seek repentance, then the Almighty will not accept their repentance. The basic criterion for repentance is that someone turns their back on the past; at the pulpit we tend to express this with a Hebrew word, *teshuvah*, meaning 'turning back to God'. Meanwhile *meshuvah* means backsliding, turning away; changing a single letter can represent quite different worlds.

The whole of morality can often depend on what example a rabbi or priest gives. Just as at the doctor's a patient can sense if the doctor is their friend or would just like to see the back of you and bring in the next person, so one can sense the same in the case of a priest. Personal behaviour is extremely important for such sensitive emotional questions.

ESV: It is important not only in small communities or in the family but also in society as a whole that if the state or an individual makes a mistake, they should own up to it. So, *mea culpa, mea maxima culpa* plays a key role, as there is no forgiveness either from a family or from a society without contrition and repentance. I am convinced that it is a real human virtue if someone can accept that they have erred, as this means they have inner integrity.

SS: Someone has to be serious when they say that what they did was genuinely a mistake. This is the starting point. If they are not serious about it, it is worthless.

PE: I would like to start at the beginning, namely with whom we are asking forgiveness from. If we think in terms of the category of sin, then only God can forgive. Atonement with another human being belongs to what Chief Rabbi Schweitzer quoted, that Jesus himself quoted: 'Therefore if thou bring thy gift to the altar, and there rememberest that thy brother hath ought against thee […] first be reconciled to thy brother, and then come and offer thy gift.' (Matt 5:23-24.) Of course there is need for this kind of atonement, but this is not yet the plane of absolution. Nowadays it has become fashionable to put this all on the social plane, and to say that we should ask for forgiveness, especially collectively or in others' name, for this is the easiest; let us ask for forgiveness, as otherwise there is no catharsis. This cannot be forced, and only God can cleanse us of sin.

ESV: I am talking about honest repentance…

PE: Repentance and forgiveness belong primarily to the relationship between man and God. Making amends, compensation for damage done, reconciliation – these are more the aspects that belong directly to the social dimension. It is certain that the notions of reconciliation and rapprochement are crucial ones, and we cannot do enough to see that these make progress within this country and this whole region, as we see it to be a holy issue.

Reconciliation? Mercy? This is also an interesting word, as this is the other word alongside justice always to appear in the Biblical approach, *hesed* and *tzedakah*, mercy and justice, or as they put it in medieval times, *misericordia et iustitia*. Over and above strictly proportional justice, there must be space in human relations for mercy, and to understand mercy as meaning all good acts beyond what is obligatory. For example, if I am due something, but I eschew it, or I help someone even though I am not obliged to. It has a thousand and one forms, which we usually list as the corporal and spiritual works of mercy; I suspect that the list of *mitzvahs* includes the very same things.

Pope John Paul II said that without mercy humanity would completely fall into the hands of evil (Cf. e.g. Homily of the Holy Father John Paul II, Krakow, 17 August 2002). The hope that humanity might be able to escape the clutches of evil is in God's mercy which we must imitate. We do not have to fear each other so much within a society, nor should we fear confronting our common situation. There are reserves in the human soul for forgiveness, mercy and generosity. I do not think that everyone demands in every detail and to the last penny that which it is unrealistic to get or to win. Most people are measured and discriminating, and understand what is possible and what is not, and if this can be pointed in this direction by the intelligentsia, by the literate, not in the direction of conflict, then I see this as a realistic route for the life of the community to be reinforced in its values and its ethics on the basis of truth and justice. And this may just bring material benefits with it in the end.

ESV: I agree, but I would mention that there intellectual atonement exists, too. We can understand the behavior of someone who is repentant, and social conscience also exists, which has an effect on the individual's actions, repentance and acknowledgement. We must not hand over everything to evil, to sin, because if there can be no repentance, then we divide the world between the good and the bad; it would be the worst mistake – indeed, a sin in itself – to divide up the world, the society of the world. I put great stead by intellectual understanding, which includes not only that deeply human characteristic of loving and understanding others but also – and my phrasing here is deliberate – that measured, intentional use of cold reason that we could also call calculation, even if it might sound pejorative. Society, the economy, the powers-that-be, the financial world all have need for this.

There is just such a motivating inner strength within society that says you have repented, come, we will take you back into our flock. It is not only religion that can provide this, not only the good Pastor can gather his children back up into his flock, but society can, too.

JS: An amnesty is example of this.

PE: To this day the Italian ministry of justice is called the *Ministero di Grazia e Giustizia*.

SS: Yes, the relation between repentance and forgiveness is an important one. Forgiveness obviously results in and of itself in the bad being lessened, as there is one fewer consequence; there is no negative response to the bad. And if there is no contrition, this is like when a landmine is pushed a little deeper into the soil, so it won't explode underneath everyone who goes by, but the landmine is not deactivated or removed, either.

ESV: My sense is that we have talked about the roots of European civilization being provided by the Old and New Testaments and we have also discussed what Greek philosophy gave us with democracy. Ultimately, this has all radiated out to the whole of the world.

JS: May I raise a provocative issue? Professor Vizi was just throwing his weight behind a book by Alfred Pasternak, who was my student at the Jewish high school...

ESV: Alfred Pasternak's book is called *Inhuman Research*; it is about the medical experiments carried out in the concentration camp. It was written by a world-famous professor of medicine, who is a corresponding member of the Hungarian Academy of Sciences, an American and Hungarian dual citizen, and a Holocaust survivor.

JS: The book takes 130 or so individuals who in addition to joining the SS were also German professors, so not just anyone. These people conducted the most abominable experiments on prisoners; for example, one doctor, in order to find a way to cure a certain infection that had afflicted the soldiers in the war, deliberately infected defenceless people, and then was either able to cure them, or he wasn't. Can we forgive this, because we teach neighbourly love? It is a wild question, but where is the boundary of human forgiveness, and where do we step into a space which is – as our concept of Biblical ethics teaches us – supranatural? Where is the line where we say that this is where the potential for human forgiveness comes to an end, and from here on only God can have mercy?

PE: Catholic theology has always distinguished between divine and human forgiveness, between God forgiving and rescinding sin as sin, on the one hand, and the Christian's obligation to forgive, on the other; for in the Lord's Prayer we pray, 'And forgive us our trespasses, as we forgive those who trespass against us'. At the same time, Catholic theology acknowledges justified self-defence, also in a collective sense, at the level of society; that is, it does not consider the validity or justification of criminal law to be at odds with a Christian's obligation to forgive. Obviously I should not retaliate an offence to my own person out of private revenge, but I am nevertheless entitled to justified self-defence, while the justified self-defence of a community can in certain instances be an obligation.

JS: Yes, but right now we are past justified self-defence; this would have been if we had been in a position to defend ourselves when they infected these children. At the time we were not able to do this, the children died, the doctors survived, the sin was committed, and so is condemnation and punishment – which seems to contradict absolution, because they were condemned and punished – still justified if this happens later?

ESV: In such instances there can be no forgiveness because, on the one hand, the experimental subjects did not give their consent, and on the other hand, these are crimes against humanity. *De jure* there can be no forgiveness for crimes against humanity.

JS: This is Professor Vizi's declaration. What is the church's declaration?

PE: In a legal sense there is no statute of limitations for these sins. In a moral sense we must forgive only those sins committed against our own person. I would like to reflect on Father Sajgó's comment about the landmine being dug deeper into the soil. If someone repents their own sin, this is a condition for God forgiving them, but I have to forgive them, even if they do not repent; in fact I have to forgive them even if they have not asked for forgiveness.

JS: In the interests of scholarship and theology, and in my own interests, I will be more forceful. An entirely trustworthy lady told me she had seen my father in 1944, going through the crowd, a towel on his head, probably wet, because he couldn't take the strong sun. He went, was thrown on a cattle truck, and murdered. My position on this is that whoever it was who forcibly sent my father there…

PE: According to traditional Catholic moral theology – this will be strange and dialectical, but also quite certain, as over our long history we have never managed to say anything else – one: I pray for the spiritual salvation of the murderers; two: if I am a witness in a trial, I will tell it as it was, they were guilty, and so they will be executed. According to traditional Catholic moral theology, the collective obligation of self-defence and personal forgiveness are compatible.

JS: But I can no longer be acting in self-defence…

PE: The objective of the sanctions of criminal law is not just prevention, but the restoration of a just order, and so to a certain degree it can be revenge, or it can be a collective prevention, a general prevention, to stop others doing it, and so on. Put simply, sometimes it can be adequate justification for meting out a punishment that it discourages others from carrying out the criminal act in question. In this connection one must always distinguish ethical sin from a criminal act in the legal sense, an act that contravenes criminal laws.

ESV: It is everyone's personal right to forgive someone, but this is their private concern; society cannot forgive. The interests of society are guarded by its laws, so in this sense, there is no forgiveness. To take the example Chief Rabbi Schweitzer gave (and there are many other examples in the book): in such instances, there is no forgiveness on the part of society, nor can there be. This is the elemental interest of society.

PE: I partly agree with this on the plane of moral theology, too, but I would phrase it by saying that society has an obligation to defend itself on the basis of justice. Society is a not a subject of forgiveness. When we speak in theological terms, then we either talk about God, who wipes away our sins with his forgiveness, or we talk about ourselves, individual people, who can forgive in our hearts the other person trespassing against us. Society is not a subject for this; society's job is to maintain the just order of life. But private forgiveness can also assist collective conciliation.

SS: While on this theme, let us talk about the story of Cain and Abel, and the marking of Cain…

JS: There is a general misunderstanding about the latter: Cain is marked to stop him being harmed, but in the public mind the mark of Cain is used in a sense antithetical to that in the Scriptures.

SS: What role does the notion of the semblance of God play in the question of morality?

JS: *B'tzelem Elohim* – the one carrying God's image.

SS: If God is infinite mercy itself, then how does man, as resembling God, become merciful, when this is the goal?

JS: God is merciful, but can also punish. Various information on both characteristics is available in the Scriptures. The Scriptures also mention God's mercy: 'I [...] will be gracious to whom I will be gracious, and will shew mercy on whom I will shew mercy' (Exod 33:19). But we can also read in the Bible of God condemning, and punishing.

SS: Can we separate forgiveness from condemnation, and from the burden of the consequences of the sin committed?

JS: I think that there are very few of us human beings capable of satisfying every ethical requirement; the average person is not capable of this. In point of fact, the court has to be aware of all of this, when someone stands there before it – that this person is this much to blame, this much innocent, and to sentence them accordingly.

SS: I would take another step… Say the innocent person has been killed, condemnation and execution has also happened; what happens to the memory of person concerned?

JS: There is also mention in the Scriptures of this wild people of the plain, the Amalekites, who appear in the second book of Moses. You left Egypt, followed the road, were tired, and they attacked the weak and those who fell behind; the Scriptures tell you to wipe even their memory. It is the best and the most we can do, to wipe evil memories from our heads. Forgiveness is a different thing; for that, we need to be prophets.

SS: So forgiveness can only happen for prophets?

JS: No, there are things where it can work for ordinary humans, but for mass murder, the infection of innocent children, for deliberately perpetrated murders, I for my own part – not *ex cathedra*, like the Pope – say that these were sinful, cursed people. I don't believe that someone strongly demanded that you infect a ten-year-old child, so that you could investigate the prevention of this or that infection, and that it was just bad luck that they died.

All I can say is *sunt certi denique fines*. There are limits. Take great care not to say things from the pulpit that you wouldn't be able to stand up for out on the high street.

ESV: It would be good if politicians followed that advice; they, too, speak from the pulpit. Just to a much bigger audience.

PLK: Is there a need for the church in today's world?

ESV: In the modern world, there are essentially two institutions that traditionally preserve values – that is, institutions that are conservative in this sense and also create values. One is the historical churches, and the other is the academic world, science, and scholarly academies. In the case of the churches, in addition to preserving values, I must provide some justification for what I just said – for there being values created, as well. Among other things, the teaching of ethics and morality, the passing on of these to the next generation, is the task of the church; these cannot be inherited genetically. One cannot inherit human characteristics or the relationships between people in society, or the relationship between humankind and the environment, just as one cannot inherit knowledge. These all have to be taught, again and again, from one generation to the next. And the churches have an important role in this teaching and passing on of knowledge in the field of ethics. Academe, on the other hand, is always presenting newer and newer truths by uncovering the secrets of society and of nature and thereby creates values. This attitude and this calling is hard to reconcile with the extraordinarily fast progress of the world, with the phenomenon of growing materialism that characterizes the world today. The omnipotence of mammon, of money, struggles to accept a 'conservative' institution, which paradoxically is liberal, as the creation of something new always demands liberal methods.

PLK: But why did all this become so intense in today's society?

ESV: We just held the annual meeting of Academia Europaea, which has 2000 academics as members, from the whole of Europe, from a pool of 400 million people. Its president is philosophy professor Jürgen Mittelstraß, and its founding president is Sir Arnold Bergen, who worked in my specific field – that is, he is a doctor and brain researcher, pharmacologist, and not just a fellow of the Royal Society, but its vice president. During our discussion, it transpired that this is not just a Hungarian phenomenon, in which these two institutions are under attack from all corners, but a European or even a world phenomenon. This is just as much the case in Britain as it is in France or Germany. It turned out that the reason for this is the morality that they represent. The basis for the workings of the academic community is the ethos of truth; the ethical message of this ethos is that you should always search for and try to find truth. Meanwhile, the teaching of the church concerns how society should live, how people should live, and what basic rules they have to follow to remain human even in what might occasionally be inhuman circumstances. And all this in this accelerated world in which we lose our relationships with one another, our human relationships, where there is no time to look at what is around us, to see how beautiful the world is, nature is, or in this world that has shrunk into a village thanks to technology, television, the internet, and the era of the mobile phone. In today's world, the form of behavior embodied by the historical churches and by science and scholarship – that is, rationalism – that demands a particular form of attitude and behavior – the search for truth – is hard to accommodate into a mercantile worldview. So, I and many others think that churches and scholars need to speak out and tell the world: Beware! Watch out, humanity, because there are values which have not only to be protected but also developed!

PE: I think that the attitude of protecting and carrying values, which is something that science and, in part, the communities of historic churches, actually perform in practice, and which can be illustrated with the very simple example of implementing the academic and historical religious communities, is also of economic benefit, as without it the human community cannot survive. Here we are talking about very real, brutal needs; it is just that when we look at our lives from a purely financial point of view, then we only think in the short term. There was a time, in the 19th century, when people went to look for gold in Alaska; they only took bread and lard with them, and were surprised when by the end of the season they had contracted scurvy. So what we are talking about is a bit like the fact that you also need vitamin C; that is, there are things in the world, in the universal reality, which are perhaps not profitable economically in the short term, but if we do not take these into account, then in the medium term – even in economic terms – they will cause a disaster. We can talk about how sociologists have shown that within a given society trust is an economically measurable source of productivity, so it is not simply the case that the economy or everyday life is only borne by short-term financial calculations. So I think that we are the bearers of a slightly longer-term view. The Catholic church, like other Christian churches, but particularly so, deliberately inherited the notion of the people of God; in the books of the New Testament the first collective Christian identity appears by saying that you are the chosen people, the royal priesthood, the holy nation, as the epistle from Saint Peter says to its readers, that is, the early Christian community (1 Pet 2:9). Saint Paul uses the same tone, in fact, when in one of his epistles he bids farewell to his readers by wishing peace for Israel (Gal 1:16). Put simply, there is intellectual historical continuity between the notion of Israel in Christ's time and the notion of the early Christian church. I think that the *punctum saliens* is about who can be a member of this. The great debate among the first generations was about whether those arriving from the pagan world could join the people or not, and what role faith should play in whether someone could become a member of this people. At the same time, the idea of an alliance is unchanged, and so the Catholic church sees itself as the partner of the Lord in this alliance; the whole Easter mystery is about this, in point of fact. There are religions of reason, there are speculative religions, but Judaism and Christianity are religions which are community in nature from the outset, by their nature, they are borne by a community, and by necessity they form a community, if you will, a brotherhood among their members. I could also add that the ideal of fraternity in the French Revolution can in this sense precisely be traced back to the Judeo-Christian religious heritage. So our faith is a communal one and one that builds communities; the passing on of tradition is part of the operation of this community. This again is an ancient thing; Saint Paul the Apostle, for example, introduces the Last Supper or his description of the Resurrection with a rabbinical turn, that I pass this tradition on to you, which I myself received as a tradition, and then goes on to describe the event itself (1 Cor 11:23; 15:3). This kind of tradition is what connects us to God's revelation, and it is the Church, as a community, which carries this tradition. In this sense, this type of conveyance of values which we were just discussing is for us a particularly conscious and acknowledged calling and mission.

The question can arise – and this is one reason it is worth confronting this issue from this angle – of how the Hungarians are related to all this. If we are the chosen people, as a community of Christians and a holy nation, then what does this nation have in common with nations in the modern sense? This is a real Christian theological problem, the solution to which is to be found in part in the history of the concept of the nation. Today the idea of nation tends to be the one from the era of the Enlightenment, in which the political structure, language, culture and geographic area all come together; previously nation had a much broader meaning, and the notion of a religion as a nation is one such older idea of nation, but which, as does the concept of Israel, still includes sovereignty. From the outset, Christians considered themselves a sovereign religious tribal community, though they accepted the authority of the Roman state; for example, they claimed the right to their own judicial system. Again, Saint Paul writes, in line with the traditions of the time: how can you turn to a pagan judge with your litigation cases? Isn't there a wise man amongst you capable of settling them? (1 Cor 6:1-6.) In other words, they demanded complete sovereignty as regards their own calling and their own religious life. The intellectual historical connection to the concept of Israel also enlightens the question why there are still apostolic nuncios to this day, or why it is the Apostolic Holy See which maintains international contacts and not the Vatican City State; the Apostolic Holy See, meanwhile, is the entirety of the governing bodies of the Catholic Church. Thus, as a religious community, the Catholic Church has considered itself an international legal subject since ancient times.

To return to traditions and national cultures, in Europe's history we see that during and after the fall of the Roman Empire the Christian faith spreads among the various barbarian tribes, as the result of which so-called Christian Europe emerges. But these peoples do not lose their languages, nor their national cultures; it is precisely under the influence of Christianity that their unique national cultural profiles emerge, which are still preserved by the European national cultures of today. Christianity does not render cultures bland or make them homogenous; rather, it gives them a special inspiration to develop further according to their own brilliance. And this question of enculturation continues to present is a big problem in Africa and Asia.

JS: The Jewish congregation is not and never has been, as a denomination, in a position to talk of influences like those Professor Vizi and Cardinal Erdő have discussed, as neither its numerical size nor its historical past have been such that it might have affected or given direction to the national attitude with its thinking.

ESV: My emphasis was on the fact that the historical churches effectively provide an ethical foundation for society, as this is not something that can be inherited genetically. The internal morality of the churches, irrespective of whether they are Jewish, Catholic or Protestant ones, plays a key role in the life of the state, the nation, and society as a whole. And I would particularly highlight that the Jewish community has played an especially significant role in Hungarian culture and Hungarian science and scholarship, particularly in the 20th century.

JS: Essentially since the Compromise of 1867. Beyond theological differences, I would say that the ethical profile of the nation is determined by what Professor Vizi has already mentioned, nurturing and education, these two things which are so interconnected and so important. Jewish schools, most of which, because of the small size of the community, were elementary schools; these were present everywhere, from the smallest villages to the big cities. They were in a slightly neglected state, but this was exactly the educational foundation which allowed the rabbinical seminary to come into being, and to a certain extent the teacher training college, too. This was the starting point for the systematization of the school system which up to then was perhaps diffuse and neglected. For – if my memory serves me correctly – as early as 1830 there was an official visitor to the Jewish school in Bonyhád in south-east Hungary. A photograph has survived of Ferdinand V visiting the Jewish school in Pozsony [today Bratislava, Slovakia]. There was a school in almost every village, and they would begin teaching the Bible almost immediately after starting to teach reading in Hebrew. The teaching of Judaism was difficult then and is difficult now, as we first have to struggle with reading in Hebrew, the Hebrew language and Hebrew translation if we want to use the original text, and if a teacher focuses on this, then not much material can be covered, as so much time is spent on grammar. In essence, though, the Jewish school and the Jewish family primarily established a family-centric attitude, one in which the father's role was considerable. In a traditional Jewish family, on Friday evenings, when the weekly celebration begins, the head of the household returns home from the temple; according to traditional customs, the women would not go to the temple in the evenings, only at great festivals. My own childhood memory from my grandfather's house was that he would come home from the temple and bless first his daughters and then me, his grandson, as I was sitting there, too. This was a hallowed moment which would return every Friday evening, when my grandfather said the Aaronic Blessing over the whole family. The regulation stipulating the ritual of kosher cooking would ultimately show that religious thought would intervene in everyday life and its rhythm; it is a different question why, in the third book of Moses, the Scriptures do not allow the eating of certain forbidden animals, and how this develops and continues through into the post-Biblical religious laws. The essence of it is that even eating, what I eat and how, has religious function – even the table. The same is true for the family – though it may be true elsewhere as well that the place of the head of the household is sacrosanct. We had an everyday dining room, as well as a larger dining room for Saturdays, but grandfather's place, where he sat – no one would have thought to sit in daddy's seat. The same was true for the teacher's place: if a different rabbi happened to go into where a rabbi would teach, he would not usually sit in the same place – so great was the respect for knowledge. There was a world-famous professor at the rabbinical seminary, Bernát Heller, who studied under the first generation of teachers there, including Wilhelm Bacher, who taught Biblical studies and rabbinical literary history. And Heller, although he received his degree as a teacher of French from the École Normale, then got his doctorate in Budapest with a thesis entitled 'The Relationship of the Evangelical Parable and the Agada', and became a seminary lecturer, never sat on the professor's chair – he said that was for Professor Bacher, and would not sit in his place. Respect of this magnitude for the family and for teachers is a tradition dating back to the time of the Mishnah; for in the period of the Tannaim, the Mishnah was the first summary of Jewish laws, which was finalized in around 200 CE. In the Mishnah, which combines religious law, private law and financial law in a single volume, there is also, interestingly, mention, among other things, of something which I imagine must still have been relevant in Hungarian villages in the last century, in the form of the institution of the town crier: the town crier beat on a drum and announced the latest news. The Bava Metzia chapter or tractate of the Mishnah mentions how if someone's animal was on the loose, and the local rabbi's animal was also on the loose, which of the two had to be announced first. They had time to fantasize about such problems! The Mishnah says that the rabbi's animal has to be announced first, as the other man had his father to thank for his physical existence, but his teacher to thank for his eternal salvation and eternal life, and so he owed his teacher this much. So almost above even the honour of one's parent, which was a commandment in the Torah, stood the honour for the teacher, who embodies the intellect and scholarship. The tradition of respect is there throughout Jewish history, one consequence of which is that in so-called Orthodox congregations children are to this day sent to Bible school at the age of three or four, where they learn the basic translation of the Bible and quite a few commentaries from Shlomo Yitzhaki, or Rashi, the greatest medieval Bible commentator. Of course they learn to read and pray in Hebrew, too. And this, in traditional Jewish communities, is the equivalent of kindergarten and elementary school. Then children are sent to the so-called yeshivah, where they learn the Talmud; many children would go there, of whom only a small proportion would become rabbis; here the basic idea was that every adult Jew had to be aware of the ideas, practicalities and literature of Judaism, at least broadly speaking, but the practicalities in detail, before they set up a family of their own. This remains the case in Orthodox synagogues, and this is what I myself experienced in Bonyhád. I was the rabbi of Pécs, and the counties of Tolna and Baranya were assigned to me, with few members of the community. One day as I was returning to Pécs early in the morning, I got off the train at Bonyhád, and went in to the morning service there. In Bonyhád, in the depths of winter, the temple was already heated by six-thirty in the morning; there was some nice tea, and there were already people sitting there, studying the Scriptures and the Talmud: this was their lesson for the day, their daily task. The Talmud is like patrology: it has a beginning but no end. It is for this reason that there was a world alliance between the two World Wars, which introduced the Daf Yomi, which simply meant that they took out a calendar, and went through it, marking in turn, for each day, which volume and which page of the Talmud they would read that day. On that day, all those who were members of this Daf Yomi world organization would read the same section from the Talmud. What is even more elegant, and few know about it, is how, long before anyone had this idea of coordinated daily Talmud study, Lipót L w, by then rabbi of Szeged, and his son Immánuel L w, a student at the Lehranstalt rabbinical seminary in Berlin, agreed that they would read a particular page from the Talmud on each particular day, so they would be together in spirit. In Jewish thinking this is how far this communal spirit went. Of course, if to a lesser extent, this has been followed by modern Jewish schools, for example the Jewish grammar schools. I had the good fortune of attending one for eight years; the Hebrew language and the Bible were fundamental there, too, and Hebrew grammar was taught just as Latin grammar was.

ESV: Over Hungarian history, alongside European culture, ethics was also taught in these schools, lycées, colleges and grammar schools.

JS: Obviously these grammar schools, the yeshivahs, only dealt with Hebrew studies, while Jewish high schools also included the Bible to some degree, and taught all the other material like any other high school.

ESV: It is no coincidence that a good number of Hungary's Nobel Prize winners attended either the Fasori high school or a Jewish grammar school, Piarist grammar school, or some similar school.

JS: Families also play a large role in raising the ethical niveau. There are festivals, like the Passover festival, the introduction to which, where the story of the Flight to Egypt is told as part of a dinner, would, before the War and the deportations, have usually have been a family celebration. But after families fell to pieces, in many families this is now a community festival, and so each congregation celebrates it, but it has a family feel to it. In point of fact this is the strengthening of family feeling, or respect for parents, and so on; to the extent that this is a force for building national identity, and that is what it is, then to this extent Judaism does contribute to educating the nation.

ESV: I would again underline the fact that Hungarian Jewry has played a very significant role in Hungarian science and academe and in Hungarian culture in general.

JS: And in Hungarian linguistics, too: Bernát Munkácsi was an academician, as was Ödön Beke, my Hungarian teacher; Fokos-Fuchs, who worked as the director of the Jewish high school, was a Finno-Ugric linguist and academician.

ESV: Islamic scholar Ignác Goldzieher, and great poet Miklós Radnóti, and many, many others. This also proves how incredibly welcoming Hungarian culture is. We should not forget about that.

PE: Alongside national culture, which is a very imposing image with regard to the Jewry and Hungarian national culture, too, I also sense another point, namely what we heard about the teacher's chair, and the respect shown for it. This is a symbol of tradition being handed on. And the substance of this tradition is such a universal value that it is for benefit of the whole of humanity. The passing on of our religious tradition, if I can say so, of what is in no small measure our common religious tradition, is one such fundamental community-building force. What does this have to do with the teacher's chair? Jesus talks of Moses' seat, where the Pharisees sit (Matt 23:2-3). Later in Christianity, meanwhile, the *cathedra Petri*, the chair of Saint Peter, is the intellectual historical continuation or successor of this as an idea – the authority of the person sitting in the chair, because of the chair. To this day, in our cathedrals – which are called cathedrals for a reason, because of the cathedra, the chair – there is a chair for the bishop, which no one else may sit in. For example if we enter Saint Stephen's Basilica in Budapest, there are two thrones: one, on the right hand side if we face the altar, is carved of beautiful wood. If there is a guest bishop leading the liturgy, this is their place. But if the cathedral's own bishop is doing so, there is the cathedra on the left, with the coat of arms of whoever the bishop presently is. The same is true in all cathedrals; this cathedra is the symbol of the Apostolic Magisterium, that is, the passing on of a religious tradition which, I believe, genuinely mediates universal values. It can also be seen as having some minor consequences: for example, the most prestigious sermons at the most celebratory masses are given by the bishop sitting down. I sit down to speak when ordaining priests, or bishops. At celebratory masses, the Pope does not only sit to give his sermon because of his age, because it is hard for him to stand, but with a view to the decorum of the occasion and the importance of teaching, for this is the teacher's chair. In this way the respect for this religious tradition survives to the present day in Christian liturgy.

JS: When I was first in Prague, the chief rabbi there was a kind old man who said to me: 'Sit wherever you like, but not here, as this is where Rabbi L w of Prague sat, and no one has sat there ever since.' So for centuries we have had this tradition of the chair, which I saw in Prague because of this old rabbi who is no longer with us.

SS: In a democratic system, everyone's faith is not merely important in as far as it does not trample on others' rights, and this is not the only reason the existence of individual churches matters; the role of a single yeshivah or of religion teaching is crucial in the way that the whole democratic apparatus can be strengthened by reinforcing the values which are preserved and presented there.

ESV: Let us dare to say it: it is in the state's interest, the nation's interest. So those who attack these institutions that preserve and present values, such as the churches or the Hungarian Academy of Sciences, as the repository of science and scholarship, are really just questioning our future, as they only have an interest in what material and other interests and values are accessible to them at the given moment. In the long run, these institutions have had an incredibly important role to play in the past, and they will continue to do so in the present and the future. If someone questions the very significance of academe, of research – and there are people in important state roles with responsibility who do question it – then they are effectively denying the future. And just as it is very important for citizens to keep to certain ethical norms for the operation of a state, of a country, it is also in the interests of the state to support the institutions that contribute to this, and this includes the church. Another thing I have not said is that both of these institutions provide a public service, *ergo* they take tasks off the state's hands.

PE: I would not dare put it like that, for two reasons. One: it is my conviction that we are older than the state, that we deal with people at a more fundamental level than the state does. Also, if I remember right, then when Abraham came out of the city of Ur, it did not matter which country he was a citizen of, but rather, someone had invited him to leave his father's house, and come. So I think that we are more fundamental than the state is, and so I do not think that we get our tasks from the state. Under current Hungarian law, which states that a public body is one which serves state or local government tasks, the churches – unlike the Academy of Sciences – do not really see it as an ambition of theirs to qualify as public bodies, because we think that our mission was given by the calling of our founder, and we do not want the state to tell us what our mission is. At the same time, almost as a by-product, it is enormously useful to the state that we do what we do, without being commissioned to do it. For the purposes of the state we are, or we should be, something akin to clean water or clean air, or a healthy natural environment – there is great need for it, and the state should protect it, but the state doesn't create it.

ESV: Dear Cardinal Erdő, I merely said that you do a public service. You do not take it over from the state, you do not get it from the state, you simply do it voluntarily. Can I give an example? You yourself often announce how charitable aid provision has an irreplaceable role in helping the poor and the needy, and how spiritual guidance is a key part of it. The state cannot provide these services *eo ipso*, but it has to acknowledge that there are institutions whose mission it is to do these tasks, and so my opinion is that it is the state's obligation to support these institutions in the tasks they perform.

PE: Here, however, there appears a very brutal postmodern phenomenon, namely the institutionalization of these charity services. The same is true of medical sciences, as it happens. The more that science progresses, the more opportunities there are, the more expensive solutions become available, the more complicated institutions come into being, and the ethical problem becomes ever greater of who will pay for all of this, or of whether a society has to make decisions about whose life or good health deserves this much and that much of public funds, and whose does not. Even scientific progress brings new pressing problems, which are connected to the institutional and bureaucratic nature of charity activity or activity that supports people. Bureaucracy is more and more of a burden on us, and I think that we are less and less able to perform such tasks with our own resources, simply out of spontaneous enthusiasm; so it really is the case that if the state would in fact like the churches really to participate in these services according to the criteria the state prescribes, then it really should help in this. There is an attitude within the church which rejects this. The Sisters of Mother Theresa, for example, say that they will not take on any form of social or health services which requires official state recognition, and for which state money is given, which here in Hungary makes things rather difficult for them, because if they are considered an institution, then they require various permits. They are this keen to emphasize the spontaneous, personal form of charitable assistance. We on the other hand are aware that we cannot do without the other, and we do not reject cooperation in this sphere, either, to the extent that with our modest resources we are capable of it, of course. What is certain is that this is not an activity that is part of religious life, but at most the particular expression of the motivation and selflessness that faith inspires.

PLK: Is it not possible for the church to say of something that it should be paid for?

PE: We have indeed said this up to now, as we are not in a position to pay ourselves. If the state wishes us to perform a particular activity it regards as of public value in institutional form, that is, according to given criteria, and we have not historically inherited a share of wealth which can allow the operation of this, nor have enough material income from our community for this, then the question of citizens' equality arises. Namely that any Hungarian citizen be treated or educated with the same conditions in an institution operated by us as in an equivalent institution operated by the state of the same nature and which satisfies the same criteria, as all citizens have paid their taxes equally. There should be no discrimination between them, and so it should not be that the state institution is free while we have to ask people to pay a fee out of their own pocket as we have no other financial sources. The services that the church provide have been forcibly blurred into a single commercial category, as if tickets for organ music and the offering of a mass could be in the same category. These are fundamentally different things. There are external conditions, like heating, floral decorations, Persian rugs, the organist playing, and so on, which we provide as a service as might anyone else. And there are specifically holy things, holy goods, for example the mercy of holy mass or the serving of sacraments, and in this instances it is a much bigger problem for us than for civil society or for secular society of how we can come to be asking for or accepting money, as this would represent simony, that is the greatest sin in the Christian tradition, the sin of Simon Magus, if we want to sell spiritual goods for money. As a result, there is canonical casuistry dating back over thousands of years, literature I will only sketch out now very briefly, about how this is not remuneration in return for a service, but rather that on such occasions the gift thus accepted is a modal donation, that is, a donation connected to a mandate. So, in the moment someone might start to see this from the outside as a service, we would naturally emphasize our eternal principle that this is for free. But as far as I know it is permissible to accept donations, especially in a country where it is said that the church should live on donations.

PLK: Then at least there is not anything to tax, either.

PE: That there is no tax on church gifts and collections is not a special privilege; this is the same all over the world. I do not know whether those who proposed such a tax in Hungary are aware of this. Or, from a different perspective, we can look at the American model, which, in its particular context, I approve of. There are many advantages to the American model of church financing; the principle is that the faithful should maintain the church. True, they do not pillage the church's resources every thirty years, and so the church has a capital accumulation to start with. And what privileges they have! For example, charity dinners. They are not only able to write off against tax all that people contribute to the church, which everyone gives in return for a paper of acknowledgement that tax can be exempted, but the church has a right to hold a dinner for as many people as they can fit in their grand hall and for as much money as they want, in return for the payment of a one-off seventy-dollar licence fee. So, for example, they can sell the two-dollar bottle of beer for eight dollars; it is possible that the customer buys the first bottle with the intention of making a contribution to the church, but this is legal, and enjoys this concession. When in America the church has such concessions, it would be easy to say that they live off the contributions of the faithful. That is an entirely different system. Not to mention the fact that they do not have the same value of historical built heritage in their control or on their shoulders as here in Central Europe. The historical and social relations are entirely different, which we have to take into account with respect, and I think that it is tolerance that really helps in this, if within a given country we view one another in such a way as to try to understand what situation they are in, rather than finding our way through the use of ideologies. Then it will transpire that all of us here, believers, non-believers and representatives of the various churches, are very, very much in the same boat.

SS: You mentioned as a unique American characteristic that the church is not robbed from time to time; neither do they rob the civil society from time to time which supports it.

JS: The Mishnah, which I just mentioned, and which is in point of fact a legal compendium, has a tractate, the Sayings of the Fathers or *Sententiae patrum*, which publishes not legal but ethical axioms. In this we read that there are three pillars to Jewish life: one is the Torah, the study of the Scriptures; the second is to serve God, that is, prayer; the third is humanitarian acts. Judaism teaches that religious actions, *ergo* religious obligations, also mean that one should play an active role in humanitarian acts as their abilities and opportunities allow.

ESV: When I attended the Sacred Heart – that is, when I was part of a religious community – then the way to Jesus' heart was to do a good deed every day, which would open a window. My understanding is that you have something similar.

JS: I don't know of this in particular, but, fundamentally, to do a good deed, to help the poor, is not just some spontaneous decision, but a religious, ethical commandment. When someone is called up to the Torah, and a paragraph is read to someone from the Torah, for which they say a blessing, and then ask for a blessing, then the proper thing is for them to donate some sum to some charitable cause. This is part of the practice of life, almost an obligation.

SS: This exists in all religions in some form; giving, alms, are also very important in Islam, in Hinduism and in Buddhism. An interesting question relating to ethics and to sin is how this relates to human liberty, also considering that a democratic community, a society, is an association of free people, and provides the assurance of freedom. Ethical deficiency or ethically reprehensible behaviour can also be understood as something that limits someone's freedom, as they allow themselves more and more to be tied up by sin, and so become more and more restricted by these bonds, and means they have less and less of the liberty in which to enjoy a healthy society and to contribute to it.

ESV: Liberty is precisely having the choice between good and evil.

SS: Yes, but everything has its consequences. If I choose evil, this means I have restricted my liberty.

ESV: Human beings are human precisely by dint of having choices. In the animal kingdom, there is no such choice; rather, instincts rule there. For us, as cortical creatures, our limbic system and our cortical workings make the absolute freedom of choice possible. This is why we can have criminal law in the first place: the first question will be whether the person in question was in their right mind, whether they were able to decide on their course of action. In a word, whether they were free. This is a hugely important basic principle, which is characteristic only of homo sapiens.

JS: This can be corroborated by the Bible. In the first pages of Genesis, we read: 'If thou doest not well, sin lieth at the door. And unto thee shall be his desire, and thou shalt rule over him.' (Gen 4:7.)

PE: I would return to the issue of liberty. In its statement which begins *Dignitatis humanae*, the Second Vatican Council, in which the church recognizes for the first time and in celebratory fashion the right to freedom of religion in its own universality, it does not justify this by saying that man is free to do what he wants, and that it does not matter what we believe; rather, it does so by saying that God calls upon us as individuals and with our own human dignity, that is, God wants us freely to accept his will, freely to recognize him, and accept him and follow his will. Of course, this assumes by necessity that God also gives us the opportunity to deviate from his will; the freedom of choice is ours. Liberty is not a negative concept, as it is fashionable nowadays to see it, namely that it releases us from this law or that obligation; rather, the essence of liberty is the positive opportunity that we ought to make the most of according to our own human dignity.

PLK: Does all sin originate from the Devil?

PE: Sin is the act with which someone knowingly and deliberately does not submit to God's will. It requires an individual, and this can be a human individual, but we believe, in line with the Biblical tradition, in the existence of angels and demons; so spiritual creatures, which also have personal freedom, have also been given the chance to reject God's will, and so sin is possible not only in the relationship between God and man, but in that between God and any creature with reason and free will.

There can be many reasons for human sin; it is freedom, after all, which is the condition for its existence. But what draws us to sin? The temptation of the devil or Satan – or our own bad propensities. What does it mean for us to have bad propensities? In Catholic theology, the teaching of the original sin mentions that as a result of the original sin our reason became vague and our will began to tend to evil; that is, there is an inner maladjustment, which Saint Augustine terms concupiscence, while Saint Paul says of this that while I know I should do good, I nevertheless do wrong: 'But I see another law in my members, warring against the law of my mind, and bringing me into captivity to the law of sin which is in my members' (Rom 7:14-15). Mankind has a feature which displays the disorder of its nature, and which leads us to sin, which brings us together with sin. There can be external circumstances, the temptation of other people, or a social situation from which it is hard to find a way out; this is this thing which South American theologians term structural sin, for example, when a whole society is characterized by corruption. It is very hard for one person to become independent from an entire system which we think not to be ethical. In such instances it more or less becomes a burden on one, and it is almost clear, as Father Sajgó put it, that the web of sins can tangibly restrict one's freedom to choose, especially at the level of the society.

ESV: In our secular world, sin or crime is just whatever social convention deems it to be, what the rule of law established over the centuries – or decades – judges to be so.

SS: We can again bring up the equivalence of natural ethics, which uncovers ethical principles by the light of natural reason and systematizes them, and of revealed ethics. It is clear that there are differences from time to time between the ethical consequences of the religion of revelation and what society's ethical expectations are, depending on what people think of what is allowed and what is not. But from the perspective of faith one has always to say that aren't two

Gods who created the Earth in which natural ethics lies, which guides us with what leads us towards life and what leads us to chaos and death; this is the same God who speaks to us through his revelation. Somewhere we have to state the unity of ethics, the unity and harmony of natural ethics and revealed ethics, and if they have not been squared as yet, this rapprochement of the two is an important goal.

ESV: Father Sajgó, we have just summarized that which we have been just discussing, about the relationship between the churches and the state and the academies and the state – that is, about how important the meeting or proximity of revealed ethics and the ethical rules accepted by society can be in the life of a country, a nation, or a continent.

JS: So is there *duplex veritas* in the field of ethics, or not?

PE: In no sense can there be: the creator of the world is the same as the one who revealed himself to the world. It is a different question that we do indeed tend to use ethics as system of norms, that is, we locate it on the plane of *sollen*, of what someone should do, and not on the plane of *sein*, of what they actually do; so we are not sociological observers who describe how often people tend to behave in a certain way, and how. It is another issue that we do not call this ethics in a theological sense; it might be a habit, or a regularity of behaviour, but we do not call it ethics. I would make another distinction between law and ethics: in the case of law, Gyula Moór (the Hungarian expert on jurisprudence who was a legal positivist) had a very nice definition, which was that law was the totality of the norms regulating society's behaviour, ultimately enforceable with physical coercion by the most powerful authority operating on the territory in question. In contrast with the Marxist philosophy of law, Gyula Moór realistically recognized that it is not necessarily only the state that can be the foundation for law, because if in some area there is a body that has greater physical strength than the state, then whatever this body demands, in a *de facto* empirically observable way, becomes the law. I never needed to explain this to my friends from Sicily; they understood at once what

Professor Moór was talking about. No doubt, there can be differences with this, and this is not the same as ethics, but in an ideal case, indeed, in a necessary case, the framework of the law, as sanctioned by the state or as sanctioned by the authority with the greatest physical potential, builds upon ethics, and not on empirical ethics, but on ethics based on an awareness of values, on the plane of *sollen*, what should be done. In this sense again all I can say is that the legislator is not sovereign: one cannot create legislation arbitrarily, hoping it will work; it has to be built on reality and on the needs emerging from reality.

SS: On the subject of ethics, there is in the Catholic understanding of it an aspect which is not always accepted: the one in which we teach that the community of the church, the universal church at one with the bishops, with the Pope of Rome, is infallible on matters of ethics, and that as a special instance of this the teaching of the Pope of Rome can in a certain carefully-defined way display ethical infallibility.

PE: This can only be an appendix to what I said about the teacher's chair. If someone is not teaching as a private individual, they must with complete formality represent the tradition they have been mandated with passing on, the tradition which refers to and comprises the mediation of the revelation. Originally, from the 1st and 2nd centuries onwards, this was called *traditio apostolica* or *apolostike paradosis*. An entirely special and celebratory form of expression of this is when the Pope speaks ex cathedra. Why do we say ex cathedra? Sitting in Saint Peter's teaching chair, with the authority of the head of the Apostolic body, he bears witness to the revelation and tradition emerging from Christ. In this sense the Pope has a unique charisma – let us call it infallibility – on questions of faith and ethics, but that statement must be made with very special formalities. When the Catholic faith speaks of Papal infallibility, then this does not refer to everything, but merely to that which is in the Christian message from the outset. The function of this is very important; indeed, the First Vatican Council, when it first defined this, it announced that when the Pope states something in such and such circumstances on matters of faith and ethics and as something determined in a final and binding fashion, then this bears the infallibility with which

Christ wanted to bestow his church (First Vatican Council, Const. Pastor aeternus, nr. 4: Denzinger-Hünermann, nr. 3074). The church, as God's people, has the gift and the charisma of preserving, until the end of history and in pure form, the divine revelation or the tradition which it received from Christ, and the mechanism and revelatory form of this is what we have been talking about, whose superficial and distinctly modern questioning has been the characteristic of the end of the 19th century or the 20th century. That this did not need previously to be dogmatized only goes to show that the authority of the teacher and the prestige of tradition was enough in and of itself. As was already said in Antiquity: *Roma locuta, causa finita*.

SS: This is mentioned as the gift of remaining in truth.

ESV: In science and scholarship, we have never accepted this notion of *ex cathedra*. Aristotle still claimed this, but after the Middle Ages – with Copernicus, Galileo and the refutation of the geocentric worldview – the view of the world became an anthropocentric one. So, we do not accept *ex cathedra* opinions, just as we do not accept the principle of acquiring the complete truth. As regards the conflict between the part and the whole, science is of the opinion that it is possible to acquire partial pieces of knowledge from the whole, or to strive towards complete truth from partial details, but there can be no talk of becoming acquainted with the complete truth. This is the basic motif of the progress of science; if we did not claim this, if we did not think this, then science would not make progress.

PE: *Nota bene*: in a certain sense, this is true of the study of theology, too.

ESV: I do not agree with that, Cardinal Erdő, as that is dogma.

PE: Catholic theology, although based on the Magisterium, on the tradition represented by the Magisterium, nevertheless poses creative new questions, and looks for ways to accommodate new situations. A very common scholastic expression since the Middle Ages is *salva reverentia magistri*, that is, 'respect to my master, and yet I would like to say that...' That is, deviating from what my teacher has taught me. This kind of research freedom within the framework of the magisterium exists even in theology, of course not quite as it does in the world of profane subjects.

ESV: However, it never rejects the fundamental dogma.

SS: Just as natural sciences never reject fundamental equations. $a^2 + b^2 = c^2$ is also dogma.

PE: In theology the term dogma was not originally used in the plural. Dogma referred to the deposit of faith, the entirety of the inheritance of faith; later, during the debates, specific articles became crystallized, which were then fixed in obligate fashion, claiming that anyone who did not claim these did not claim this faith. There have been dogmas ever since the debates around certain articles made it inevitable to tie down certain truths, forcibly, in the form of definitions. This is a process of development which to the present day has not come to a close. So, in this regard, the fact of the progress of dogma has since the 19th century brought with it an ideological change to Catholic theology, that is, reflection on the development of dogma has appeared. The first to deal with this properly was Cardinal Newman, but it was later, at the turn of the 20th century, in part in connection with modernism, that this became a subject of debate.

JS: There was a teacher of theology in Budapest who did not accept the infallibility of the Pope: Péter Hatala, who then taught Semitic philology at the university's faculty of humanities; I know, because my grandfather was his doctoral student. I was recently in a village called Taliándörögd in Veszprém county, where my wife joined a group of friends which was sorting through the old books of the parish church which were of no interest to anyone. My friend there showed me a book: Péter Hatala, 'My Confession of Faith' (*Az én hitvallásom*). I told him that there wasn't a person in the whole of Taliándörögd who would know who Péter Hatala was, but I do, through the family, and I asked him to give me the book. So I brought it; it's a thin volume, but I haven't read it yet. The point is his confession of faith: he rejected the Pope's infallibility, and so left the church.

PE: He joined the Old Catholic Church.

SS: After the First Vatican Council, many left the church, led by Döllinger; they became the Old Catholic Church.

PE: Péter Hatala rejected it. My honourable predecessor, János Simor, did not reject it, but at the emperor's instruction, together with all the other bishops from the Austro-Hungarian Empire, left the Council before the voting took place. Pope Pius IX even said to them, with a play on Simor's name, 'Simor, Simor, behold, Satan hath desired to have you, that he may sift you as wheat' (Cf. Luke 22:31).

SS: There has repeatedly been mention of the importance of love in ethics. Any kind of law, system of norms, regulation, etc., will only function to the extent that it has some effect on that inner force known as love or affection. Seen on the ontological plane, it is very interesting that even Christianity names as the truest characteristic of mystery the fact that God is love itself. Thus if his being is definitive in everything, his being is the source of everything, from a universal, ontological point of view, then it is clear that in an absence of this any ethical law, system of norms, anything, which exists, will not work. As Jesus says, the commandment of love is the first and great commandment, love for everything, for what is invisible and what is visible, for what is made and unmade.

JS: I think that all believers quietly agree with the Bible's teaching that 'love covereth all sins' (Pro 10:12).

PE: According to our faith, those gifts from God which lead a person to love, or to find the appropriate norms, also operate in the non-believer, when they look for the truth about the world's affairs. So I do not think that someone could not be ethical without explicit faith. This is precisely what gives hope that a working social consensus really can come into being on the most basic of normal human values, because even those who do not share a faith in God, if they think in an honest way and consistently look for truth without compromise, can recognize basic things from the structure of reality, which matches what we stand for and respect on the basis of our own personal faith. For me it is a question of faith that we have to put our hopes in this possibility, even if if sometimes it seems to be harder and harder, or that people no longer believe in the old categories of natural law, or that they no longer see them as during the era of Enlightenment. From a doctrinal perspective, for me as a Catholic, it is my obligation to believe that a consensus on basic ethical norms and values is possible in a society, irrespective of religious denomination.

ESV: Perhaps I can provide a piece of neurobiological evidence for this. Saint Francis of Assisi said that love is the human property that we will have more of the more of it we give away. In today's words, when I love someone else, or share my love with others, I feel that I will be happier, too. There is a neurochemical center of happiness, which is part of the limbic system – in the animal kingdom, interestingly, this is mostly connected to the sense of smell – which, in humans, is a special center where a chemical material is released, which if released in great quantities makes one feel satisfied, or happy. It is very interesting that there is a cognitive possibility for stimulating this center. One such cognitive possibility is visual, or a response in the form of gratitude, words or caresses, in the form of love or affection, when the cognitive signal follows a path from the cortex and enters the limbic system, where this particular chemical material can gradually be released. Although it might be strange that I am providing evidence for what Saint Francis of Assisi said with a neurochemical scientific result, this certainty does exist. It is no accident that those suffering from being unloved turn to recreational drugs, as their effect works through precisely this center.

There is a great difference between natural happiness and man-made happiness evoked by drugs. Naturally induced happiness is when I recognize my wife, my family, through seeing memories, or an association with a sound or even a smell, though even seeing a photo can produce a sense of happiness. The short-lived 'sense of happiness' induced by recreational drugs is not connected to such memory images and cannot be repeated, so the affected person has no choice but to take the drug again and again. This is why Baudelaire, who himself took drugs, in his book 'Artificial Paradises' (*Les Paradis artificiels*) says that if you step through a gateway through the use of drugs, you will never be the same person, even if you come back through it – and we see the same in Aldous Huxley's *Brave New World*. This is slavery to drugs, as brain researchers put it. Baudelaire did not understand it scientifically, but he put it precisely. This is why humanity must stay on the natural path to happiness and must not stray from this path because once you step through the gateway, you cannot return.

SS: How can someone who has fallen from innocence manage to return?

PLK: Where does love reside, according to Judaism?

JS: It is hard for me to answer that. It must reside in everyone's own heart, own emotional world; if not, they are all the poorer for it. In vain does the Torah instruct me to love my neighbour, if I am forced to withstand an effect from someone that is utterly at odds with this, then I can at best be tolerant to them. But I must strive to find what is good in them, what is lovable in them. I am often asked: how are you always able to say good things about people at their funeral? How does this work, how do you find something good to say about everyone? There is a very good rabbinical answer to this, which I have passed on to my students: before I bury someone, a family member of the deceased comes, I talk with them, from beginning to end, from every angle, and in the end it is certain that from the 50, 60 or 80 years of anyone's life, I can find ten minutes' worth of things appropriate to say. So we all have something good in us, something that can be loved.

ESV: There is no doubt that the Kádár regime, but especially the Rákosi regime before it, caused enormous moral destruction. Hungarian society was simply not prepared, either morally or economically, for what came after it from one moment to the next – namely, that it would have to confront economic fundamentalism. And with this an era arrived in Hungary in which freedom primarily meant the infinite space for and mobility of capital – that is, capital and financial freedom – not the freedom for human values to blossom. It is in this sense that there is an ethical and value crisis in Hungary much more than there is an economic crisis. When examining this, of the trinity of the state, the historical churches and academe, the latter two must not be omitted, because they are at once preservers and creators of values.

The Old and New Testaments raise generations on ethics and the truths of human life and transcendence. The innovation of the modern age is the 'third' alliance established between nature and mankind, the alliance of becoming acquainted and being acquainted through knowledge and science. Scholars and scientists always have to form this alliance anew. Their task is to uncover the social and natural laws, to discover the truths of humanity's life and environment.

This task brings with it a new responsibility: instead of monopolizing knowledge, we must make use of the opportunities presented by the information revolution and make knowledge and culture accessible and consumable by all. Technical methods, the new techniques of recording and transmitting images and sounds, television, computers, the internet, are all a help in this. In a globalizing world interwoven with information and communication networks, the equality of opportunity for acquiring knowledge can increase. In the 'knowledge-based' society, all this can make the global spread of a new type of democracy possible, but this will only be a real blessing for people if we provide moral lessons along with this knowledge. This is the great possibility and challenge of the 21st century.

PE: The organic union of faith and science is needed for us to provide an ethical response to the exceptionally complex economic, scientific and social questions of our age, for us to discover the right human behaviour in these situations. Our faith communicates to us the consequences of the created character and intelligence of nature, and also ethical norms discovered from a God who reveals himself. But the implementation of these without a scientific-level knowledge of material reality is distinctly uncertain. And so, however great an effort it requires, today's theologians must pursue a dialogue with the highest level of human science and scholarship, in order to mediate the ethical laws learned from our faith to society in a convincing and authentic way. But this difficulty must not discourage us. If Christ gave us a mission that is for the whole world and for people of all ages, then he also gives us the flexibility and the mercy always to rise up to this wonderful challenge again and again throughout history.

•   •   •

Brought to a close at the end of October 2006 – this is what we could write in the epilogue to this volume, at the end of a series of conversations that took place over almost half a year. It was on Palm Sunday that, after lengthy deliberations, the blessing was given for this book to come into being. Except that we do not wish to bring anything to a close. These wide-ranging conversations, the dialogue between three world-class thinkers, raise as many questions as they answer. In the eternity of an incalculable world, what is calculable is showing humanity an ever more anxious face. It is equally hard to experience and understand its signs and its phenomena. In this, honest words, a respect for knowledge, and the ethics of faith will all be of assistance. We, who followed every twist and turn of the above conversations, can conclude with a clear conscience that every word written here was written in this spirit.

The Publisher